EXCHANGE RATES, MONEY AND OUTPUT

The macroeconomic performance of the industrialised countries since 1970 has been anything but brilliant. Low growth of output, increasing unemployment, high and variable inflation rates and interest rates, volatile exchange rates, these are the hallmarks of the 1970s and the early 1980s.

The first part of the book analyses how inflation, oil shocks and tax policies in major European countries have affected the supply of industrial output. At the same time it develops and tests the Lucas-supply equation for open economies. The results of this analysis suggest that both the changes in the terms of trade (due to oil shocks) and tax policies have negatively affected industrial output in the EC countries.

The second part of the book studies the financial side of the EC economies. Models of the money and banking sectors of the EC countries are developed and tested. These models are used to analyse various policy issues. In particular, how effective is the official management of exchange rates in Europe? How do exchange rate and monetary policies interact? What has been the nature of the financial interdependence within the EMS? In a final chapter the uneasy economic interdependence between the USA and Europe is studied. One conclusion of this analysis is that the present exchange rate regime combines the disadvantages of both the fixed and flexible exchange rate systems, thereby exacerbating conflicts between the USA and Europe.

Paul De Grauwe is Professor of Economics at the University of Leuven, Belgium. He has been visiting professor at the Universities of Paris, Michigan, Brussels and Tilburg and at the Wharton School (University of Pennsylvania). He obtained his Ph.D. in economics from Johns Hopkins. He worked as a research fellow at the Brookings Institution (1972–73), and as an economist at the International Monetary Fund. His publications include *Macroeconomic Theory for the Open Economy*, and *Exchange Rates in Multicountry Econometric Models* (co-editor with Theo Peeters.

Michele Fratianni is Professor of Business Economics and Public Policy at the Graduate School of Business of Indiana University and visiting professor of economics at the University of Leuven, Belgium. He has served as economic adviser with the EC in Brussels from 1976 to 1979; Senior Staff economist with the US President's Council of Economic Advisors from 1981–2; and adviser to the Italian Ministry of the Budget. His publications include *Bank Credit, Money and Inflation in Open Economies* (co-editor with Karel Tavernier) and *One Money for Europe* (co-editor with Theo Peeters).

Mustapha K. Nabli is Professor of Economics and Econometrics at the Faculté de Droit et Sciences Economiques at Tunis. He obtained his PhD in economics from UCLA. He has worked as a research associate with the National Bureau of Economic Research (1976–8), the EC Commission (1977–9), University of Leuven (1980–3) and the Ministry of Planning in Tunisia (since 1982). He has been visiting professor at the University of Southern California and the University of Toulouse. His publications are in the field of econometrics, international economics, and economic development.

EXCHANGE RATES, MONEY AND OUTPUT

The European Experience

Paul De Grauwe
Catholic University of Leuven
Michele Fratianni
Indiana University
Mustapha K. Nabli
University of Tunis

M
MACMILLAN

First published 1985 by
THE MACMILLAN PRESS LTD
London and Basingstoke
Companies and representatives
throughout the world

Printed in Hong Kong

British Library Cataloguing in Publication Data
Grauwe, Paul De
Exchange rates, money and output.
1. Macroeconomics—Mathematical models
2. European Economic Community countries—
Economic policy—Mathematical models
I. Title II. Fratianni, Michele
III. Nabli, Mustapha K.
339′.094 HC241.2
ISBN 0–333–36877–0

Contents

List of Tables viii
List of Figures x
Acknowledgements xii

1 Introduction 1

PART 1 OUTPUT, MONEY AND INFLATION IN OPEN ECONOMIES

2 The Theory of Output and Inflation with Rational Expectations in Open Economies **7**
I Introduction 7
II The Aggregate Supply Function 8
III Aggregate Demand 11
IV Solution Equations 11
V Short- and Long-run Effects 14
VI The Non-Traded Sector 20
VII Summary 21

3 Supply of Output and Inflation in EC Countries **22**
I Introduction 22
II Description of Data 24
III Supply of Output with Fixed Nominal Wages 28
IV The Rational Expectations Hypothesis 30
V The 1970s with Quarterly Data 38
VI Conclusions 43

Appendix: Forecasting Exogenous Variables 46

PART II EXCHANGE RATES AND THE FINANCIAL SECTOR

4 Interest Rate Parity and Imperfect Substitutability **53**

I Introduction 53

II Interest Rate Parity 54
III The Forward Rate, The Expected Spot Rate and Risk Premiums 65
IV Summary 67

5 The Theory of the Financial Economy 70

I Introduction 70
II A Portfolio-balance Model With a Banking Sector 70
III Outside Domestic Bonds and Interventions in the Exchange Market 80
IV The Rational Expectations Solution 85
V Summary 87

Appendix: Derivation of the Rational Expectations Solution 88

6 Modelling the Financial Markets: Empirical Findings 90
I Introduction 90
II Empirical Specifications 91
III Modelling Spot Exchange Rates and Expectations 97
IV Estimation Problems and Methods 102
V Estimation Results for Five Countries 105
VI The Financial Model of the United Kingdom 112
VII Simulation and Tracking Performance 120

Appendix: Tables 124

PART III EXCHANGE RATE AND MONETARY POLICIES AND WORLD FINANCIAL INTERDEPENDENCE

7 Policy Choices Under Different Exchange Rate Regimes 143
I Introduction 143
II The Model under Free Floating 143
III The Effectiveness of Intervention in the Exchange Market 148
IV Conclusion 156

8 Monetary Interdependence within the European Monetary System 159
I Introduction 159
II Main Features of the EMS 159
III The EMS and Exchange Rate Stability 160
IV Intervention Policies in a Multi-country Setting 166

V Expectations and Monetary Control within the EMS 170
VI Conclusion 171

9 Monetary Policy in an Interdependent World 173

I Introduction 173
II Interdependence During the 1970s: Some Empirical Observations 173
III Interdependence During the 1970s: The Commom Shock Explanation 176
IV Interdependence During the 1970s: A Monetary Explanation 177
V US Policies, 1979–82, and the European Economy 183
VI US Policies, 1979–82, and the European Economy: Some Empirical Observations 188

10 Summary and Conclusion 192

Appendix Data definitions and sources 196
Bibliography 230
Index 237

List of Tables

2.1	List of variables used in Chapter 2	9
3.1	Increase in taxation of labour and oil as a percentage of *GDP* from 1970 to 1980	23
3.2	Fixed wage supply of output (2 SLS), annual data, 1957–80	29
3.3	Rational expectations equations for expected inflation rates, annual data, 1959–80	32
3.4	Unexpected inflation rates equations, annual data, 1959–80	34
3.5	Supply of output equations in level (2 SLS) and rational expectations, annual data, 1959–80	35
3.6	The effect of the tax wedge for Italy and France	37
3.7	Rational expectations equations for expected inflation rates, quarterly data, 1971(I)–1980(IV)	40
3.8	Output supply equations, quarterly data, 1971(I)–1980(IV)	41
3A.1	Vector autoregressive models of exogenous variables	49
4.1	Descriptive statistics on interest rate parity, quarterly data, end of period, 1973(I)–1980(IV)	55
4.2	Autoregressive pattern of *X*, 1973(I)–1980(IV)	60
4.3	Interest rate parity tests	63
4.4	Simple market efficiency hypothesis	68
5.1	List of variables used in Chapter 5	71
5.2	Multipliers of the financial economy	77
6.1	List of variables used in the financial model	92
6.2	Short-term (*S*) and long-term (*L*) elasticities in the demand for monetary assets	107
6.3	Short-term (*S*) and long-term (*L*) elasticities of banks' demand for assets	110
6.A	The German financial model	126
6.B	The French financial model	128
6.C	The Italian financial model	130
6.D	The Dutch financial model	132
6.E	The Belgian financial model	134
6.F	Definitions and identities used in the models for Germany, France, Italy, the Netherlands and Belgium	136

6.G The UK financial model 137
6.H Within sample tracking performance of financial models 139

8.1 Real effective exchange rate changes 162
8.2 Mean absolute yearly change of real exchange rates 162
8.3 Inflation rates (CPI) in EMS countries 164
8.4 Growth rates of money stock (M_1) in EMS countries 165
8.5 Change in stock of international reserves, the money base and the money stock (M_2) 170
9.1 Correlation matrix of yearly growth rates of real GDP (1962–81) 174
9.2 Correlation matrix of yearly rates of inflation 175
9.3 Mean and standard deviation of yearly inflation rates, 1960–80 175
9.4 Loss of manufacturing output from 1973 to 1980 due to oil price increase 176
9.5 Regression results of equation (9.1) 178
9.6 Regression results of equation (9.2) 180
9.7 Correlation of growth rates of international reserves and rates of change of dollar (1971–82) 181
9.8 Correlation of growth rates of international reserves and growth rates of the money stock M_1 181
9.9 Change in the money-stock (M_1), foreign exchange reserves and in the dollar exchange rate, in percentage 189
9.10 Terms of trade, dollar exchange rates and oil price, 1980–2 190

A.1 Germany 199
A.2 Belgium 206
A.3 France 210
A.4 Italy 214
A.5 The Netherlands 217
A.6 United Kingdom 223
A.7 List of variables and sources used in the real sector (in Chapter 3) 227

List of Figures

2.1 Devaluation 14
2.2 Rise in intermediate goods terms of trade 17
2.3 Increase in the tax wedge 18
2.4a Effect of increase in t_1 in labour market 19
2.4b Effect of increase in t_2 in labour market 19
3.1 International prices, 1958–80 24
3.2 Evolution of main variables for Belgium, 1958–80 25
3.3 Evolution of main variables for France, 1958–80 26
3.4 Evolution of main variables for Italy, 1958–80 27
3.5 Evolution of manufacturing output and prices in the United Kingdom, 1971(I)–1980(IV) 38
4.1 Deviations from IRP: United Kingdom XE and XD, 1973(I)–1980(IV) 58
4.2 Deviations from IRP: Germany XE and XD, 1973(I)–1980(IV) 59
5.1 The money and credit markets 75
5.2 Increase in the monetary base 78
5.3 Increase in the foreign interest rate or expected depreciation of the domestic currency 79
5.4 Increase in reserve requirements 79
5.5 Increase in the stock of domestically-held foreign bonds 81
5.6 Increase in the stock of domestic bonds 83
6.1 Covered with respect to DM and uncovered Eurodollar rate 100
6.2 Exchange rate expectations: Germany 101
6.3 Exchange rate expectations: the United Kingdom 102
6.4 Decision tree of the non-bank private sector 115
7.1 Change in dollar exchange rate after 10 per cent price shock 144
7.2 Change in money base after 10 per cent price increase 145
7.3 Change in M_2 after 10 per cent price increase 146
7.4 Change in dollar exchange rate after permanent Increase of Eurodollar interest rate 147
7.5 Change in dollar exchange rate after temporary increase in Eurodollar interest rate 147

7.6 Change in dollar/DM rate after 10 per cent price increase 150
7.7 Change in dollar/FF rate after 10 per cent price increase 150
7.8 Change in M_2 after 10 per cent price increase (Germany) 151
7.9 Change in M_2 after 10 per cent price increase (France) 151
7.10 Change in dollar/DM rate after 1 per cent increase in Eurodollar rate 152
7.11 Change in dollar/FF Rate after 1 per cent increase in Eurodollar rate 152
7.12 Change in loan rate after 1 per cent increase in Eurodollar interest rate (Germany) 153
7.13 Change in M_2 after 1 per cent increase in Eurodollar interest rate 154
7.14 Change in dollar/DM rate after 1 per cent increase in Eurodollar interest rate (sterilised and non-sterilised) 155
7.15 Change in dollar/DM rate after 1 per cent increase in Eurodollar interest rate (active non-sterilised intervention) 156
8.1 Change in dollar/DM rate after 1 per cent increase in Eurodollar interest rate 168
8.2 Change in dollar/FF rate after 1 per cent increase in Eurodollar interest rate 169
8.3 Change in loan rate (Germany) after 1 per cent increase in Eurodollar interest rate 169
8.4 Change in dollar/DM rate after 1 per cent increase in Eurodollar interest rate (link Belgium–Germany) 171
9.1 US policy mix and aggregate demand in Europe 184
9.2 Aggregate demand and supply in Europe 185
9.3 US policy mix and aggregate demand in Europe: flexible exchange rates 186
9.4 Aggregate supply and demand in Europe: flexible exchange rates 187
9.5 Aggregate supply and demand in Europe: managed float 188

Acknowledgements

The research project is the outcome of several years of association at the Catholic University of Leuven. It was made possible by a generous grant from the Belgian Ministry of Science (Geconcerteerde Onderzoeksactie GOA 80–85/1). We have benefited immensely from the advice of Eric de Souza at several stages of our research. Much of our research would not have been possible without the aid of Kent Matthews, who provided us with the rational expectations simulation program developed at the University of Liverpool and helped in its implementation at Leuven. In addition, Matthews developed and tested the UK financial model. Our gratitude goes also to Marc Janssens, José Mont, Marc Rosiers and Guy Verfaille for outstanding research assistance and to Paul Zonderman for computing assistance. Marc Janssens, in addition, undertook the onerous task of attending to the details of the final work. Finally, we are grateful to Eva Crabbé for the speed and the enthusiasm with which she typed the manuscript, and to Vic Van Eycken for the administrative organisation of this project.

PAUL DE GRAUWE
MICHELE FRATIANNI
MUSTAPHA K. NABLI

1 Introduction

The macroeconomic performance of the industrialised countries since 1970 has been anything but brilliant. Low growth of output, increasing unemployment, high and variable inflation rates and interest rates, volatile exchange rates; these are the hallmarks of the 1970s and the early 1980s. In this book we examine in detail some aspects of these macroeconomic problems in six European countries: Belgium, the Netherlands, France, Germany, Italy and the United Kingdom.

In Part I of the book we analyse how money growth and inflation, the terms of trade and exchange rates, and increasing tax burdens have affected supply decisions in manufacturing in these countries. In particular two main issues are addressed. The first is the extent to which the successive oil shocks and the 'labour tax shock' have exerted an adverse effect on aggregate output in Europe. The second concerns the empirical basis of the new business cycle theory which stresses the importance of unanticipated monetary shocks in explaining output fluctuations, in the context of the European open economies.

In Chapter 2 we develop a theoretical model for the supply side of the real sector along the lines of a Lucas-type supply equation extended to an open economy, in a rational expectations framework. This equation emphasizes four determinants of the supply of manufacturing output: inflation 'surprises', external final goods terms of trade, oil-price variations, and taxation of labour. The model exhibits also an institutional feature of European economies which is wage indexation. The model is then tested in Chapter 3, with data from the six countries both annual for the period 1957–80, and quarterly for the 1970s. In the empirical analysis we investigate, in particular, the effects of money growth and exchange-rate variations on inflationary expectations and actual inflation, and output.

Part II of the book deals with the financial side of the economy. There, we construct a theoretical framework and empirical models enabling us to analyse financial interdependence among the major European countries and to study how the changed environment of the 1970s has affected monetary and exchange rate policies. The chosen paradigm is one of imperfect substitutability among assets, denominated in different currencies. We subject this paradigm to extensive empirical testing in Chapter 4, and we find enough evidence to support it. These empirical tests provide justification for specifying, in Chapter 5, a financial model of the portfolio balance type, whose theoretical properties are investigated. The chosen structure is used in Chapter 6 to specify and estimate econometric models of the financial markets of the six countries. The prototype model includes about ten behavioural equations and essentially solves for interest rates, a number of monetary aggregates and the spot exchange rate, given the expected future exchange rate. The latter is determined using the rational expectations hypothesis. The model includes in particular, a money market, a bank credit market, and a bond market. The open economy characteristics of the European countries are emphasised by the explicit modelling of the demand for foreign assets, capital movements and balance of payments equilibrium, and the effects of foreign interest rates on the demand for domestic assets.

In Part III the models, developed and estimated in Part II, are employed for a study of monetary and exchange rate policies in the context of a world of changed financial interdependence. The analysis imposes the condition that expectations of exchange rates are formed rationally, in the sense that they are consistent with the model. This characteristic allows us in particular to study the effectiveness issue of economic policies in a world where people incorporate the existence of these policies in their decision-making process. In Chapter 7 we raise the question of how foreign and domestic disturbances affect the financial side of the economy under different exchange rate regimes, and we investigate the effectiveness of official intervention in the foreign exchange market. The latter is a question to which we repeatedly return in this last Part of the book. Sterilised and non-sterilised interventions are considered and their relative effectiveness evaluated. Then in Chapter 8 we ask the question 'how successful has the European Monetary System been in fostering exchange rate stability?' The econometric models of the EC countries are used with a linkage procedure to ascertain the effects of the new exchange rate arrangement on monetary relations in the EMS, and the role of official interventions in the exchange markets.

Chapter 9 deals with the new monetary and financial relations since the early 1970s. The problem arises because the international arrangements today combine features of the fixed and flexible exchange rate regimes, thus complicating the understanding of financial interdependence. Too often interdependence is analysed assuming the polar cases of either fixed or flexible exchange rates. We offer some suggestions about the ways the system of managed exchange rates has altered the nature of international monetary interdependence. The nature of the transmission of monetary shocks from the United States to other countries, in particular Europe, is analysed, and illustrated with a case study of the 1979–82 period.

In the last chapter the results of the book are summarised and we offer some concluding remarks.

Part I
Output, Money and Inflation in Open Economies

2 The Theory of Output and Inflation with Rational Expectations in Open Economies

I INTRODUCTION

The objective of this chapter is to develop a theoretical framework of the real sector of a small open economy which will then be tested in Chapter 3 using annual and quarterly data from six EC member countries.

The model includes several crucial aspects of open industrial economies. First, the economies export on the whole manufactured goods while importing both manufactured goods and raw materials used as intermediate goods in the production process.[1] To the extent that domestically and foreign produced goods are imperfect substitutes, there will be changes in the terms of trade which will in turn affect the domestic real sector.

Second, it is possible in an open economy, apart from misperceptions of the current price level, to generate an aggregate supply curve which is positively sloped with respect to domestic prices. This result derives from the behavioural postulate that, while the demand for labour responds to the domestic price level, the supply of labour responds to the overall expected price level.

Third, several industrial economies have institutionalised to different degrees wage indexation schemes which insulate labour from the effects of forecast errors in the overall price level (cf. Braun (1976) for example). The intuitive implication is that wage indexation tends to reduce changes in output attributable to misperceptions of the current overall price level.

Fourth, the share of government in EC countries has dramatically increased in the post-war period, an increase accompanied or sparked by a rise in transfer payments. Since the latter alter the existing distribution of property rights and hence incentives, there is a presumption that output has been affected by the rise in the relative growth of government.

In particular, we shall investigate the implications of the so-called wedge problem, the gap existing between the cost of labour paid by firms and the net-of-tax wage received by workers. When government-provided services are valued as being less than the taxes paid to government, firms and workers either reduce the work effort (that is, trade leisure for work) or seek alternative arrangements which effectively lower the tax burden. This is the motivation underlying the growth of the underground economy. In either case efficiency is reduced which results in a lower growth rate of 'normal' output.

Finally, economic agents behave rationally in the Muth (1961) sense, that is they form expectations consistent with the underlying model. The above considerations suggest that the Lucas (1973) aggregate supply function, which has been widely used in recent years, is too restrictive for open economies and thus requires appropriate modifications.[2] This will be done in Section II of this chapter. Section III introduces aggregate demand. The properties of the model are analysed in the remaining sections of the chapter.

II THE AGGREGATE SUPPLY FUNCTION

We begin our theoretical discussion with the supply side of the model which stresses, among other things, the role of intermediate goods.[3] The representative firm in our open economy produces a final good Y under the following production function

$$Y = AN^{\alpha_1} H^{\alpha_2}, \quad \alpha_1 + \alpha_2 < 1 \tag{2.1}$$

where A is fixed input, N labour, H the imported intermediate good. Y is imperfectly substitutable for the final good produced abroad. There is a downward sloping demand schedule for Y. Firms maximise

$$P_d Y - NW(1 + t_w^1)^{\delta_1} - P_h H \tag{2.2}$$

where P_d and P_h are the prices of Y and H and W is the nominal wage rate, t_w^1 is the tax on wages in the form of social security contributions, insurance premiums against accidents and sickness etc. paid by the employer. The value of the parameter δ_1 indicates how the firm values government services (including subsidies) generated by the tax. When $\delta_1 = 0$ there is no wedge problem; when $\delta_1 = 1$ the wedge is complete. First-order conditions yield

$$a + \alpha_2 h + \bar{\alpha}_1 + (\alpha_1 - 1)n = w - p_d + \delta_1 \tau_1 \tag{2.3a}$$

$$a + (\alpha_2 - 1)h + \bar{\alpha}_2 + \alpha_1 n = p_h - p_d \tag{2.3b}$$

with lower case letters denoting natural logarithms, $\tau_1 = \log(1 + t_w^1)$ and $\bar{\alpha}_i = \log(\alpha_i)$. (A complete list of variables and symbols used in this chapter is given in Table 2.1). The demand schedules of the two inputs are obtained by solving simultaneously (2.3a) and (2.3b):

$$h = h_0 + a_1(p_d - w) + b_1(p_d - p_h) - a_1\delta_1\tau_1 \tag{2.4}$$

$$n = n_0 + b_2(p_d - w) + a_2(p_d - p_h) - b_2\delta_1\tau_1 \tag{2.5}$$

where

$$h_0 = (a + \bar{\alpha}_2 - \alpha_1\alpha_2 + \alpha_1^2)/(1 - \alpha_1 - \alpha_2)$$
$$n_0 = (a + \alpha_2^2 + \bar{\alpha}_1 - \alpha_1\alpha_2)/(1 - \alpha_1 - \alpha_2)$$
$$a_1 = \alpha_1/(1 - \alpha_1 - \alpha_2) > 0$$
$$a_2 = \alpha_2/(1 - \alpha_1 - \alpha_2) > 0$$
$$b_1 = (1 - \alpha_1)/(1 - \alpha_1 - \alpha_2) > 0$$
$$b_2 = (1 - \alpha_2)/(1 - \alpha_1 - \alpha_2) > 0$$

Factor demands depend positively on the fixed input and the two relative prices. The intermediate good is supplied at the foreign currency

TABLE 2.1 *List of variables used in Chapter 2*

All variables are expressed in natural logarithms unless otherwise indicated

y	= output
a	= fixed input
n	= units of labour services
h	= units of intermediate good
p	= the overall price level, i.e. the consumer price level
p_d	= price of domestic final goods in domestic currency
p_f	= price of foreign final goods in domestic currency
e	= the exchange rate, the domestic price of foreign currency
p_h	= price of intermediate good in domestic currency
t_w^1	= tax rate on the nominal wage rate paid by employers
t_w^2	= tax rate on the nominal wage rate paid by wage earner
τ_1	= $\log(1 + t_w^1)$
τ_2	= $\log(1 + t_w^2)$
m	= stock of money
I	= nominal impulses other than money
b	= wage indexation parameter
v_d, v_s	= error terms
$\underset{t-1}{E}$	= mathematical expectation conditional on information set Ω_{-1}
Ω_{-1}	= information set which includes all lagged variables up to $t-1$

* indicates that variables are denominated in foreign currency.

price p_h^* which is given for the small open economy. The domestic price of h is simply $p_h^* + e$ where e is the log of the exchange rate expressed as the domestic price of one unit of foreign currency.

Labour supplies services according to the following wave-setting function

$$w_t = \underset{t-1}{E}(p_t|\Omega_{-1}) + b\left[p_t - \underset{t-1}{E}(p_t|\Omega_{-1})\right] + \delta_2 \tau_{2t}. \tag{2.6}$$

Labour contracts are negotiated at the end of period $t-1$ at which time workers make their best forecast concerning the overall price level for period t. The forecasts are conditional on the information set Ω_{-1} which includes the history of all variables up to $t-1$. Nominal wages respond fully to changes in the overall expected price level. In addition, workers may bargain for indexation clauses which will insulate them from the effects of forecast errors in the general price level. The degree of protection is reflected in the value of $0 \leqslant b \leqslant 1$; when $b = 1$ wages adjust completely to changes in the current but unknown price level. Finally, workers may seek higher nominal wages the higher the level of taxes on wage income. The extent to which this is done depends on the valuation of government-provided services (including transfers) relative to taxes paid. Let δ_2 measure the wedge and $\tau_2 = \log(1 + t_w^2)$ where t_w^2 is the tax rate on wage income, then the tax-push effect on the supply side of the labour market is given by $\delta_2 \tau_2$. As in the case of δ_1, the parameter δ_2 can acquire values from zero to unity.

The price level is defined as a weighted average of the domestically- and foreign-produced final goods prices

$$p = \lambda p_d + (1 - \lambda) p_f \tag{2.7}$$

where $p_f = p_f^* + e$. The domestic economy is a price-taker in the foreign-produced goods market.
Equations (2.1), (2.4), (2.5), (2.6) and (2.7) yield

$$y_t = a_0 - a_1 \tau_t + a_1 (1 - b)(p_t - \underset{t-1}{E} p_t) + (a_1 [1 - \lambda] + a_2)(p_{d,t} - p_{f,t})$$
$$- a_2 (p_{h,t} - p_{f,t}) + v_{s,t} \tag{2.8}$$

where $a_0 = a + \alpha_1 n_0 + \alpha_2 h_0$, $\tau = \delta_1 \tau_1 + \delta_2 \tau_2$ and $v_{s,t}$ a white-noise error term.

This is a Lucas-type aggregate supply function extended to our open economy. The first term on the right-hand side of (2.8) gives the 'normal' level of output in the absence of tax-induced disincentive effects captured in the second term; the third term is the Lucas price level misperception effect; the last two terms capture the impact of the final goods terms of trade and the intermediate goods terms of trade on domestic output supplied. An increase in domestic goods prices relative to foreign goods prices raises y supplied; an increase in the intermediate good relative to foreign final goods prices lowers it. Indexation lowers the effect of the surprise variable on output supplied, disappearing altogether when $b = 1$. Note that the closed-economy Lucas supply curve is obtained from (2.8) by setting $b < 1$, $\lambda = 1$ and ignoring intermediate goods. It is also illustrative to consider the supply of output with an exogenously determined nominal wage rate, $\bar{w}$,

$$y = a_0 - a_1\tau + a_1(p - \bar{w}) + [a_1(1-\lambda) + a_2](p_d - p_f) - a_2(p_h - p_f) \tag{2.9}$$

which differs from (2.8) in that the term $a_1(1-b)(p_t - \underset{t-1}{E}\, p_t)$ has been replaced by $a_1(p - \bar{w})$.

III AGGREGATE DEMAND

We postulate that aggregate demand depends positively on real cash balances, $m_t - p_t$, and other real impulses, $I_t - p_t$, and negatively on the final goods terms of trade. This formulation, which is fairly standard, allows a variety of outcomes and in particular it is neutral with respect to the issue of whether monetary or fiscal impulses dominate[4]:

$$y_t = \beta_1(m_t - p_t) - \beta_2(p_{d,t} - p_{f,t}) + \beta_3(I_t - p_t) + v_{d,t} \tag{2.10}$$

with $v_{d,t}$ being a white-noise error term. Although equation (2.10) is simply stated here it could be derived from a standard Keynesian aggregate demand.

IV SOLUTION EQUATIONS

Equations (2.1), (2.4), (2.5), (2.6), (2.7) and (2.10) form a system which solves for the six endogenous variables y, h, n, w, p and p_d for given values of p_f^*, p_h^*, m, I and e. The exchange rate e is parametrically given in this real sector model. Since our primary interest at this stage is the behaviour of prices and output, we will use equations (2.8) and (2.10) to obtain first, using the terminology of Wallis (1980), the 'non-observable' reduced form equation for p_d

$$p_{d,t} = \frac{1}{D}\{-a_0 + a_1\tau_t + \beta_1 m_t + [a_1(1-\lambda)b + (\lambda - 1)(\beta_1+\beta_3) + \beta_2]p_{f,t} + a_2 p_{h,t} + a_1(1-b)\underset{t-1}{E}p_t + \beta_3 I_t + v_t\} \tag{2.11}$$

where $D = a_1(1-b\lambda) + a_2 + \beta_2 + \lambda(\beta_1+\beta_3) > 0$
$v_t = v_{dt} - v_{st}$

which is homogeneous of degree one with respect to m_t, p_{ft}, p_{ht}, $\underset{t-1}{E}p_t$ and I_t. All these variables exert a positive impact on p_d except for p_f which has an ambiguous sign. Complete indexation removes the effect of the expected price level on p_d. The overall expected price level can be decomposed in a domestic $\lambda\underset{t-1}{E}p_{d,t}$, and a foreign component, $(1-\lambda)\underset{t-1}{E}p_{f,t}$. The domestic component is internally generated by the model; that is, take the conditional expectation of both sides of (2.11) and solve for $\underset{t-1}{E}p_{d,t}$

$$\underset{t-1}{E}p_{d,t} = \frac{1}{a_1(1-\lambda)+a_2+\beta_2+\lambda(\beta_1+\beta_3)} \times\{-a_0 + \beta_1\underset{t-1}{E}m_t + a_1\underset{t-1}{E}\tau_t + [a_1(1-\lambda)+(\lambda-1)(\beta_1+\beta_3)+\beta_2] \times\underset{t-1}{E}p_{f,t} + a_2\underset{t-1}{E}p_{h,t} + \beta_3\underset{t-1}{E}I_t\} \tag{2.12}$$

which again is homogeneous of degree one in nominal variables $\underset{t-1}{E}m_t$, $\underset{t-1}{E}p_{f,t}$, $\underset{t-1}{E}p_{h,t}$ and $\underset{t-1}{E}I_t$. Note that the sign of $\underset{t-1}{E}p_{f,t}$ remains potentially ambiguous and that $\underset{t-1}{E}p_{d,t}$ is independent of the indexation parameter b.

The unexpected level of domestic goods prices depends on the unexpected components of the underlying exogenous variables:

$$p_{d,t} - \underset{t-1}{E}\, p_{d,t} = \frac{1}{D}\{a_1(\tau_t - \underset{t-1}{E}\,\tau_t) + \beta_1(m_t - \underset{t-1}{E}\,m_t)$$
$$+ [a_1(1-\lambda)b + (\lambda-1)(\beta_1+\beta_3) + \beta_2]$$
$$\times (p_{f,t} - \underset{t-1}{E}\,p_{f,t}) + a_2(p_{h,t} - \underset{t-1}{E}\,p_{h,t})$$
$$+ \beta_3(I_t - \underset{t-1}{E}\,I_t) + v_t\} \qquad (2.13)$$

To obtain the 'observable' reduced form for p_d, where only exogenous and expectations of exogenous variables appear on the right hand side, we replace (2.12) in (2.11) to obtain:

$$p_{d,t} = -\frac{a_0}{D'} + \frac{\beta_1}{D}(m_t - Em_t) + \frac{\beta_1}{D'}Em_t + \frac{a_1}{D}(\tau_t - E\tau_t) + \frac{a_1}{D'}E\tau_t$$
$$+ \frac{\beta_3}{D}(I_t - EI_t) + \frac{\beta_3}{D'}EI_t + \frac{a_2}{D}(p_{ht} - Ep_{ht}) + \frac{a_2}{D'}Ep_{ht}$$
$$+ \frac{1}{D}[a_1(1-\lambda)b + \beta_2 + (\lambda-1)(\beta_1+\beta_3)](p_{ft} - Ep_{ft})$$
$$+ \frac{a_1(1-\lambda) + \beta_2 + (\lambda-1)(\beta_1+\beta_3)}{D'}Ep_{ft} + \frac{1}{D}(v_{st} - v_{dt}) \quad (2.14)$$

where $D' = a_1(1-\lambda) + a_2 + \beta_2 + \lambda(\beta_1+\beta_3)$
and the $t-1$ on the expectations variables has been dropped to simplify notation.

Finally, substituting (2.12) and (2.13) in (2.8) we derive the 'observable' reduced-form equation for output:

$$y_t = \frac{a_0\beta^*}{D'} + \frac{a^*\beta_2}{D}(m_t - Em_t) + \frac{[a_2 + a_1(1-\lambda)]\beta_1}{D'}Em_t$$
$$- \frac{a_1\beta^*}{D}(\tau_t - E\tau_t) - \frac{a_1\beta^*}{D'}E\tau_t + \frac{a^*\beta_3}{D}(I_t - EI_t)$$
$$+ \frac{[a_2 + a_1(1-\lambda)]\beta_3}{D'}EI_t - \frac{a_2\beta^*}{D}(p_{ht} - Ep_{ht}) - \frac{a_2\beta^*}{D'}Ep_{ht}$$
$$- \frac{\beta^*}{D}[a_1(1-\lambda)b - \frac{a^*}{\beta^*}(\beta_2 + (\lambda-1)(\beta_1+\beta_3)](p_{ft} - Ep_{ft})$$
$$+ \frac{1}{D'}[a_2\beta^* - (a_2 + a_1(1-\lambda)(\beta_1+\beta_3)]Ep_{ft}$$
$$+ \frac{1}{D}(\beta^* v_{dt} - \beta^* v_{st}) \qquad (2.15)$$

where $a^* = a_1(1-b)\lambda + a_1(1-\lambda) + a_2$ and $\beta^* = \beta_2 + \lambda(\beta_1 + \beta_3)$ are the slopes of the supply and demand curves for output with respect to p_d.

It may surprise that money has non-neutral effects: indeed both the unexpected and the expected component of m appear on the right hand side of (2.15). This non-neutrality, however, stems from the fact that the real sector takes the exchange rate as parametrically given. In the fuller model the exchange rate adjusts to changes in m and the impact of Em on p_d is compensated by the impact of Em on e. It remains, however, the possibility that these two effects may not be quantitatively the same; which, in turn, implies changes in real exchange rates and hence a non-zero impact on y. Needless to say, exchange rate arrangements such as the EMS facilitate the emergence of non-neutralities.

V SHORT- AND LONG-RUN EFFECTS

Devaluation

It is instructive at this point to trace in detail the short-and long-run impacts on p_d and y of a few shocks. With the short-run effects we mean the effects of unanticipated shocks. The long-run effects here relate to the fully anticipated effects. We begin with a devaluation, and concentrate on the short-run effects first. Figure 2.1 will aid the discussion. The *ss* and *dd* curves are respectively the supply and demand schedules (see

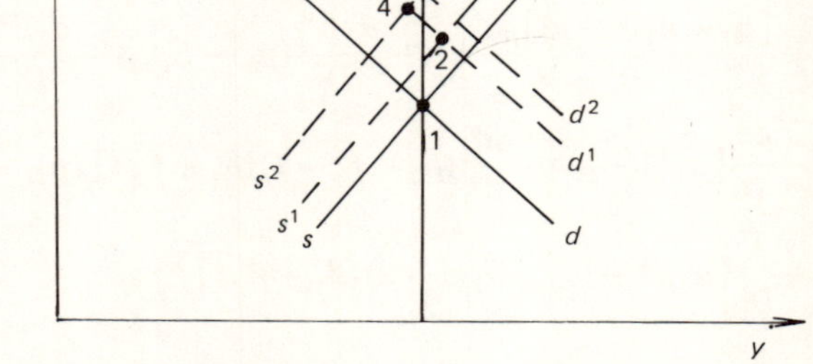

FIGURE 2.1 *Devaluation*

equations (2.8) and (2.10)). Their slopes are unambiguously positive and negative. The vertical line is the 'normal' output condition which depends on a_0, the tax wedge and the intermediate goods terms of trade $p_h - p_f = p_h^* - p_f^*$. An unexpected devaluation (i) lowers the terms of trade $p_d - p_f$, (ii) raises the unexpected foreign goods prices in domestic currency $p_f - \underset{t-1}{E}\, p_f$ and (iii) lowers real cash balances and the real value of other impulses. Shock (i) causes the supply curve to shift to the left; shock (ii) to the right; combined they exert a depressive impact on output supplied, this impact is stronger the higher the degree of indexation.[5] Shock (i) causes the demand curve to move to the right; shock (iii) to the left; combined they exert an ambiguous impact on output demand. Only if the substitution effect prevails over the real cash balance and other real impulse effects will the demand schedule shift to the right.[6] To make a devaluation work the shift in demand has not only to be positive, but also larger in absolute value than the shift in the supply schedule. This is the situation we have assumed in Figure 2.1 with the short-run equilibrium point 2. The likelihood that point 2 may be realised, as opposed to a short-run equilibrium point to the left of the normal output line, depends among other things on the degree of indexation. Stated differently, the positive output effect arises from the inflation surprise, with workers not having fully anticipated the effect of the devaluation when bargaining for their wages. As a result real wages decline.

The long-run (fully anticipated) effects of a devaluation are substantially different from the short-run (unanticipated) effects. Assume first that the *nominal* money stock m_t and the nominal budgetary impulse I_t remain fixed. In that case the devaluation has a permanent negative effect on output. This can be seen from the solution equation (2.15). Setting $p_{ht} = Ep_{ht}$ and $p_{ft} = Ep_{ft}$ yields for the output effect of the fully anticipated devaluation:

$$-\frac{1}{D'}(a_2 + a_1[1-\lambda][\beta_1 + \beta_3]) < 0$$

In terms of the graphical representation of Figure 2.1 the economy ends up in a point like 4, which is to the left of the initial position. The counterpart of this result for the domestic price level p_d is that it increases less than the rate of devaluation. (For a similar result see R. Marston (1983)).

This long-run result may seem surprising. It can easily be understood, however, when one takes into account that by assuming a fixed nominal money stock, the devaluation permanently reduces the real money stock. It does the same with the real fiscal impulse $I_t - P_t$. As a result, a permanent deflationary effect on aggregate demand is introduced.

The long-run neutrality proposition of the devaluation is reinstated if one assumes that the nominal quantities m_t and I_t increase in the same proportion as the devaluation. This can be shown using equation (2.15), where we allow Em_t and EI_t to change in the same proportion as the variables Ep_{ht} and Ep_{ft}. We find that the sum of the coefficients is zero. Graphically the economy moves to a point like 3 in Figure 2.1. The devaluation has no effect on output, and increases the domestic price level in the same proportion.

The conditions under which the nominal money stock and the fiscal variable change have not been spelled out here. They depend, among other things, on the effects of the devaluation on the balance of payments. In general one expects that the nominal money stock increases at least if the devaluation leads to a surplus in the balance of payments. We do not pursue this matter here.[7]

Another way to understand the long-run neutrality result of a devaluation is as follows. The condition for a permanent positive *supply* effect of a devaluation is that the latter improves the terms of trade (the term $p_d - p_f$ must increase in the supply of output equation (2.8) to increase the supply). However, to increase aggregate *demand* permanently (assuming the real money stock to be kept unchanged) the terms of trade $(p_d - p_f)$ should decline. Since in the new equilibrium point demand must equal supply it follows that this can only be achieved if the terms of trade return to their initial level, thereby bringing demand and supply of output also to their initial level. Any other outcome would lead to inequality between demand and supply. For example, if the devaluation should lead to a deterioration of the terms of trade ($p_d - p_f$ declines) this would lead to excess demand for the domestic good, because aggregate demand increases and aggregate supply declines. This would tend to push up the domestic price level until equilibrium between demand and supply is restored.

Changes in terms of trade

Consider now the case of an unexpected increase in the price of intermediate products relative to manufactured goods, that is, a rise in $p_h^* - p_f^*$, with a maintained exchange rate. The supply curve shift, measured along the y axis, is proportional to $-a_2$ (cf. point 2 in Figure

2.2); as the increase in p_h^* becomes incorporated into a permanent component the supply will further shift to the left (point 3). At this point the total impact on output is $-a_2\beta^*/(a_1[1-\lambda]+\beta^*+a_2)$ where β^* is the slope of the demand curve measured from the horizontal axis. All along we have kept the demand curve unchanged by assuming that the outflow of money prompted by a current account deficit is sterilised and that p_f^* is unaffected by p_h^*. The normal output line will move to the left in response to the rise in the intermediate goods terms of trade $p_h^*-p_f^*$ which is an external shock comparable with a tax levied by a foreign government. A further shift of the vertical line is to be expected when the capital stock adjusts to the new values of $p_h^*-p_f^*$.[8] In summary, the increase in p_h^* produces the familiar phenomenon of stagflation.

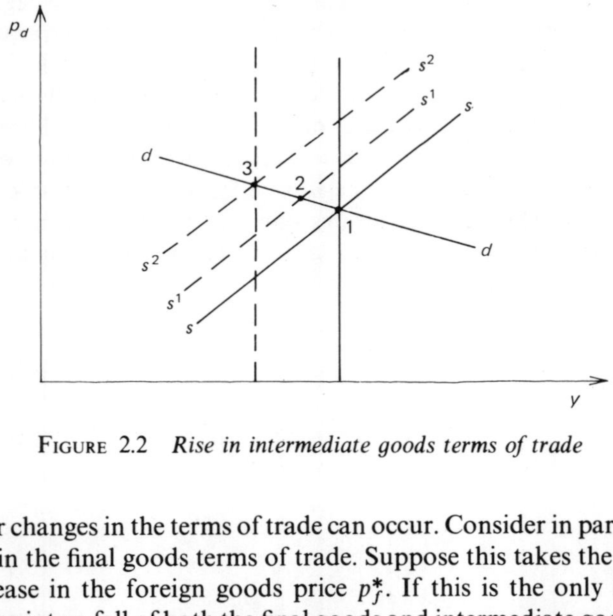

FIGURE 2.2 *Rise in intermediate goods terms of trade*

Other changes in the terms of trade can occur. Consider in particular a change in the final goods terms of trade. Suppose this takes the form of an increase in the foreign goods price p_f^*. If this is the only shock it translates into a fall of both the final goods and intermediate goods term of trade. The effect of such a fully anticipated shock can be found from equation (2.15). Output will change as given by the expression

$$\frac{1}{D'}[a_2\beta^*-(a_2+a_1(1-\lambda)(\beta_1+\beta_3))]$$

which can be positive or negative. This ambiguity in the long-run effect of an increase in the foreign goods price is the result of the ambiguity of this shock for the aggregate supply decision. (See equation 2.8). The increase in p_{ft} reduces the intermediate goods term of trade $(p_h - p_f)$. In other words the relative price of intermediate goods (oil) declines, thereby raising aggregate supply. At the same time the increase in p_f deteriorates the final goods term of trade $(p_d - p_f)$. This leads to a permanent decline in the supply of output.

The Tax Wedge

An increase in the tax wedge has macroeconomic effects which are qualitatively similar to a deterioration in the intermediate goods terms of trade. The supply curve shifts upwards. If the increased labour tax rate is used to finance transfers, the demand effects are likely to be negligible as the reduced after-tax income is compensated by increased transfers. The economy moves from point 1 to point 2 in Figure 2.3. Here also the 'normal' output level will decline permanently. Note that the size of this negative effect on output depends on the utility workers and firms attach to government services and transfers relative to the disutility of paying taxes. If the former is low the negative effect of the taxation on output will increase. This point illustrates how the degree of efficiency of the public sector has direct implications for the workings of the private sector.

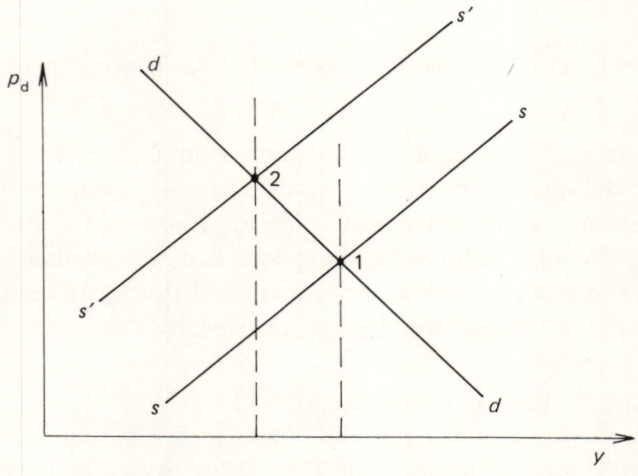

FIGURE 2.3 *Increase in the tax wedge*

The effect of an increase in the tax wedge on domestic output depends, *inter alia*, on the degree of price-takership of the domestic producers in the foreign markets. With an increasing degree of price-takership (a flatter demand curve) an increase in the tax wedge has larger negative effect on domestic output.

The following additional results are noteworthy. An increase in the tax wedge improves the terms of trade of the country. This is so because by raising taxation on labour domestic output is reduced. To the extent that the domestic producers are not complete price-takers this increases the price of the domestic good. This positive terms-of-trade effect is reduced with an increasing degree of price takership. The similarity of this result with results obtained in the literature on optimal tariffs is obvious. In general any measure that restricts domestic output improves the terms of trade, provided the country has some market power in the world markets. The latter is measured by the shape of the demand curve.

The implications of a higher tax wedge in the labour market are illustrated in Figures 2.4a and 2.4b where N^d and N^s represent the demand for labour–equation (2.5)–and the supply of labour–equation (2.6)–respectively. An increase in the tax rate on the nominal wage paid by employers (τ_1), generates a downward shift in the demand for labour, as shown in Figure 2.4a; an increase in the tax rate paid by workers (τ_2) generates an upward shift in the supply of labour, as shown in Figure 2.4b. In either case measured employment falls. To the extent that there exist 'underground' markets (that is, labour markets permitting tax

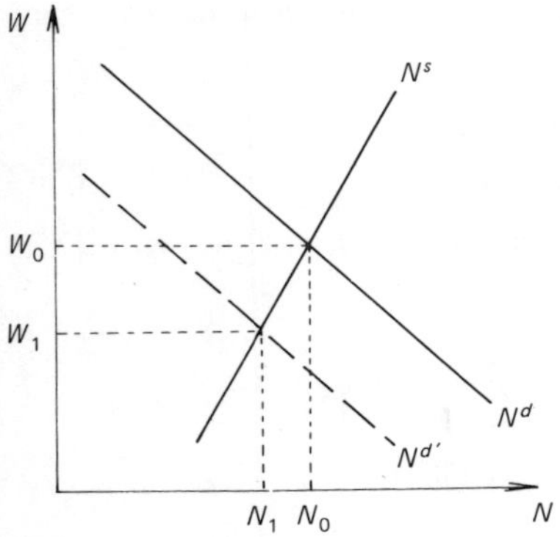

FIGURE 2.4a *Effect of increase in τ_1 in labour market*

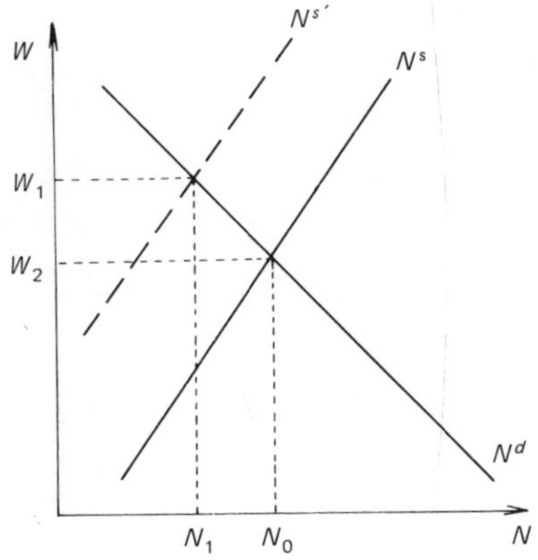

FIGURE 2.4b *Effect of increase in τ_2 in labour market*

evasion) part or all of the loss in employment in the 'above-ground' market will spill over to the 'underground' market. This substitution, however, is constrained by the expected cost borne by those engaging in tax-free activities and the technology of production. There are three activities which legitimately escape taxation: leisure, production of goods for own consumption (for example, gardening and house repairs) and barter of services.[9] In sum, measured employment is expected to decline as a result of higher taxes. The effect of the latter on wages received by workers is ambiguous. Taxes paid by employers tend to lower W, taxes paid by workers tend to raise W. This result has intuitive appeal. Firms seek to minimise labour costs, i.e. $W(1+t_w^1)N$. An increase in t_w^1 has the same significance as an equivalent rise in W. Thus, other things the same, the wage rate W offered to workers declines. On the other hand, unless government-provided services are valued as much as private consumption, workers will react to a rise in taxes on their wages by raising W.

VI THE NON-TRADED SECTOR

Even in economies as open as the ones we are considering the weight of p_d and p_f in the overall price level is less than 50 percent. Food and services – our measure of non-traded goods – form too big a sector to be ignored without serious consequences in the empirical work.

Denoting with p_0 the log of the 'non-traded' goods price level we redefine the overall price level as:

$$p = \lambda_1 p_d + \lambda_2 p_f + \lambda_3 p_0 \tag{2.7'}$$

Keeping p_0 exogenous, the supply of output now responds to a new relative price – the internal terms of trade, $p_0 - p_d$:

$$\begin{aligned} y_t = a_0 - a_1\tau_t + a_1(1-b)[p_t - Ep_t] + (a_1\lambda_2 + a_2)(p_d - p_f) \\ - a_2(p_h^* - p_f^*) - a_1\lambda_3(p_0 - p_d) + v_s \end{aligned} \tag{2.8'}$$

Equation (2.8′) replaces (2.8). The reduced-form for p_d with (2.7′) becomes:

$$\begin{aligned} p_{d,t} = \frac{1}{D}\{ -a_0 + a_1\tau_t + \beta_1 m_t + [a_1\lambda_2 b - \lambda_2(\beta_1+\beta_3) + \beta_2] \\ \times p_{f,t} + a_2 p_{h,t} + a_1(1-b) \underset{t-1}{E}\, p_t + \beta_3 I_t \\ + \lambda_3[a_1 b - (\beta_1+\beta_3)] p_{0,t} + v_t \} \end{aligned} \tag{2.9'}$$

which replaces (2.11). The unit homogeneity properties of p_d with respect to all nominal magnitudes are maintained. An increase in the price of 'non-traded' goods relative to traded goods lowers manufacturing output which is our proxy of the rate of traded good production. A rise in p_0 has an ambiguous effect on p_d under an indexation regime, whereas it is negative when $b = 0$.

VII SUMMARY

This chapter has developed a model of the real sector of a small open economy. Domestically-produced output, domestic prices and the overall price level are explained in terms of foreign prices, money, the fiscal impulse, exports and the exchange rate. The model incorporates rational expectations and derives a modified Lucas-type supply of output which depends not only on the unexpected rate of change of the overall price level, but also on the final goods, intermediate goods and internal terms of trade, and on the level of taxation of labour income.

NOTES

1. The oil-producing United Kingdom and the natural-gas producing Netherlands are two exceptions.
2. Argy (1978), in his comment to the papers by Fratianni (1978), Fourçans (1978) and Korteweg (1978) who adopt the standard Lucas-supply function, argues the same point. For another recent attempt at extending the Lucas-supply function to open economies see Marston (1983).
3. On this point we have been particularly influenced by the papers of Bruno and Sachs (1979), Leiderman (1981) and Darby (1981).
4. See for example the studies cited in note 2. Argy and Spitäller (1980) derive and estimate such an equation, see their equation (10).
5. The shift of the ss curve measured along the y axis is equal to $-ba_1(1-\lambda) -a_2$.
6. I.e. if $\beta_2 + (\lambda - 1)(\beta_1 + \beta_3) > 0$, shift measured along the y axis.
7. Since substitutability among goods rises over time p_d approaches p_f in the long run.
8. Darby (1981) discusses the implications of an oil-price increase on output after the stock of capital has fully adjusted.
9. The barter of services does not escape taxation in all countries. Belgium, for example, enforces a law that makes mutually-provided services subject to the full range of taxes.

3 Supply of Output and Inflation in EC Countries

I INTRODUCTION

The theory of Chapter 2 explains domestically-produced output, domestic prices and the overall price level in terms of foreign prices, money, the exchange rate and other impulses. The central feature of the theory is the Lucas supply of output extended to an open economy which incorporates, in addition to inflation-rate misperceptions, terms-of-trade effects, the 'tax wedge' and wage indexation.

European countries have been subjected to two types of shocks during the 1970s. The first were the oil-price increases of 1973–4 and 1979–80 that dramatically worsened the terms of trade of most European countries. The second shock, introduced more gradually, resulted from large increases in taxation of labour income (income taxes and social security contributions) during the same period.

Table 3.1 measures the size of these two shocks in relation to *GDP*. The first column gives the increase of income taxes and social security contribution as a percentage of *GDP* for the industrialised countries, and the second column the increased value of oil imports also expressed as a percentage of *GDP*. The latter figure is used as a broad indication of the OPEC-imposed 'oil tax'. The table illustrates that both supply shocks have been substantial, particularly so for the small European oil importers where during 1970–80, taxation on labour increased by 5.8 percentage points, in contrast with an increase in the oil tax by 3.8 percentage points.

Most theoretical and empirical research has concentrated on the macroeconomic effects of the oil-price shocks.[1] Relatively little has been done to measure the macroeconomic implications of the second supply shock, a gap we intend to fill.

The chapter is organised as follows. Section II presents the stylised facts germane to our hypothesis. Section III deals with estimation of a supply of output equation that includes, relative prices but maintains nominal wages as parametrically given, for instance, equation (2.9).

TABLE 3.1 *Increase in taxation of labour and oil as a percentage of GDP from 1970 to 1980*

	Labour	*Oil*
European oil importers:		
Austria	6.3	2.7
Belgium	7.8	5.5
Denmark	2.9	3.0
Finland	1.9	5.7
France		2.8
Germany	5.1	3.0
Ireland	9.2	5.6
Italy	4.6	3.3
Netherlands	5.1	4.1
Sweden	8.3	4.4
Switzerland	7.0	2.2
Average	5.8	3.8
Standard deviation	2.3	1.3
Other industrialised countries:		
Canada	1.2	1.7
Japan	5.4	4.2
UK	−0.2	0.8
US	3.0	2.7
Average (all countries)	4.6	3.4

NOTE The first column (labour) represents the increase in income tax and social security contribution as a percentage of *GDP*; the second column represents the increased value of oil imports as a percentage of *GDP*. For countries producing domestic oil (Canada, UK, US) the increased value of oil imports is a bad proxy for the increased OPEC-induced oil tax.

SOURCE IMF, *International Financial Statistics*, and OECD (1981b, p. 14).

In Section IV we introduce the misperception term. Inflation expectations will be measured using all information available up to the time the researcher intends to make his 'rational' forecasts for the period in question. The Lucas open-economy supply model, that is, equation (2.8) is tested at first employing yearly data from 1957 to 1980. In Section V we use quarterly data for the period 1971(I)–1980(IV) to provide additional evidential material bearing on the model's implications. The quarterly estimation differs from the annual estimation in that the expected values of the exogenous variables are generated through vector-autoregressive models rather than ARMA models. Conclusions are drawn in Section VI.

II DESCRIPTION OF DATA

To test the main implications of this theory we employ alternatively annual data for the period 1957–80 and quarterly data for the period 1971(I)–1980(IV) from six European countries: Belgium (B), France (F), Germany (G), Italy (I), the Netherlands (N) and the United Kingdom (UK). Data Appendix A.7 provides a complete description of data, sources and sample periods. In the remainder of the section we describe the salient features of the yearly data. For a visual inspection, the reader can refer to Figure 3.1 for the evolution of international prices and Figures 3.2–3.4 for the evolution of three country-specific data.

Not knowing the outcome of our findings, we employed three

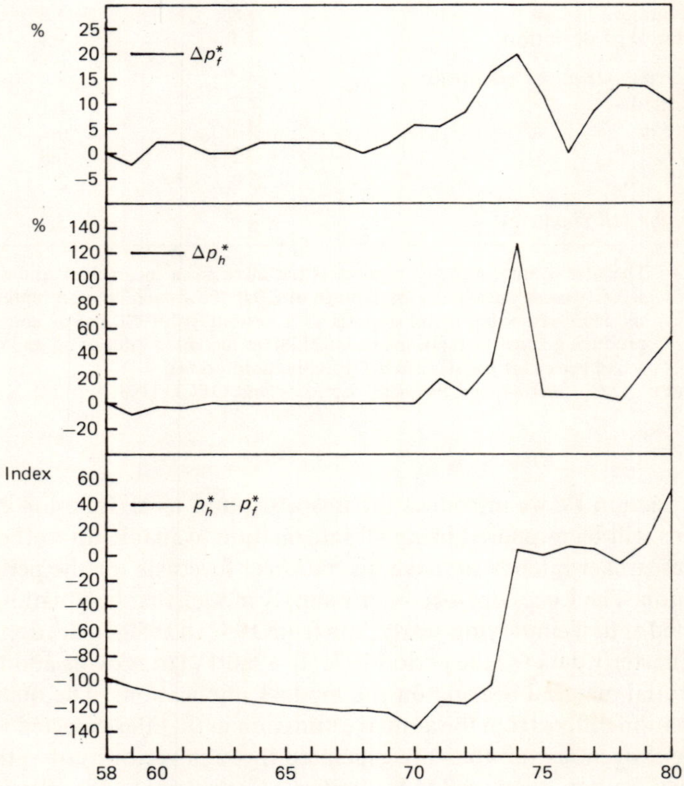

FIGURE 3.1 *International prices*

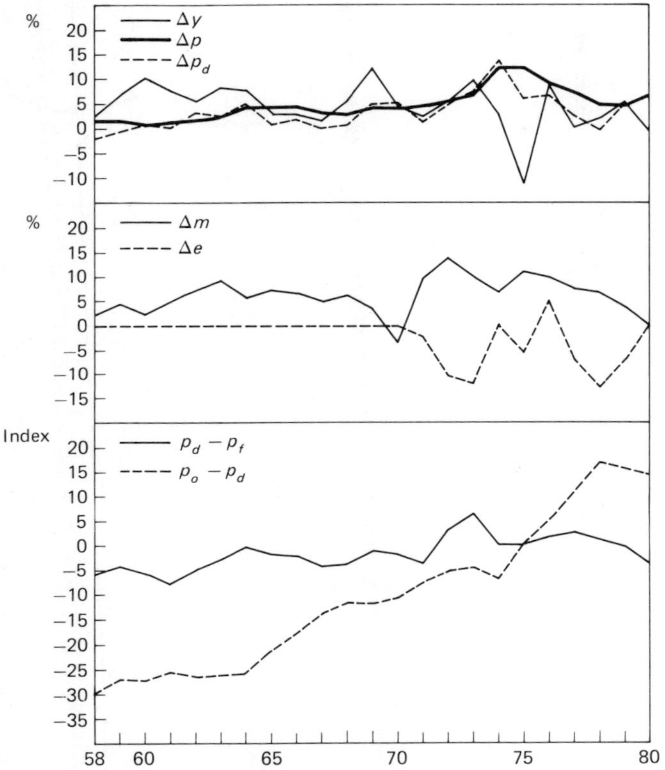

FIGURE 3.2 *Evolution of main variables for Belgium*, 1958–80

different definitions of output.[2] After preliminary tests we chose an index of manufacturing production. The growth rate of this series, which is very variable, displays a downward trend for the 1970s and a sharp drop in 1975. These features are common to the six countries, although to different degrees. Similarly, prices of domestic final goods were approximated by three different series.[3] In the end, because of data limitations, we concentrated on the wholesale price index for France, Italy, the Netherlands, the UK, and on domestic goods prices published by the United Nations for Belgium and Germany. However, we carried some tests using Germany for which the three indexes are available, and found little sensitivity of the results to the type of index chosen. Δp_d has a distinctive upward trend in the 1970s and peaks in 1974 and again in 1980.[4] The rate of change in the overall price level, the consumer price

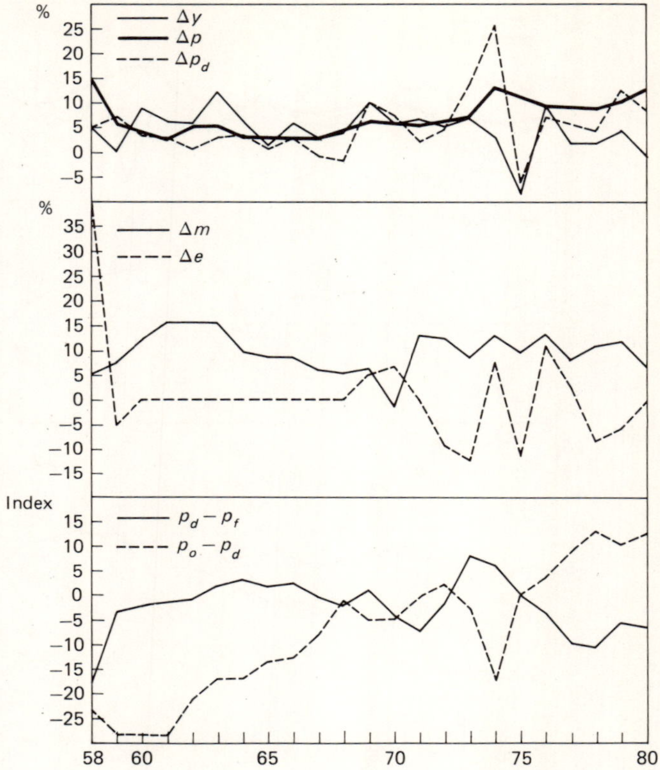

FIGURE 3.3 *Evolution of main variables for France*, 1958–80

index, also peaks in 1974 and 1980 and displays the same trend of Δp_d, although its variance is substantially smaller. The general impression one gets from a 'visual' study of Δy, Δp_d and Δp is that the six countries under consideration have shared a similar cycle, an observation which is consistent with a common shock affecting these economies in roughly the same manner. We shall have more to say on this in Chapter 9.

Moving from endogenous to exogenous variables, we note that the price of foreign goods measured in dollars (Δp_f^*) displays a movement resembling Δp_d with peaks occurring in 1974 and in 1980; Δp_f^* has pronounced autoregressive characteristics. Petroleum prices in dollars (p_h^*) decline from 1957 to 1970, then rise dramatically in 1974, and less so, in 1980. The intermediate goods terms of trade, $p_h^* - p_f^*$, are dominated by the behavior of p_h^*. The exchange rate, the domestic price of the dollar,

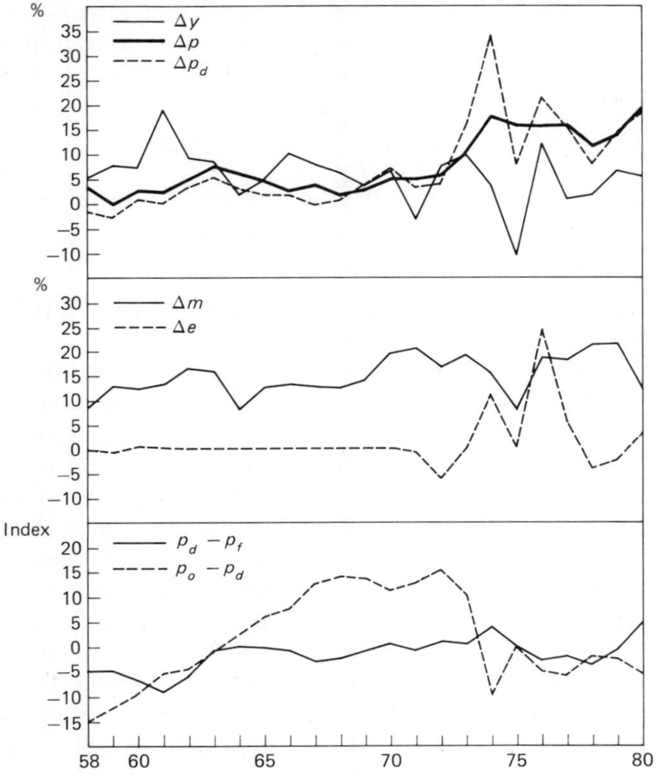

FIGURE 3.4 *Evolution of main variables for Italy*, 1958–80

has the distinctive features of a random walk: the past history of Δe seems to yield no information concerning its future course. The final goods terms of trade, $p_d - p_f$, appear volatile.

Germany, Belgium and the Netherlands exhibit very similar variations in their terms of trade: strong peaks in 1964, 1973–4 and 1977–8, and sharp drops in 1960–1, 1968, 1975 and 1980. France and Italy on the other hand, show a different pattern: peaks in 1964 and 1973–4, and troughs in 1968 and 1977–8. The UK terms of trade exhibit a totally different pattern: an upward trend from 1957 to 1970 with a sharp rise in 1968, fluctuating between 1970 and 1974, sharply increasing during the period 1975–7 and decreasing thereafter.

The money stock is defined exclusive of time deposits and is measured as yearly averages; its growth rate is highly volatile. Our variable I, impulses other than money, consists of the fiscal impulse, ΔF, and the growth rate of exports at current prices, Δxc. The fiscal impulse was calculated so as to eliminate the induced part due to changes in income, that is:

$$\Delta F = \{\Delta G - [\Delta T - \left(\frac{T}{GDP}\right)_{-1} \Delta GDP]\}/GDP_{-1}$$

GDP = Gross Domestic Product at current prices
G = Nominal government expenditures
T = Nominal tax revenues

for which we could not detect any systematic part. Therefore this variable was dropped in the study.

There is no single aggregative quantitative counterpart of what we have called the tax wedge. In an initial attempt we approximate τ with the ratio of total transfer payments of general government to nominal GDP. Clearly not all transfer payments reduce incentives to work and output. Some transfers are received by the same individuals who bear the cost of the transfers: they lower, albeit inefficiently, the effective tax rate. Only those transfers who take from A and give to B can be argued to lower work incentives and reduce overall efficiency. Some preliminary results are reviewed below and some difficulties are pointed out.[5] The transfer payment ratio has been rising at unprecedented rates during our sample period. It goes from 0.09 in 1957 to 0.22 in 1979 for Belgium; 0.14 to 0.23 for France; 0.09 to 0.17 for Italy; 0.09 to 0.29 for the Netherlands; 0.14 to 0.17 for Germany and 0.06 to 0.13 for the United Kingdom. With the exception of Germany this ratio cannot be distinguished from a simple time trend in a statistical sense. For France and Italy the tax wedge was measured alternatively by the ratio

$$\log \frac{1 + \text{social security contributions rate paid by workers}}{1 + \text{social security contributions rate paid by employers}}$$

which is an approximation of $\tau_2 - \tau_1$.

Our variable I, impulses other than money, consists of ΔF – which we have already discussed – and Δxc, the growth rate of exports at current prices. The movement in Δxc did not reveal any systematic component.[6]

III SUPPLY OF OUTPUT WITH FIXED NOMINAL WAGES

Table 3.2 shows the estimates obtained by 2SLS applied to (2.9) suitably modified to incorporate p_0. A time trend captures the growth of the fixed

TABLE 3.2 *Fixed wage supply of output* (2 *SLS*). *Annual data*, 1957–80

Country	C	t	$\hat{p}-\bar{w}$	$\hat{p}_d-p_f$	p_h-p_f	$p_o-\hat{p}_d$	*SE*	*DW*
Belgium	−196.8	0.102	0.517	1.237	−0.048	−1.474	0.029	1.87
	(6.62)	(6.78)	(1.77)	(2.71)	(1.80)	(6.67)		
France	−174.6	0.090	0.610	0.167	−0.096	−0.452	0.043	1.23
	(5.03)	(5.16)	(1.23)	(0.84)	(1.71)	(1.46)		
Netherlands	−21.5	0.013	−0.874	−0.824	−0.086	0.698	0.031	2.36
	(1.20)	(1.47)	(5.38)	(2.71)	(4.30)	(2.29)		
Italy	−276.9	0.142	1.461	0.598	−0.254	−0.923	0.045	1.27
	(5.17)	(5.26)	(3.72)	(1.22)	(1.95)	(1.36)		
Germany	10.6	−0.003	−1.026	−0.147	−0.027	0.265	0.034	1.86
	(0.31)	(0.17)	(4.38)	(0.37)	(0.37)	(0.51)		
United Kingdom	−42.1	0.023	−0.474	0.051	−0.159	−0.309	0.043	1.09
	(2.34)	(2.60)	(1.65)	(0.44)	(2.54)	(0.87)		

NOTES
1. All variables are in natural logarithms, except t which is $t = 1957, \ldots, 1980$ and C is the constant term.
2. Numbers in parenthesis under each coefficient are Student t-values.
3. Statistical indicators are:
   $\bar{R}^2$: Coefficient of determination adjusted for degrees of freedom when relevant
   SE: Standard error of equation
   DW: Durbin-Watson statistic.
4. Variables with a ^ indicate that they are fitted values from a first-stage regression equation.

input; the tax wedge proxy was dropped. The results indicate that on the whole the terms of trade matter and in the direction suggested by theory. There are exceptions such as the sign of the coefficient of $p_d - p_f$ and $p_0 - p_d$ for the Netherlands and Germany. Altogether different is the outcome for $p - \bar{w}$. With the exception of Italy and less significantly for Belgium, the fixed-money wage hypothesis is rejected. For Germany and the Netherlands $p - \bar{w}$ has even a significantly negative sign. We use the structure of (2.9) as a benchmark for comparing the findings of the rational expectations hypothesis inclusive of the tax wedge.

IV THE RATIONAL EXPECTATIONS HYPOTHESIS

Our estimation procedure is first to generate the expected value of p_d and p from the underlying variables of the model. This process permits us to transform the unobserved endogenous Ep_d and Ep in 'observable' variables $\widehat{Ep_d}$, $\widehat{Ep}$. The rational expectations estimates $\widehat{Ep_d}$ and $\widehat{Ep}$ and the unexpected underlying exogenous variables will be employed to generate $\hat{p}_d$ and $\hat{p}$, that is, the estimates of p_d and p. Finally, using $E\hat{p}_d$, $E\hat{p}$, $\hat{p}_d$ and $\hat{p}$ we estimate the output equation (2.8) which will yield classical two-stage estimates of the parameters. Thus, estimation of the supply of output equation is based on limited information methods for structural equations estimation. Only in the estimation of the price equations do we use the overall structure of the model and the rational expectations hypothesis. Since we do not impose all resulting constraints in the actual estimation we test rational expectations only in the weak sense: the estimates of the coefficients are consistent with rational expectations but we do not provide positive evidence for their existence. On this point see Wallis (1980, pp. 66–69) and Wickens (1982, p. 59).[7]

Rational expectations and the inflation rate

Equation (2.12) provides the basis for estimating the expected domestic price level. In first differences it can be rewritten as:

$$E\Delta p_d = f(E\Delta Z) \tag{3.1}$$

where $E\Delta Z$ is a vector consisting of $E\Delta m$, $E\Delta\tau$, $E\Delta p_f$, $E\Delta p_h$, $E\Delta p_0$ and $E\Delta I$. $E\Delta Z$ is quantified by the systematic component of univariate time series (ARIMA) models for annual data and vector autoregressive (VAR) models for quarterly data. The difference in technique was dictated by the fact that there were too few observations in the annual data to justify the employment of VAR. The non-white noise part of the models yields an estimate $\widehat{E\Delta Z}$.

The expected rate of domestic price inflation is obtained from the regression:

$$\Delta p_d = \hat{A}_0 + \hat{A}_1 \widehat{E\Delta Z} + \widehat{\text{error}}\ (u_t) \tag{3.2}$$

where $\widehat{E\Delta p_d} = \Delta p_d - \widehat{\text{error}}$

A similar procedure holds for $E\Delta p$. Recalling that:

$$E\Delta p = \lambda_1 E\Delta p_d + \lambda_2 E\Delta p_f + \lambda_3 E\Delta p_0 \tag{3.3}$$

and using (3.1) we derive:

$$E\Delta p = \lambda_1 f(E\Delta Z) + \lambda_2 E\Delta p_f + \lambda_3 E\Delta p_0$$

Since $E\Delta p_f$ and $E\Delta p_0$ are included in the vector $E\Delta Z$, we obtain

$$E\Delta p = g(E\Delta Z) \tag{3.4}$$

where g depends on f, λ_1, λ_2 and λ_3.

Using the ARIMA or VAR models for Z we can transform the non-observable form (3.4) into a testable equation of the type (3.2):

$$\Delta p = \hat{B}_0 + \hat{B}_1 \widehat{E\Delta Z} + \widehat{\text{error}}\ (u_t) \tag{3.5}$$

We refer the reader to the appendix to this chapter for estimates of $E\Delta Z$. Here a few general comments suffice. Using annual data, $E\Delta m$ is best measured by an AR(1) process for four countries; the hypothesis of Δm being white noise for Germany and the Netherlands could not be rejected. Δe, Δp_h^* and Δxc are also white noise. Δp_f^* follows an AR(3) scheme; Δp_0 and AR(1). Finally, no systematic component could be detected in the fiscal impulse.[8] These findings restrict the vector $E\Delta Z$ to $E\Delta m$, $E\Delta p_f^*$ an $E\Delta p_0$. The estimates of (3.2) and (3.5) are reported in Table 3.3. The results show that the expected part of the inflation rate is relatively small and money seldom turns out to be significant.[9] The expected foreign price, on the other hand, always has a positive effect, although not always significant. On the whole estimates for $E\Delta p$ are better than those for $E\Delta p_d$, where 'better' is judged on standard statistical criteria. This is mainly due to Δp_0 which is a component of Δp. A favourable outcome for the hypothesis is that homogeneity conditions are satisfied in many instances.

The estimates for $E\Delta p_d$ and $E\Delta p$ of Table 3.3 are employed to explain the current rate of inflation. The procedure followed is that implied by (2.13): we regress $\Delta p_d - E\Delta p_d$ and $\Delta p - E\Delta p$ on the unexpected value of

TABLE 3.3 *Rational expectations equations for expected inflation rates. Annual data, 1959–80*

Country	*Dependent variable*	C	$\widehat{E\Delta m}$	$\widehat{E\Delta p_f^*}$	$\widehat{E\Delta p_o}$	$\bar{R}^2$	*SE*	*DW*
Belgium	Δp_d	−0.042	1.048	0.269	−0.073	0.28	0.028	1.55
		(1.51)	(2.08)	(1.80)	(0.24)			
	Δp	−0.018	0.333	0.226	0.582	0.71	0.016	1.54
		(1.08)	(1.13)	(2.59)	(3.31)			
France	Δp_d	0.014	−0.343	0.353	0.756	−0.004	0.064	2.43
		(0.10)	(0.31)	(1.18)	(0.61)			
	Δp	−0.052	0.264	0.364	1.025	0.61	0.020	2.00
		(1.25)	(0.78)	(3.93)	(2.66)			
Netherlands	Δp_d	−0.004	−0.200	0.124	0.954	0.41	0.023	1.81
		(0.09)	(0.31)	(1.03)	(2.65)			
	Δp	−0.005	0.065	0.073	0.894	0.47	0.019	2.20
		(0.13)	(0.12)	(0.74)	(3.02)			
Italy	Δp_d	−0.199	1.186	0.467	0.855	0.47	0.064	2.33
		(1.13)	(0.99)	(1.21)	(2.19)			
	Δp	−0.187	1.211	0.170	0.892	0.83	0.024	2.05
		(2.80)	(2.66)	(1.16)	(6.00)			
Germany	Δp_d	0.059	−1.110	0.236	1.245	0.23	0.034	1.62
		(0.44)	(0.73)	(1.36)	(1.41)			
	Δp	0.073	−0.858	0.123	0.728	0.53	0.011	1.57
		(1.59)	(1.64)	(2.06)	(2.39)			
United Kingdom	Δp_d	−0.065	0.144	0.813	0.960	0.57	0.042	2.51
		(1.65)	(0.37)	(3.76)	(1.83)			
	Δp	−0.035	0.281	0.680	0.613	0.53	0.39	2.24
		(0.96)	(0.76)	(3.33)	(1.23)			

NOTE Cf. notes to Table 3.2.

the model's determinants, that is, $\Delta Z - E\Delta Z$. In other words:

$$u_t = h(\Delta Z - E\Delta Z) + \varepsilon_t, \quad \varepsilon_t = \text{error term} \tag{3.6}$$

The estimates of these regressions are presented in Table 3.4. All unanticipated variables, except for money and to a lesser extent exports, affect the unanticipated rates of inflation. The model explains a large fraction of the latter variable. In sum, our evidence is consistent with the notion that the larger portion of the rate of inflation is unanticipated which can be traced back to unanticipated changes in foreign prices, exports and non-traded goods prices. Unanticipated money has a tenuous impact on the unanticipated rate of inflation. This does not rule out that unexpected money growth influences Δp_d and Δp through Δp_0. This point will be taken up again when discussing quarterly data.

Estimates for Output

Having estimates for $\Delta p - E\Delta p$ and p_d we are now in a position to fit the data to equation (2.8) so as to incorporate simultaneously the formation of rational expectations and the endogeneity of p_d. The tax wedge variable τ, ignored for the moment, is discussed below. The estimates using equation (2.8) in level are shown in Table 3.5.[10] We have also estimated output equations in growth rates but since their results were generally inferior to their level counterparts they are not reported here. From Table 3.5 we can see that the coefficient of the rate of inflation comes out highly significantly for France and Italy, but marginally significantly for Germany and the Netherlands. It is not statistically different from zero for Belgium a country with virtually complete indexation and the United Kingdom. Italy and the United Kingdom apart, both the final goods and intermediate goods terms of trade exert the impact predicted by theory.

The evidence concerning the internal terms of trade is more mixed: strong and conforming to theory for Belgium, opposed to what theory predicts for the Netherlands and Italy, and inconclusive for France, Germany and the United Kingdom.

Despite the weakness of specific empirical results, we assess that for four countries the overall evidence is favourable towards an hypothesis that stresses the role of relative prices, including the unexpected rate of inflation, in explaining the cycle of manufacturing output. It follows that the traditional Lucas-supply equation does not do as well as a model that, in addition to misperception of the price level, includes internal and

TABLE 3.4 *Unexpected inflation rates equations. Annual data, 1959–80.*

Country	*Dependent variable*	*C*	$\Delta m - \widehat{E\Delta m}$	$\Delta p_f^* + \Delta e - \widehat{E\Delta p_f^*}$	$\Delta p_o - \widehat{E\Delta p_o}$	Δxc	$\bar{R}^2$	*SE*	*DW*
Belgium	$\Delta p_d - \widehat{E\Delta p_d}$	−0.002	0.092	0.330	0.691	0.088	0.69	0.014	1.11
		(0.29)	(0.90)	(3.63)	(3.52)	(1.53)			
	$\Delta p - \widehat{E\Delta p}$	0.008	0.095	0.199	0.637	−0.035	0.78	0.007	1.37
		(2.18)	(1.92)	(4.51)	(6.70)	(1.28)			
France	$\Delta p_d - \widehat{E\Delta p_d}$	−0.061	0.250	0.364	0.144	0.452	0.64	0.035	1.44
		(3.16)	(1.21)	(2.44)	(0.49)	(3.75)			
	$\Delta p - \widehat{E\Delta p}$	−0.005	−0.002	0.103	0.360	0.043	0.49	0.013	1.77
		(0.73)	(0.03)	(1.87)	(3.31)	(0.97)			
Netherlands	$\Delta p_d - \widehat{E\Delta p_d}$	−0.001	−0.022	0.112	0.396	0.038	0.10	0.021	1.91
		(0.09)	(0.16)	(0.91)	(1.32)	(0.44)			
	$\Delta p - \widehat{E\Delta p}$	0.001	0.011	0.018	0.946	−0.005	0.96	0.003	2.39
		(0.57)	(0.53)	(0.91)	(19.63)	(0.39)			
Italy	$\Delta p_d - \widehat{E\Delta p_d}$	−0.013	0.073	0.722	0.466	0.012	0.62	0.036	1.38
		(0.52)	(0.32)	(3.42)	(1.42)	(0.08)			
	$\Delta p - \widehat{E\Delta p}$	0.011	−0.097	0.275	0.500	−0.094	0.69	0.013	1.99
		(1.35)	(1.24)	(3.79)	(4.44)	(1.77)			
Germany	$\Delta p_d - \widehat{E\Delta p_d}$	−0.026	0.109	0.148	1.059	0.308	0.42	0.024	1.47
		(1.88)	(0.51)	(1.10)	(2.40)	(2.92)			
	$\Delta p - \widehat{E\Delta p}$	−0.0006	0.001	0.043	0.773	0.021	0.72	0.005	1.62
		(0.18)	(0.03)	(1.34)	(7.40)	(0.85)			
United Kingdom	$\Delta p_d - \widehat{E\Delta p_d}$	−0.016	−0.121	0.069	0.270	0.136	0.36	0.034	2.79
		(1.16)	(0.68)	(0.74)	(2.35)	(1.40)			
	$\Delta p - \widehat{E\Delta p}$	−0.007	−0.125	0.067	0.390	0.066	0.51	0.025	2.54
		(0.74)	(0.95)	(0.97)	(4.35)	(0.92)			

NOTE See notes to Table 3.2.

Table 3.5 *Supply of output equations in level (2 SLS and rational expectations). Annual data, 1959–80.*

Country	C	t	$\widehat{\Delta p - E\Delta p}$	$\hat{p}_d - p_f$	$p_h - p_f$	$p_o - \hat{p}_d$	$\bar{R}^2$	*SE*	*DW*
Belgium	−147.09	0.076	0.028	0.096	−0.088	−1.207	0.99	0.031	1.80
	(8.15)	(8.40)	(0.03)	(0.38)	(4.27)	(2.92)			
France	−114.81	0.060	1.346	0.579	−0.130	−0.180	0.99	0.031	1.75
	(10.10)	(10.51)	(2.01)	(2.45)	(4.84)	(0.83)			
Netherlands	−62.58	0.034	0.765	0.141	−0.116	1.029	0.98	0.043	1.67
	(2.53)	(2.72)	(1.36)	(0.39)	(3.76)	(2.34)			
Italy	−95.75	0.050	1.200	−0.321	0.033	0.834	0.98	0.048	1.36
	(7.80)	(8.20)	(2.05)	(0.80)	(0.42)	(2.70)			
Germany	−74.29	0.039	1.688	0.305	−0.104	0.480	0.97	0.043	1.70
	(3.32)	(4.53)	(1.66)	(1.12)	(1.92)	(1.02)			
United Kingdom	−48.24	0.026	−0.445	−0.131	−0.067	0.249	0.89	0.046	1.10
	(4.31)	(4.74)	(0.91)	(1.47)	(1.47)	(1.11)			

Note See notes to Table 3.2.

external relative prices as well as wage indexation. The misperception term will be shown to be even less important with quarterly data than yearly data. The results of Table 3.5 bear on this point: two out of three relative prices are highly significant for Belgium, France and the Netherlands, whereas one out of three is significant for Germany. The evidence for Italy, on the other hand, is more consistent with a fixed-wage hypothesis than with the modified Lucas-supply curve. The evidence for the United Kingdom is the least conclusive: one relative price is correctly signed, another is not, but both have too high a standard error to draw solid inference.

The Tax Wedge

So far our discussion has omitted any references to the tax wedge τ. When τ, measured by the ratio of transfer payments to gross domestic product, was introduced in equation (2.8) it was found to be negative – but too weak statistically – for four countries and strongly positive for Germany. The standard errors of the regressions did not fall except for Germany, whose structure of coefficients was adversely affected by the introduction of τ. The way we measure τ may make it highly co-linear with other variables and subject to simultaneity bias. To remedy these potential weaknesses we proceeded in an alternative manner for two countries, France and Italy, for which data are available. Using data from the national income accounts we obtained a series of total gross wages paid by the manufacturing part of the industrial sector (Italy) or by the entire industrial sector (France). In the notation of Chapter 2 this series can be labelled $NW(1+t_w^1)$. Independent series were obtained for 'labour' tax rates paid by employers and social security contributions rates paid by workers. Thus we were able to quantify the two tax parameters, τ_1, and τ_2, that influence respectively the demand and supply of labour (cf. Figures 2.4a and 2.4b and the discussion thereof).[11] For convenience we rewrite the labour market in the functional form (the sign above the variables indicates the direction of the influence):

Demand for labour

$$N = N^d \left(\overset{-}{\frac{W_n}{P}(1+t_w^1)}, \overset{+}{Y} \right) \tag{3.7}$$

Supply of labour

$$N = N^s(\overset{+}{W_n/EP}, \overset{-}{(1+t_w^2)} \tag{3.8}$$

where W_n is the productivity-adjusted wage rate, from which we can express changes in equilibrium nominal wage rates as being positively related to the actual and expected inflation rate, changes in output, changes in t_w^2 and negatively to changes in t_w^1. Imposing equality between Δp and ΔEp, we can test for the effects of the tax wedge on the labour market through the following regression:

$$\begin{aligned}\Delta w_n &= \Delta w - \Delta p - \Delta\log \text{(labour productivity)}\\ &= \alpha + \beta\ \Delta\log \text{Unemployment}_{-1} + \gamma\Delta y + \delta[\Delta\tau_2 - \Delta\tau_1]\\ &\quad + \text{error term}\end{aligned} \tag{3.9}$$

where τ_1 and τ_2 are defined in Table 2.1.

Equation (3.9) states that changes in real wages adjusted for productivity (Δw_n), not only depend on cyclical variables such as unemployment ($\beta < 0$) and output ($\gamma > 0$), but also on changes in the tax variables $\Delta\tau_2 - \Delta\tau_1$. The parameter δ has a precise interpretation, for the formulation (3.9) forces the effect on nominal wages of tax changes working through the supply side (Figure 2.4b) to be quantitatively the same as the tax effect working through the demand side (Figure 2.4a). It follows that δ is equal to the ratio of the elasticity of the supply of labour with respect to $(1 + t_w^2)$ to the difference of the logarithmic slopes of N^s and N^d in relation to the wage rate.[12] The fraction is constrained to be $0 < \delta < 1$. The estimates of (3.9) are shown in Table 3.6. The French regression performs better than the Italian regression both in terms of explanatory power and significance of the coefficients. The French $\hat{\delta}$ is statistically in the neighbourhood of unity; the Italian $\hat{\delta}$ is only marginally significant and does not justify definite inferences. Both, however, suggest that there is something to the argument that a tax wedge affects negatively measured employment.

TABLE 3.6 *The effect of the tax wedge for Italy and France (See equation 3.9)*

Dependent variable	$\hat{\alpha}$	$\hat{\beta}$	$\hat{\gamma}$	$\hat{\delta}$	$\bar{R}^2$	*DW*	*SE*
France	−0.044	−0.092	0.412	0.881	0.86	2.56	0.01
1964–80	(2.64)	(4.04)	(2.77)	(9.30)			
Italy	0.003	−0.235		1.007	0.17	2.29	0.05
1960–79	(0.32)	(2.28)		(1.37)			

NOTE For Italy γ was not statistically significant, and was dropped.

V THE 1970s WITH QUARTERLY DATA

The 1970s – characterised by two oil shocks, sharp changes in the terms of trade, steady increases in the relative share of government, and high and variable rates of inflation – are the ideal years to test our model.

The yearly data, while providing us with an over-all appreciation of the power and limitations of the theory, could not focus on what is widely believed to be a turbulent period for industrialised economies. Needless to say, turbulent periods are more difficult to explain than tranquil periods. This fact must be faced and accounted for in addition to the other fact that quarterly data have more noise than yearly data. The point is illustrated by Figure 3.5 which shows the one-quarter difference of the logarithm of manufacturing output (Δy), the over-all price level (Δp) and the domestic price level (Δp_d) for the United Kingdom from 1971(I) to 1980(IV).

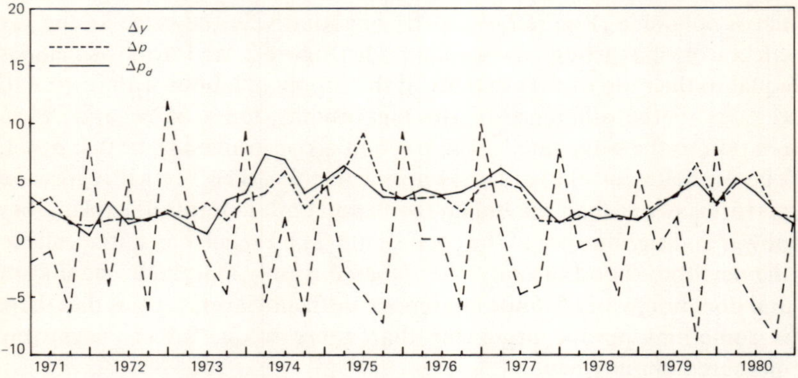

FIGURE 3.5 *Evolution of manufacturing output and prices in the United Kingdom,* 1971(*I*) *to* 1980(*IV*) (*percentage*)

Our estimation procedure for quarterly data is the same as for annual data except that the elements of $E\Delta Z$ of equation (3.1) are now quantified by the systematic component of VAR models rather than ARMA models. More precisely, fourth-quarter difference in the log of the money stock, the exchange rate, exports, government expenditures, the 'tax wedge' and the non-traded goods price level were regressed on their first and second-lagged values and on the fourth-quarter logarithmic difference of world prices of manufactured goods, oil prices and the US money stock. For Δp_f^* and Δp_h^* the information set was restricted to the first and second-lagged values of Δp_f^*, Δp_h^* and the US Ml money stock. The results are summarised in the appendix to Chapter 3.

The explanatory power of VAR is substantially higher than ARMA models, suggesting that the information set given to people in making estimates of the annual $E\Delta Z$ was too restrictive. On the other hand, we cannot claim that our VAR procedure has included all relevant information. This was not possible statistically given the still relatively few degrees of freedom afforded by forty quarterly observations.

There is little point in dwelling on the importance of individual coefficients because their significance is intimately connected with the presence or absence of other explanatory variables. We find it more worthwhile to look instead at general patterns. The table in the appendix to this chapter shows for what country a given variable is significant in the sense that the student's t statistic is at least 1.5. Some results have an immediate intuitive explanation, for example, the impact of past exchange rate changes on the growth rate of the domestic money stock; others less so, for example, the impact of the US money growth rate but not of its domestic counterpart on the growth of government expenditures.

Table 3.7 is the quarterly equivalent of Table 3.3 except that we have not reported the estimates for Δp_d. The general pattern of the results does not change. Money, directly, is marginally significant in a couple of countries. Indirectly, however, money affects the exchange rate and p_0 and, thus, influences Δp.

The over-all effect of the domestic money stock on the formation of inflation expectations is feeble, feebler than we had anticipated. Expected foreign prices have a positive effect in general, but with low statistical significance. Expected oil prices and government expenditures are statistically insignificant, with the exception of government expenditures for the Netherlands.

Table 3.8 is the quarterly equivalent of Table 3.5. The output equations were estimated either in log level form or in their first differences. In either case the unanticipated inflation rate was transformed from Δ_4 differences to Δ differences by adding to the fitted values of the unanticipated inflation rates (not reported) $\Delta_4 p_{t-1}$ and subtracting Δp_{t-1}. In contrast to Table 3.5 Δp_d or p_d, as the case demanded it, was entered as an actual value rather than as an estimate of the model. Results using $\Delta \hat{p}_d - \Delta p_f$ and $\Delta \hat{p}_0 - \Delta p_d$ were less conclusive than those shown in Table 3.8. To account for adjustment lags we employed either a lagged dependent variable assuming a geometric lag on all variables or,

TABLE 3.7 *Rational expectations equations for expected inflation rates. Quarterly data, 1971(I)–1980(IV)*

Country	*Dependent variable*	*C*	$\widehat{E\Delta_4 m}$	$\widehat{E\Delta_4 p_f^*}$	$\widehat{E\Delta_4 p_o}$	$\widehat{E\Delta_4 p_h^*}$	$\widehat{E\Delta_4 g}$	$\widehat{E\Delta_4 e}$	$\bar{R}^2$	*SE*	*DW*
Belgium	$\Delta_4 p$	0.004	0.004	0.061	0.632	0.004	−0.001	—	0.49	0.006	1.21
		(1.33)	(0.14)	(1.73)	(5.74)	(0.59)	(0.13)				
France	$\Delta_4 p$	0.002	0.028	0.042	0.798	0.004	0.004	—	0.41	0.006	1.55
		(0.44)	(0.92)	(1.18)	(4.97)	(0.63)	(0.64)				
Netherlands	$\Delta_4 p$	0.006	0.013	0.022	0.596	—	0.022	−0.002	0.51	0.005	1.64
		(2.55)	(0.86)	(0.70)	(5.23)		(2.84)	(0.07)			
Italy	$\Delta_4 p$	0.003	0.009	0.118	0.849	−0.007	0.004	—	0.58	0.010	1.54
		(0.51)	(0.22)	(1.97)	(7.14)	(0.61)	(0.33)				
Germany	$\Delta_4 p$	0.004	0.039	0.020	0.591	0.005	−0.011	—	0.65	0.004	1.75
		(2.42)	(1.58)	(0.85)	(6.09)	(1.08)	(1.37)				
United Kingdom	$\Delta_4 p$	0.001	0.117	0.074	0.719	0.006	0.019	—	0.54	0.011	1.69
		(0.17)	(1.59)	(1.05)	(7.06)	(0.44)	(0.54)				

NOTE See notes to Table 3.2.

TABLE 3.8 *Output supply equations. Quarterly data, 1971(I)–1980(IV)*

Country	Equation
Belgium	$\Delta y = \underset{(2.38)}{0.038} + \underset{(2.56)}{0.231}\,\Delta\tau + \underset{(0.79)}{2.713}\,(\widehat{\Delta p - E\Delta p}) + \underset{(1.12)}{0.253}\,(\Delta p_d - \Delta p_f)$ $- \underset{(1.39)}{0.146}\,(\Delta p_h - \Delta p_f) - \underset{(2.91)}{3.306}\,(\Delta p_o - \Delta p_d) - \underset{(4.41)}{0.906}\,\Delta y_{-1}$ $\overline{R}^2 = 0.34$ $SE = 0.064$ $DW = 2.15$
France	$y = \underset{(25.02)}{3.946} - \underset{(0.14)}{0.002}\,\tau - \underset{(0.23)}{0.120}\,(\widehat{\Delta p - E\Delta p}) + \underset{(0.69)}{0.051}\,(p_d - p_f)$ $- \underset{(2.20)}{0.046}\,(p_h - p_f)_{-1} - \underset{(5.31)}{0.847}\,(p_o - p_d)_{-1} + \underset{(5.34)}{0.668}\,(p_o - p_d)_{-2}$ $\overline{R}^2 = 0.99$ $SE = 0.016$ $\rho = \underset{(3.06)}{0.492}$
Netherlands	$\Delta y = \underset{(3.08)}{0.016} - \underset{(2.47)}{0.397}\,\Delta\tau + \underset{(0.86)}{1.405}\,(\widehat{\Delta p - E\Delta p}) + \underset{(2.32)}{0.674}\,(\Delta p_d - \Delta p_f)$ $- \underset{(3.51)}{0.939}\,(\Delta p_d - \Delta p_f)_{-1} - \underset{(2.75)}{0.106}\,(\Delta p_h - \Delta p_f)_{-1} - \underset{(0.97)}{0.605}\,(\Delta p_o - \Delta p_d)$ $\overline{R}^2 = 0.95$ $SE = 0.026$ $\rho = \underset{(30.58)}{-0.971}$
Italy	$y = \underset{(17.67)}{3.726} + \underset{(10.60)}{0.011}\,t + \underset{(0.054)}{0.003}\,\tau + \underset{(2.34)}{2.286}\,\tfrac{1}{2}\,[(\Delta p - E\Delta p)_{-1}$ $+ (\Delta p - E\Delta p)_{-2}] - \underset{(2.23)}{0.388}\,(p_d - p_f) + \underset{(2.17)}{0.336}\,(p_d - p_f)_{-2}$ $+ \underset{(2.34)}{0.086}\,(p_h - p_f)$ $- \underset{(3.55)}{0.171}\,(p_h - p_f)_{-1} - \underset{(5.28)}{1.554}\,(p_o - p_d)_{-1} + \underset{(6.47)}{1.365}\,(p_o - p_d)_{-2}$ $\overline{R}^2 = 0.95$ $SE = 0.026$ $DW = 1.52$

TABLE 3.8 *Continued*

Country	*Equation*
Germany	$\Delta y = 0.009 - 0.341\ \Delta\tau - 5.379\ \tfrac{1}{2}\,[(\Delta p - E\Delta p)_{-1} + (\Delta p - E\Delta p)_{-2}]$ (1.32) (4.40) (1.98) $+0.797\ (\Delta p_d - \Delta p_f) - 0.001\ (\Delta p_h - \Delta p_f)_{-1} - 1.138\ (\Delta p_o - \Delta p_d)$ (3.24) (0.03) (2.08) $\bar{R}^2 = 0.88$ $SE = 0.038$ $DW = 2.23$
United Kingdom	$y = 2.575 + 0.004\ t - 0.526\ \tau - 1.765\ (\widehat{\Delta p - E\Delta p}) + 0.097\ (p_d - p_f)$ (3.25) (2.62) (3.49) (2.90) (3.53) $-0.031\ (p_h - p_f) - 0.379\ (p_o - p_d)$ (2.44) (1.99) $\bar{R}^2 = 0.80$ $SE = 0.024$ $DW = 2.37$

NOTE When equation estimated correcting for serial correlation, the value of ρ is given.

alternatively, one and/or two-period lagged explanatory variables. The best results are reported in Table 3.8.

The most striking finding of the quarterly estimates is the poor showing of the Lucas effect which is nowhere significantly positive, whereas it is significantly negative for the United Kingdom. Italy has a positive coefficient for the lagged error of forecast, but for Germany it is negative. The appearance of past values of $(\Delta p - E\Delta p)$ in the equations is inconsistent with the misperception theory but is consistent with the thesis that the economy suffers from inertia. There are three different pieces of supporting evidence in favour of the hypothesis: the oil terms of trade, the internal terms of trade and the tax wedge. The degree of confidence in these results varies from one variable to another. The strongest evidence is for $p_o - p_d$, significant in five out of six countries, and $p_h - p_f$, significant in four out of six countries.[13] The evidence concerning the external terms of trade is broadly supportive to the hypothesis: a positive effect is detected using the unlagged variable for Belgium, France, Germany, the Netherlands and the United Kingdom. In the case of the Netherlands this effect is followed by a stronger negative lagged effect. For Italy an initial negative lagged one-period effect is accompanied by a positive effect of equal magnitude one period later. The tax wedge, on the other hand, appears with the predicted negative sign in Germany, the Netherlands and the United Kingdom, but for Belgium – a country not different from the Netherlands in many respects – it goes the other way. The quarterly data are more favourable towards τ than the yearly data, a finding that agrees with the sharp growth of the public sector in the 1970s. In sum, the evidence is quite supportive to the effects of relative prices – in particular oil and internal terms of trade – and the tax wedge but is negative with respect to the misperception factor.

VI CONCLUSIONS

The theory of the real sector developed in Chapter 2 was tested using annual and quarterly data for six EC countries: Belgium, France, Germany, Italy, the Netherlands and the United Kingdom. The key elements of the theory were inflation surprises, terms of trade changes and the so-called tax wedge. The evidence denies any significant effect of inflation surprises to changes in output but is supportive otherwise. Variations in the terms of trade, in particular the intermediate (oil) and internal ones, have exerted a significant negative effect on output in most of the six countries under examination. The theoretically-predicted negative effect of the tax wedge was found to be significant in two countries during the whole sample period using annual data, and in three countries (Germany, the Netherlands and the United Kingdom) for the 1970s using quarterly data. What are the policy implications of these results?

There are essentially two. One is that the oil-induced supply shocks, which occurred during the 1970s, were aggravated by the simultaneous and large increase in the taxation of labour during the same period. Our results confirm the results obtained by others (Bruno and Sachs (1979)) indicating the significant negative effect of the oil shock on aggregate output in European countries. At the same time, however, these countries imposed on themselves a 'labour tax shock' which tended to make the use of labour in the supply of output less and less attractive. This negative effect appears to have been significant in three of the six countries analysed here during the 1970s. Thus these countries compounded the externally-generated supply shock by a domestic one. The first shock could not be avoided, the second shock was entirely home-made. The latter led to a decline of the 'natural' level of output which went beyond the one produced by the oil shock. In so doing it aggravated the adjustment problems faced by these countries after the oil shock.

A second implication of the results of this chapter relates to the determinants of the business cycle and the policies to follow to stabilise the business cycle. One important implication of the inflation surprise variable in aggregate supply equations is that it provides a basis for a theory of the business cycle. This theory, as developed by Lucas (1975) and Barro (1981), can be summarised very briefly as follows. Unanticipated monetary shocks lead to inflationary surprises. These then lead through the supply of output equation, to variations in output. Thus, the variability of output can be explained by the unexpected variability of monetary policies. The way to stabilise output then consists in making monetary policies more stable and predictable. The weak evidence about the output effects of inflationary surprises casts doubt about this explanation of the business cycle in the European countries analysed here. They also cast doubt about the methods to stabilise output. The link between the supply of output decisions and monetary shocks does not appear to be a strong one empirically. This also implies that stabilisation of the growth rate of the money supply is unlikely to be sufficient (although probably necessary) to stabilise output. Put differently, the evidence, using European data, is not in favour of the new equilibrium theory of the business cycle, and its policy prescription suggesting that to stabilise output it suffices to stabilise the growth rate of the money stock. This does not mean that a greater stability of monetary policies is not important or that inflation does not matter. It suggests only that the empirical basis of the new business cycle theory is weak in the EC-countries and that the traditional approach to the stabilisation of the business cycle, in particular the use of budgetary policies, should not be discarded.

NOTES

1. Noteworthy are the studies by Bruno and Sachs (1979) and (1982) and Giavazzi, Odekon and Wypsloz (1982).
2. These are as indicated in the Data Appendix A-7: index of industrial production, index of manufacturing production and value added in manufacturing.
3. See again Data Appendix A-7.
4. The 1974 values are 34.2 per cent (I), 25.5 (F), 13.5 (B), 13.2 (G), 20.4 (UK) and 9.1 (N); the 1980 values are 18.3 per cent (I), 8.4 (F), 6.07 (B), 7.7 (G), 15.0 (UK) and 7.8 (N).

5. The studies by Benjamin and Kochin (1979), Holden and Peel (1979) and Minford (1983) indicate that the natural rate of unemployment responds very strongly to changes in unemployment benefits and less to tax rates on employers and employees.
6. Korteweg (1980) finds that the volume of world imports follows an MA(2) model.
7. Note that the errors-in-variables method proposed by McCallum (1976) cannot be applied in our case because we have p_t on both sides of the equation.
8. This evidence contrasts with the findings of Fratianni (1980a) and Korteweg (1980) who define the fiscal impulse in a more detailed manner (that is, they purge the series of other induced components). Fratianni obtains that ΔF is an MA(1) process with a coefficient of 0.8 and Korteweg obtains that $\Delta(\Delta F)$ is an MA(1) scheme with a coefficient of 0.75.
9. For Germany and the Netherlands $E\Delta m$ entered as AR(1) with virtually no explanatory power. Moreover, some experiments show that using $M2$ improves the forecast of money and expected prices, but does not improve the explanation of unexpected inflation and output supply functions.
10. $\hat{p}_d = (\widehat{\Delta p_d - E\Delta p_d}) + \widehat{E\Delta p_d} + p_{d-1}$

    Notice that we actually carry out the estimation in two steps, instead of a one-step instrumental variable procedure. Therefore, standard errors of estimates are not strictly correct. Notice also that for the estimated equations reported in this chapter, the DW statistic tests show either that the null hypothesis of no serial correlation is not rejected, or in most cases the test is indeterminate. We do not discuss the issue further in the text, since there does not seen to exist a serious problem with serial correlation.
11. See Data Appendix A-7 for more details.
12. Rewrite (3.7) and (3.8) in log-linear form

$$\log N = -\alpha_1 \left[\log \frac{W_n}{P} + \log (1 + t_w^1) \right] + \ldots$$

$$\log N = -\beta_1 \log (1 + t_w^2) + \beta_2 \log \frac{W_n}{EP}$$

    where α_1, β_1, β_3 are positive coefficients.
    Set $P = EP$ and solve for $\log W_n/P$

$$\log W_n/P = \frac{-\alpha_1}{\alpha_1 + \beta_2} \tau_1 + \frac{\beta_1}{\alpha_1 + \beta_2} \tau_2 + \ldots$$

    We can derive an expression like (3.9) if $\alpha_1 = \beta_1$:

$$w_n = \delta[\tau_2 - \tau_1] + \ldots$$

    where $\delta = \dfrac{\beta_1}{\alpha_1 + \beta_2}$ has the interpretation given in the text.
13. Peculiar findings are the statistically very significant and positive coefficients of the two-period lagged internal terms-of-trade variable for France and Italy.

APPENDIX FORECASTING EXOGENOUS VARIABLES

I ARIMA PROCESSES FOR ANNUAL DATA

Standard Box-Jenkins techniques (using an IBM program) were used to identify and estimate ARIMA models to forecast the exogenous variables. The number of observations was necessarily limited on the basis of annual data, 1957–80. In all cases first order differencing of the variables (in natural logarithms) was necessary to ensure that the series were stationary.

Money Stock

The variable used is M1, as a yearly average. Through analysis of autocorrelation and partial autocorrelation coefficients it appeared that:

for Germany and the Netherlands, a white noise process for Δm, around a constant growth rate of money, could not be rejected.
for the other countries some evidence, but not very strong, appeared in favour of an AR (1) process, but for the United Kingdom the AR process was strongly significant.

Fitting AR(1) models for all countries we obtained the following estimates which were used to generate $E\widehat{\Delta m}$, even though, as expected for Germany and the Netherlands the explanatory power is almost nil:

Germany	: $\widehat{\Delta m_t} = 0.091 - 0.107\,\Delta m_{t-1}$	$\bar{R}^2 = -0.02$
(t-values)	: (7.04) (0.74)	
Netherlands	: $\widehat{\Delta m_t} = 0.066 + 0.240\,\Delta m_{t-1}$	$\bar{R}^2 = 0.01$
	(3.14) (1.09)	
France	: $\widehat{\Delta m_t} = 0.066 + 0.316\,\Delta m_{t-1}$	$\bar{R}^2 = 0.06$
	(3.04) (1.51)	
Belgium	: $\widehat{\Delta m_t} = 0.037 + 0.388\,\Delta m_{t-1}$	$\bar{R}^2 = 0.10$
	(2.40) (1.80)	
Italy	: $\widehat{\Delta m_t} = 0.103 + 0.322\,\Delta m_{t-1}$	$\bar{R}^2 = 0.07$
	(3.35) (1.62)	
United Kingdom:	$\widehat{\Delta m_t} = 0.033 + 0.559\,\Delta m_{t-1}$	$\bar{R}^2 = 0.31$
	(2.13) (3.23)	

Foreign Price

The foreign price in domestic currency (in logs) is defined as:

$$p_f = p_f^* + e$$

Attempts to estimate ARIMA models for p_f directly did not yield any results. So we decided to model p_f^* and e separately.
For the exchange rate (domestic currency price of the dollar), Δe exhibits the characteristics of white noise; it is constant up to 1971 and highly volatile during the 1970s.

As for Δp_f^* an AR(3) model was identified and estimated, using data for the period 1957–80:

$$\widehat{\Delta p_f^*} = \underset{(1.26)}{0.012} + \underset{(5.90)}{1.118}\, \Delta p_{f-1}^* - \underset{(3.20)}{0.819}\, \Delta p_{f-2}^* + \underset{(2.80)}{0.552}\, \Delta p_{f-3}^* \quad \bar{R}^2 = 0.69$$

Intermediate Goods Price

The variable used is the dollar price of Saudi oil. The analysis of the autocorrelation and partial autocorrelation coefficients did not suggest any particular model, and the coefficients were not significant. Attempts to fit AR(1) or MA(1) models did not yield positive results, so Δp_h is treated as white noise.

Exports

Like for the price of oil the analysis of the series of exports value did not yield any good ARIMA model, so we could not reject a white noise process.

Other Goods Prices

For the price index of food and services p_o an AR(1) was found satisfactory in general:

Germany : $\widehat{\Delta p_{ot}} = \underset{(2.10)}{0.013} + \underset{(3.76)}{0.641}\, \Delta p_{ot-1} \quad \bar{R}^2 = 0.38$

Netherlands: $\widehat{\Delta p_{ot}} = \underset{(2.01)}{0.017} + \underset{(4.72)}{0.699}\, \Delta p_{ot-1} \quad \bar{R}^2 = 0.50$

France : $\widehat{\Delta p_{ot}} = \underset{(3.27)}{0.044} + \underset{(2.01)}{0.341}\, \Delta p_{ot-1} \quad \bar{R}^2 = 0.13$

Belgium : $\widehat{\Delta p_{ot}} = \underset{(1.48)}{0.010} + \underset{(7.30)}{0.829}\, \Delta p_{ot-1} \quad \bar{R}^2 = 0.71$

Italy : $\widehat{\Delta p_{ot}} = \underset{(1.12)}{0.011} + \underset{(8.24)}{0.914}\, \Delta p_{ot-1} \quad \bar{R}^2 = 0.76$

United Kingdom : $\widehat{\Delta p_{ot}} = \underset{(2.62)}{0.064} + \underset{(1.26)}{0.277}\, \Delta p_{ot-1} \quad \bar{R}^2 = 0.02$

II VECTOR AUTOREGRESSIVE ANALYSIS USING QUARTERLY DATA

All exogenous variables were transformed in $z_t - z_{t-4}$, where z denotes the natural logarithms of the variable, and regressed on their first and second-period lagged values as well as the first and second-period lagged values of a rather extensive but not complete set of exogenous models. The results are summarised in Table 3A.1.

TABLE 3A.1 *Vector autoregressive models of exogenous variables. Quarterly Data*, 1971(*I*)–1980(*IV*)

Dependent variable	$\Delta_4 m_{-i}$	$\Delta_4 e_{-i}$	$\Delta_4 g_{-i}$	$\Delta_4 xc_{-i}$	$\Delta_4 p^*_{f-i}$	$\Delta_4 m^*_{-i}$	$\Delta_4 p^*_{h-i}$	$\Delta_4 \tau_{-i}$	$\Delta_4 p_{o-i}$	$\bar{R}^2$	
$\Delta_4 m$	B, UK, I, N, G	B, UK, G,	F, B, N, G	B, UK, I, N	UK, N, G	B, G	UK, I, G	F, N, G	F	F = 0.38 B = 0.63 UK = 0.79	I = 0.88 N = 0.79 G = 0.62
$\Delta_4 e$	F, N	F, B, UK, I, N, G	B, I, N	B, UK, N	UK, N, G	F, N, G	F, B, I, N, G	B, UK, N	B, UK	F = 0.66 B = 0.70 UK = 0.87	I = 0.60 N = 0.81 G = 0.76
$\Delta_4 xc$	UK, I, N	F, B, UK, I, G	I	F, B, I, N	UK, I	B	F, B, UK, I	I, N	I, UK	F = 0.71 B = 0.75 UK = 0.60	I = 0.73 N = 0.66 G = 0.50
$\Delta_4 p_o$	B, UK, G	F, B, I, G	UK, I, G	F, B, N, G	F, B, UK, G	I, G	F, UK, G, N	B, UK, I, N, G	F, B, UK, I, N, G	F = 0.90 B = 0.94 UK = 0.92	I = 0.94 N = 0.90 G = 0.86
$\Delta_4 g$	G		B, UK	B, I, G	F, B, UK, N	F, UK	F, B, UK, N, G	B, UK, I, G		F = 0.52 B = 0.69 UK = 0.93	I = 0.27 N = 0.45 G = 0.40
$\Delta_4 \tau$	UK		UK	B, UK, N, G	F, N, G	F, UK	F, UK, N, G	UK	G	F = 0.52 B = 0.32 UK = 0.47	I = 0.20 N = 0.60 G = 0.70
$\Delta_4 p^*_f$					*	*	*			0.80	
$\Delta_4 p^*_h$							*			0.69	

NOTE The table indicates with a letter whether the coefficient of either one lag or both lags of the variable shown at the top of the column was significant in the sense that its $t \geqslant 1.5$.
B = Belgium, F = France, G = Germany, I = Italy, N = Netherlands, UK = United Kingdom.
$\Delta_4 z = z_t - z_{t-4}$.
A* indicates significance of the relevant variables, in the last 2 lines.

Part II
Exchange Rates and the Financial Sector

4 Interest Rate Parity and Imperfect Substitutability

I INTRODUCTION

This chapter is intended to motivate and justify the strategy adopted in Part II; namely, modelling exchange rates within a portfolio-balance framework rather than relying on a monetary approach. The latter, by taking domestic and foreign assets as perfect substitutes, emphasises only one asset, money. In contrast, by removing the perfect substitutability assumption, the portfolio-balance approach allows current-account imbalances to affect the exchange rate via changes in the world distribution of assets denominated in different monies. The structure and implications of this view of the world are discussed in detail in Chapter 5. We leave to this chapter the presentation of evidential material supporting our choice of models.

There are many reasons why assets are imperfectly substitutable: governmental regulations, differential taxation, default risk, political risk, upward-sloping arbitrage schedules and diversification requirements. In the literature of the 1960s 'the failure of interest-rate parity to occur', in the words of Officer and Willett (1970) who surveyed the area, was accepted as evidence of differences in assets characteristics. The emergence and growth of the Eurocurrency market provided a unique opportunity for testing the interest-rate parity (IRP) condition free from the influences of direct government intervention and control, as well as taxation and political risk differences.[1] As was noted by Bilson (1978), Eurocurrency assets (that is, bank deposits) 'are identical in all respects other than the currency denomination, (and hence) efficient arbitrage should equate the covered yields on the different deposits, after due allowance is made for transaction costs'. In Section II of this chapter we review the evidence of IRP using both Eurocurrency deposit interest rates and comparable domestic bank deposit interest rates. Differences in the findings will be rationalised in terms of differences in transaction costs and differences in those characteristics mentioned above. The main point is that, regardless of the cause, domestic assets are less substitutable than Eurocurrency assets.

A second way to justify imperfect substitutability among assets of different currency denomination is to test whether or not the forward premium is a biased predictor of the one-period-ahead change in the exchange rate, the bias reflecting the so-called (exchange) risk premium. Under these conditions, risk-averse investors will absorb an increase in the supply of a given asset by demanding and obtaining a higher expected yield. In other words, risk must be compensated and assets with different currency denominations are priced differently. Hence they are less than perfectly substitutable. Research in this field is active and unsettled. While there is agreement on the theoretical importance of the risk-premium argument, the empirical findings are far from conclusive. Two recent examples are Frankel (1982) who cannot reject the null hypothesis of risk neutrality and Dooley and Isard (1982) who instead find evidence of risk premiums. This topic is taken up in Section III of the chapter.

II INTEREST RATE PARITY

Deviations from interest rate parity are defined by XD in equation (4.1a) for 'inland' interest rates and XE in equation (4.1b) for Eurocurrency rates:

$$XD = \log(1+i^*) - \log(1+i) + f - e \tag{4.1a}$$

$$XE = \log(1+i_E^*) - \log(1+i_E) + f - e \tag{4.1b}$$

where i^* = the US short-term interest rate
i = the home short-term interest rate
i_E^* = the Eurodollar short-term interest rate
i_E = the Euro-domestic short-term interest rate
e = the log of the spot exchange rate expressed in units of domestic money per US dollar
f = the log of the forward exchange rate, in units of domestic money per US dollar, at time t for delivery at time $t+1$.

XD and XE can be small or large, unpredictable or predictable. A relatively large X need not imply profit opportunities, for transaction costs could be such as to make arbitrage uneconomic.[2] The less predictable X and the smaller its absolute value the stronger the evidence in favour of IRP and hence of perfect substitutability between the two underlying assets.

Table 4.1 shows basic statistics pertaining to the two equations already

TABLE 4.1 *Descriptive statistics on interest rate parity. Quarterly data, end of period*, 1973(*I*)–1980(*IV*)

Country	*Variable*	*Mean*	*Standard deviation*	*Minimum*	*Maximum*
US	$i_E^* - i^*$	0.00173	0.00107	0.00031	0.00438
Germany	$IEG - IG$	−0.00094	0.00563	−0.02000	0.00594
	XD	−0.00138	0.00717	−0.02300	0.02722
	XE	−0.00005	0.00071	−0.00198	0.00162
	$XD - XE$	−0.00133	0.00720	−0.02220	0.02777
France	$i_E - i$	0.00503	0.00574	−0.00344	0.02375
	XD	−0.00021	0.00284	−0.00677	0.00697
	XE	0.00120	0.00188	−0.00048	0.01018
	$XD - XE$	−0.00141	0.00308	−0.00731	0.00650
Netherlands	$i_E - i$	−0.00132	0.00326	−0.01031	0.01014
	XD	−0.00289	0.00304	−0.01093	0.00655
	XE	0.00001	0.00193	−0.01022	0.00153
	$XD - XE$	−0.00289	0.00378	−0.01234	0.00890

TABLE 4.1 *Continued*

Country		*Variable*	*Mean*	*Standard deviation*	*Minimum*	*Maximum*
Belgium	Commer-	$i_E - i$	−0.00023	0.00092	−0.00407	0.00172
	cial	XD	−0.01681	0.01655	−0.05140	0.01654
	rate	XE	0.00165	0.00512	−0.01028	0.01786
		$XD - XE$	−0.01845	0.01873	−0.05185	0.02189
	Finan-	XD	−0.00179	0.00281	−0.00632	0.00709
	cial rate	XE	0.00017	0.00267	−0.00521	0.00829
	77(II)–80(IV)	$XD–XE$	−0.00195	0.00083	−0.00376	−0.00103
Italy		$i_E - i$	0.01166	0.01527	−0.01313	0.04750
		XD	0.01028	0.02408	−0.02905	0.07470
		XE	0.00263	0.00400	−0.00840	0.01029
		$XD - XE$	0.00765	0.02282	−0.02950	0.06441
UK		$i_E - i$	0.00336	0.00325	−0.00110	0.01219
		XD	0.00068	0.00750	−0.01944	0.01528
		XE	0.00022	0.00214	−0.00889	0.00359
		$XD - XE$	0.00046	0.00762	−0.01292	0.01389

shown for the period 1973–80. The data are quarterly end-of-period observations. Spot (e) and forward (f) exchange rates and interest rates on three-month Eurocurrency deposits (i_E^*, i_E) are the Friday bid closing rates published by the Harris Bank in its *Weekly Review*.

We took the closest Friday before the end of the quarter. Interest rates i^* and i are the yield on the three-month negotiable certificates of deposits published by the Morgan Guaranty Trust Co. in its *World Financial Markets*. The reader can obtain more detailed information in the Data Appendix.

Table 4.1 reveals that both the average value and the variability of XE are a fraction of those of XD.[3] These characteristics are displayed in Figures 4.1 and 4.2 where XE and XD are plotted for two important countries like Germany and the United Kingdom. The average deviation from Eurocurrency IRP for Germany and the Netherlands is very close to being zero. For the other countries it is much larger.

A particularly important aspect of equation (4.1) is the predictability of X. In most tests deviations from IRP are jointly tested with the hypothesis of market efficiency which requires that XD and XE be uncorrelated over time. In Table 4.2 we check for this by regressing X on X_{-1}, X_{-2}, X_{-3} and X_{-4}. Both XD and XE display serial correlation in many cases, XD having more than XE. In addition, the autocorrelation patterns of the two series differ, suggesting that differences between 'inland' and Eurocurrency interest rates are not constant over time.

Let us now rewrite equation (4.1) in regression form:

$$f - e = \alpha + \beta\left[\log(1+i) - \log(1+i^*)\right] + XD' \tag{4.2a}$$

$$f - e = \alpha + \beta\left[\log(1+i_E) - \log(1+i_E^*)\right] + XE' \tag{4.2b}$$

In our previous discussion we have assumed implicitly that $\alpha = 0$ and $\beta = 1$, properties for which we can test. Before doing so we modify IRP to make room for transaction costs. The investor bears four different costs: (i) the brokerage fee – expressed as a fraction of one dollar – to purchase dollars spot; (ii) the brokerage fee – again expressed as a fraction of one dollar – to sell dollars forward, (iii) the cost in purchasing the asset denominated in dollars and (iv) the cost in selling the asset denominated in domestic money. In the case of Eurocurrency deposits or domestic bank deposits the individual investor will bear the transaction cost in the form of a yield that is lower than the market yield.

It can be shown that:

$$\begin{aligned}\alpha = 0 \pm &\log(1 - \text{transaction cost on the spot market})\\ &+ \log(1 - \text{transaction cost on the forward market})\end{aligned}$$

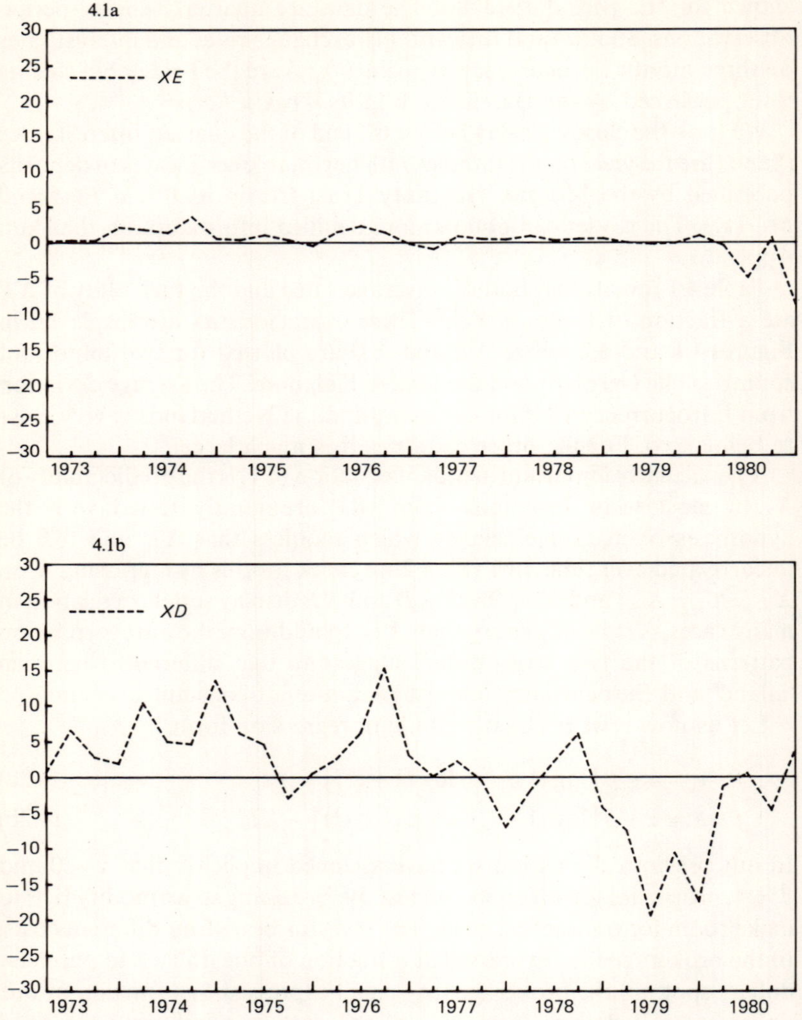

FIGURE 4.1 *Deviations from IRP: United Kingdom XE and XD, 1973(I)–1980(IV) (percentage, quarterly rates)*

and that β is very close to unity, but differs from this value depending on the value of the ratios

$$\log(1+i)/\log(1+i^*) \quad \text{and} \quad \frac{\text{transaction cost on domestic assets}}{\text{transaction cost on dollar assets}}$$

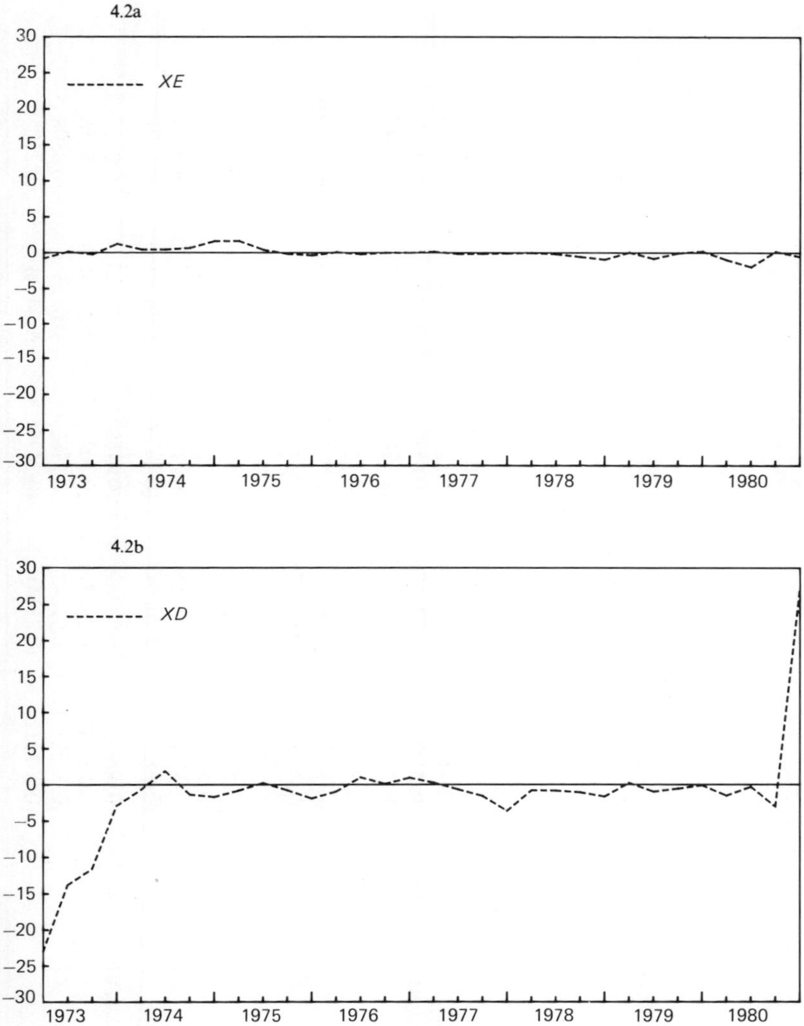

FIGURE 4.2 *Deviations from IRP: Germany XE and XD,* 1973(*I*)–1980(*IV*) (*percentage, quarterly rates*)

For more details the reader can refer to Fratianni and Wakeman (1982).

The regression estimate of α, $\hat{\alpha}$, captures the average transaction cost over the period under examination. Deviations from this average are impounded in the error term X'. During periods of high uncertainty (for

TABLE 4.2 *Autoregressive pattern of X, 1973(I)–1980(IV)*

Country	*Dependent variable*	$\hat{\beta}_0$	$\hat{\beta}_1$	$\hat{\beta}_2$	$\hat{\beta}_3$	$\hat{\beta}_4$
Germany	*XE*	−0.00009	0.46241*	−0.07438	0.17301	0.18032
		(0.00012)	(0.18733)	(0.2221)	(0.2582)	(0.2236)
	XD	−0.00091	−1.7386*	0.8539	−0.7763	0.2357
		(0.00128)	(0.9255)	(0.7266)	(0.7079)	(0.4447)
France	*XE*	0.00043	0.08188	0.12757	0.034219	0.14267
		(0.00031)	(0.1995)	(0.09454)	(0.09714)	(0.09504)
	XD	−0.00041	0.4425*	−0.2277	0.3612	−0.2167
		(0.00051)	(0.1981)	(0.2104)	(0.2087)	(0.1965)
Netherlands	*XE*	−0.00002	−0.0155	−0.00343	−0.0842	−0.16433
		(0.00041)	(0.2053)	(0.2045)	(0.2046)	(0.2055)
	XD	−0.0011	0.5285*	−0.0768	0.2899*	−0.0584
		(0.0007)	(0.2039)	(0.2050)	(0.1455)	(0.1391)
UK	*XE*	−0.00052	0.03369	0.81601*	0.28603	0.023715
		(0.00054)	(0.2857)	(0.3024)	(0.4613)	(0.4456)
	XD	0.00021	0.5164*	0.1782	−0.0525	−0.0808
		(0.00131)	(0.2114)	(0.2426)	(0.2404)	(0.2105)

Country	Dependent variable		$\hat{\beta}_0$	$\hat{\beta}_1$	$\hat{\beta}_2$	$\hat{\beta}_3$	$\hat{\beta}_4$
Belgium	Commercial	XE	0.00325*	−0.03907	−0.19408	−0.038485	−0.040958
	rate		(0.00118)	(0.1987)	(0.1736)	(0.1802)	(0.1688)
		XD	−0.0111*	0.3113	0.1269	0.0905	−0.1122
			(0.0057)	(0.2010)	(0.2071)	(0.2058)	(0.1903)
	Financial	XE	0.00051	−0.77567*	−0.52958	−0.45208	−0.22692
	rate		(0.00066)	(0.30821)	(0.3662)	(0.3669)	(0.3094)
		XD	−0.0030*	−0.4942	−0.1295	−0.2027	0.0095
	77(II)–80(IV)		(0.0014)	(0.3191)	(0.3378)	(0.3301)	(0.3084)
Italy		XE	0.00104	0.12102	0.12281	0.22797	−0.15630
			(0.00100)	(0.1993)	(0.2135)	(0.2670)	(0.2413)
		XD	0.0030	0.2529	0.3616*	−0.0150	−0.1387
			(0.0043)	(0.1757)	(0.1872)	(0.1889)	(0.1973)

NOTES 1. Numbers in parentheses are standard errors

2. A^* indicates significance at 90 per cent level.

$X = \beta_0 + \beta_1 X_{-1} + \beta_2 X_{-2} + \beta_3 X_{-3} + \beta_4 X_{-4} + \text{error}$

example, the default of a bank) transaction costs rise and so does the true α. Therefore X augments. The size and evolution of X can tell us something about market turbulence.

Although in principle separable, in practice it is impossible to distinguish changes in X' attributable to higher transaction costs from changes in X' attributable to differences in exchange rate risk. It is tempting to surmise that over a relatively long period of time occasional spurts in uncertainty concerning the fulfilment of an exchange contract need not lead to an autocorrelated X', whereas the perception that one asset is more risky than another leads the forward rate to be a biased predictor of the expected spot rate. Hence, under these circumstances X' should display serial correlation. Caution is advised in drawing too precise inferences from the serial pattern of X'. There are too many causes that can potentially affect it, from regulatory activity to political risks.

With these introductory comments out of the way, we proceed to test equation (4.2). The results are presented in Table 4.3 and deserve three principal remarks. First, $\hat{\beta}$ is statistically not different from unity – using two standard errors on both sides of the mean as a criterion – in five out of seven cases for Eurocurrency and six out of seven for inland interest rates. Differences arise instead in the $\hat{\alpha}$s and in the serial correlation properties of X'.

Insofar as the intercept is concerned, $\hat{\alpha}$ is different from zero in five out of seven cases for inland rates and in three out of seven for Eurocurrency rates. This evidence is consistent with our prior that assigns higher transaction costs to home assets than to Eurocurrency assets. Finally, serial correlation is fairly widespread for XD' (France, Germany, the Netherlands and the United Kingdom) and much less so for XE' (the United Kingdom).

The inference one draws from the last finding is not clear. Had exchange rate risk been the dominant cause of serial correlation, both XD' and XE' should be displaying it, for the risk in question is related by definition to assets denominated in different monies. Thus something else is responsible for the difference in patterns and this 'something else' includes the long list of factors mentioned in the introduction to this chapter.

In sum, the evidence presented suggests that IRP holds fairly tightly when using Eurocurrency rates and less so when using domestic rates of interest. This finding is in accord with the literature.[4]

TABLE 4.3 *Interest rate parity tests. Equations (4.2a) and (4.2b). End-of-period quarterly data, 1973(I)–1980(IV)*

Country		$\hat{\alpha}$	$\hat{\beta}$	$\overline{R}^2$	DW	X'_{-1}	X'_{-2}	X'_{-3}	X'_{-4}	*Constant*
Germany	Euromarket rates	0.00033	1.04335	0.99	1.42	0.30078	−0.0335	−0.0366	0.2770	−0.00004
		(0.00020)	(0.0184)			(0.19841)	(0.2238)	(0.3158)	(0.2845)	(0.00013)
	Domestic rates	−0.00459*	0.4757	0.23	1.03	0.1856	1.100*	−1.1513*	0.2653	0.00043
		(0.00141)	(0.1478)			(0.2624)	(0.2608)	(0.3453)	(0.2466)	(0.00076)
France	Euromarket rates	0.00107*	1.0297	0.96	1.99	0.00312	0.0749	0.0124	0.1317	−0.00033
		(0.00037)	(0.0374)			(0.1979)	(0.084)	(0.085)	(0.085)	(0.00017)
	Domestic rates	−0.00024	1.024	0.84	1.21	0.4365*	−0.2250	0.3450	−0.2110	−0.00027
		(0.00052)	(0.081)			(0.1982)	(0.2110)	(0.2089)	(0.1961)	(0.00051)
Netherlands	Euromarket rates	−0.00013	0.9663	0.94	1.93	0.0036	0.0022	−0.0698	−0.2292	−0.00002
		(0.00039)	(0.0456)			(0.2017)	(0.2006)	(0.2005)	(0.2018)	(0.0004)
	Domestic rates	−0.00287*	1.009	0.86	1.61	0.5182*	−0.0729	0.2894*	−0.058	−0.00017
		(0.0006)	(0.0724)			(0.2044)	(0.2044)	(0.1451)	(0.1398)	(0.0004)
UK	Euromarket rates	−0.00007	1.0327	0.92	1.36	0.0097	0.7634*	0.1428	0.1263	−0.0004
		(0.0006)	(0.0538)			(0.2852)	(0.2956)	(0.4646)	(0.4521)	(0.0005)
	Domestic rates	−0.00077	1.2023	0.51	0.97	0.4392*	0.2545	−0.0881	−0.0786	−0.00002
		(0.0020)	(0.2091)			(0.2146)	(0.2382)	(0.2317)	(0.2109)	(0.0013)

TABLE 4.3 *Continued*

Country			$\hat{\alpha}$	$\hat{\beta}$	$\overline{R}^2$	DW	X'_{-1}	X'_{-2}	X'_{-3}	X'_{-4}	*Constant*
Belgium	Commercial rate	Euromarket rates	0.00161* (0.00086)	1.2552 (0.1254)	0.76	1.83	−0.0022 (0.198)	−0.2491 (0.1766)	−0.0293 (0.1874)	−0.0400 (0.1773)	0.0008 (0.00085)
		Domestic rates	−0.0169* (0.0031)	1.0324 (0.4668)	0.11	1.25	0.3081 (0.2011)	0.1290 (0.2070)	0.0911 (0.2056)	−0.1141 (0.1902)	−0.0013 (0.0030)
	Financial rate 77(II)–80(IV)	Euromarket rates	−0.00008 (0.0007)	0.8755 (0.1289)	0.76	2.96	−0.3705 (0.191)	−0.2467 (0.198)	−0.2940 (0.179)	−0.1751 (0.142)	0.000014 (0.0003)
		Domestic rates	−0.0018* (0.0007)	0.8928 (0.1430)	0.73	2.77	−0.1062 (0.215)	−0.0047 (0.221)	−0.0963 (0.213)	0.0264 (0.186)	−0.0004 (0.0005)
Italy	Euromarket rates		0.00555* (0.00186)	0.8824 (0.0742)	0.82	1.13	0.1049 (0.1314)	0.1528 (0.1352)	0.0659 (0.1269)	−0.1135 (0.1102)	−0.0014 (0.0007)
	Domestic rates		0.0120* (0.0055)	0.7067 (0.3455)	0.09	1.40	0.2466 (0.1835)	0.3038 (0.1919)	−0.0420 (0.1963)	−0.2000 (0.2106)	−0.0014 (0.0040)

NOTES
1. Numbers in parentheses are standard errors
2. * indicates significance at 95 per cent level
3. The right-hand side of the table is an autoregressive equation using the estimated error terms from the left-hand side of the table.

III THE FORWARD RATE, THE EXPECTED SPOT RATE AND RISK PREMIUMS

In a portfolio model people will hold foreign assets if compensated for the additional risk that stems from the fact that consumption occurs predominantly, if not exclusively, at home. In other words domestic and foreign assets are priced differently. Denoting by Ee the expected value of the log of the exchange rate for the period $t+1$ conditional on information available up to t and by RP the risk premium we can state the condition for imperfect substitutability across assets of different currency denomination:

$$i^* - i + Ee - e = RP \tag{4.3}$$

(for simplicity we have used i and i^* instead of the precise form $\log(1+i)$ and $\log(1+i^*)$).

One way to arrive at an analytical expression of RP is to develop a 'finance-type' model where the individual maximises an expected utility function dependent on the mean and variance of portfolio returns (see Dornbusch (1983b) or Frankel (1982)). With real rates of return being stochastic RP can be expressed as

$$RP = \begin{bmatrix} \text{Degree of} \\ \text{risk} \\ \text{aversion} \end{bmatrix} \cdot \begin{bmatrix} \text{Variance–} \\ \text{co-variance} \\ \text{of expected} \\ \text{exchange} \\ \text{rate changes} \end{bmatrix} \cdot \begin{bmatrix} \text{Portfolio} & \\ \text{share} & \text{Minimum} \\ \text{in foreign} - & \text{variance} \\ \text{currency} & \text{portfolio} \\ \text{asset} & \end{bmatrix} \tag{4.4}$$

The additional risk in holding foreign-currency assets rises when the inflation rates at home and abroad become more unpredictable or when the ratio of foreign-currency assets to total non-monetary wealth rises. On the other hand, a negative co-variance between expected domestic inflation, π, and expected foreign inflation π^*, lowers RP. More importantly, if investors are neutral towards risk $RP = 0$ and the law of one price holds, that is $i = i^* + Ee - e$.

An alternative way to derive RP is to consider the model developed by Stulz (1983) where the world is characterised by one non-stochastic real rate of return, r. The market rates of interest turn out to be more complex than the well-known Fisherian relationship:

$$i = r + \pi + z \text{ var}(K) + a \text{ cov} \tag{4.5a}$$

$$i^* = r + \pi^* + z \text{ var}(K) + b \text{ cov}^* \tag{4.5b}$$

where var (K) denotes the variance of the growth of the capital stock in the world and cov and cov* the covariances at home and abroad between the growth rate of money and the growth rate of capital stock. In more intuitive terms, cov and cov* stand for the relative riskiness of domestic and foreign monetary policies. Finally, we let the change in the expected exchange rate follow expected PPP plus an expected change in real exchange rates, *re*:

$$Ee - e = \pi - \pi^* + re \tag{4.6}$$

Equations (4.5) and (4.6) yield

$$i^* - i + Ee - e = re + b\,\text{cov}^* - a\,\text{cov} \tag{4.7}$$

where the risk premium is equal to the right-hand side of (4.7). The interpretation of the solution is straightforward: a larger expected real depreciation of the domestic money or a monetary policy abroad 'riskier' than that at home raise *RP*. Where *PPP* holds perfectly then $RP = b\ \text{cov}^* - a\ \text{cov}$.

A direct implication of a risk premium is that the forward rate is a biased predictor of the expected spot rate. To see this, recall the gist of Section II. There we made a case that:

$$i^* - i + f - e = 0 \tag{4.8}$$

where the precise form log $(1 + i^*)$ and log $(1 + i)$ was dropped for notational simplicity. Substituting (4.8) in (4.7):

$$Ee - f = RP \tag{4.9}$$

Subtracting from both sides of (4.9) e and using $e_{+1} = Ee - u_{+1}$, u_{+1} being a white-noise error term we obtain

$$e_{+1} - e = (f - e) + RP + u_{+1} \tag{4.10}$$

The left-hand side of (4.10) is the one-period ahead change in the exchange rate. The right-hand side has three components: the forward premium, f–e, the risk premium, *RP*, and the 'news' term, u_{+1}. It follows that the forward premium is a biased predictor of $e_{+1} - e$. It also follows that market efficiency tests based on:

$$\Delta e_{+1} = \alpha + \beta[f - e] + \gamma RP + u_{+1} \tag{4.11}$$

with null hypothesis $\gamma = \alpha = 0$ and $\beta = 1$ are not likely to do well. Levich (1983) in his review article concludes that the empirical studies of the 1970s could not reject the simple market efficiency hypothesis of the form $e_{+1} = \text{a} + \text{bf} + \text{error}$. However, tests performed directly on (4.11) with $\gamma = 0$, rather than on its level form, have done poorly. We report in Table 4.4 estimates of α and β, as well as the serial correlation properties of the error term, of (4.11) in the absence of the non-observable risk premium. Not only $\hat{\alpha}$ but also $\hat{\beta}$ is not significantly different from zero, using the 'soft' criterion of one standard error. Also about zero is the explanatory power of f–e in tracking movements in Δe_{+1}. Thus, we concord with Levich in the assessment that the evidence is not too charitable towards simple forward market efficiency.

More important for us is how to interpret the foregoing results with reference to the non-observable risk premium. The literature presents mixed results. For example, Jeffrey Frankel who has contributed to the literature on the subject finds in the paper cited earlier that he cannot reject the null hypothesis of risk neutrality when estimating asset demand functions of the general form of equation (4.4). On the other hand, there are several studies which associate the failure of the simple market efficiency hypothesis with the existence of a risk premium that changes over time.[5] Dooley and Isard (1982) generate a risk premium by estimating a portfolio-balance model in which the expected rate of exchange is formed rationally. By so doing they are able to track Δe_{+1} more tightly than using (f–e), although errors of their model's prediction of the level of the exchange rate are serially correlated. On the whole, the evidence of the study favours the existence of risk aversion.

IV SUMMARY

This chapter intended to prepare the ground for modelling the financial sector of the economy along the guidelines of portfolio-balance theory, in contrast to a strict monetary theory of exchange rate determination. To justify the choice, we had to make the case that assets denominated in different currencies are imperfectly substitutable, either because governmental controls, fiscal treatment or political risks make them so or because investors require a risk premium in holding an asset denominated in a money other than the money exchanged domestically for consumer goods.

We found that interest rate parity (IRP) holds fairly tightly when using Eurocurrency interest rates and much less so when using domestic interest rates. We also found that the null hypothesis of simple forward market efficiency must be rejected. The inference we have drawn from our tests, as well as those available in the literature, is favourable towards imperfect substitutability across assets with different currency denominations.

TABLE 4.4 *Simple market efficiency hypothesis*, (equation 4.11, $\gamma = 0$). *Quarterly data, end-of-period* 1973(*I*)–1980(*IV*)

Country		$\hat{\alpha}$	$\hat{\beta}$	$\overline{R}^2$	*DW*	*Constant*	*u*	u_{-1}	u_{-2}	u_{-3}	*F*
Germany		0.002 (0.02)	1.705 (1.77)	−0.002	2.09	0.002 (0.01)	−0.083 (0.21)	−0.229 (0.21)	0.270 (0.20)	0.032 (0.22)	1.24
France		0.001 (0.01)	−0.206 (1.06)	−0.033	1.96	−0.003 (0.01)	−0.167 (0.23)	−0.014 (0.20)	0.096 (0.22)	−0.144 (0.22)	0.24
Netherlands		−0.007 (0.01)	0.922 (1.53)	−0.022	2.00	0.0005 (0.01)	0.057 (0.21)	−0.397* (0.20)	0.286 (0.20)	−0.162 (0.22)	1.82
UK		−0.012 (0.01)	1.448 (1.12)	0.022	1.65	−0.002 (0.008)	0.319 (0.21)	−0.255 (0.20)	0.422* (0.20)	0.049 (0.21)	2.02
Belgium	Commercial rate	−0.007 (0.01)	−0.50 (1.13)	−0.028	2.14	−0.001 (0.01)	−0.180 (0.22)	−0.299 (0.21)	0.245 (0.21)	0.032 (0.22)	1.49
	Financial rate 77(II)–80(IV)	1.005 (0.02)	4.188 (5.14)	−0.027	2.75	−0.002 (0.01)	0.132 (0.23)	0.036 (0.19)	0.196 (0.16)	0.105 (0.12)	0.77
Italy		0.009 (0.02)	0.215 (0.67)	−0.031	2.32	−0.002 (0.01)	−0.131 (0.21)	0.076 (0.21)	0.137 (0.21)	−0.209 (0.21)	0.51

NOTES 1 Standard errors in parentheses
2. A* denotes significance at 90 per cent level
3. The right-hand side of the table shows the autocorrelation pattern of the error term of the left-hand side of the table.

NOTES

1. Aliber (1973) was the first to make this point.
2. In this chapter X will be used as a general symbol denoting either XD or XE.
3. With the exception of the absolute mean value of the French XE which is about six times its XD counterpart.
4. Cf. Fratianni and Wakeman (1982) and Levich (1983).
5. These are reviewed in Frankel (1982) and in Levich (1983) who curiously misinterprets Frankel's 1982 study.

5 The Theory of the Financial Economy

I INTRODUCTION

The essential message of Chapter 4 was that financial assets with different currency denominations are imperfect substitutes. This consideration justifies modelling the financial economy according to portfolio-balance principles. The literature on this subject is of recent vintage. While Fleming (1962) and Mundell (1963) are credited with having inspired the portfolio-balance approach, it was not until the early 1970s that economists adapted James Tobin's well-known contribution to the theory of asset determination – developed for a closed economy – to an economy that desires to be a holder of net external claims (net external liabilities), that is an economy with a surplus (deficit) in its cumulative current account of the balance of payments.[1] The exchange rate, in this framework, adjusts so as to ensure that asset supplies are willing held. Thus, by its very nature, this view emphasises the short run.

Typically, portfolio-balance models of the open economy consist of two domestic assets, currency and a domestic bond supplied by the government and one foreign asset. Assets supplied by the domestic banking sector, for example, loans, are routinely disregarded. Our theory will instead incorporate a banking sector into the traditional model. This is done in Section II of the chapter. The domestic bond market, initially ignored, will be introduced subsequently. Finally, we will provide an analytical 'rational' solution for the expected exchange rate.

II A PORTFOLIO-BALANCE MODEL WITH A BANKING SECTOR

Demand Behaviour

Individuals in our economy are allowed to hold three assets and issue one liability (a negative asset): domestic currency, BP; domestic bank deposits, D; foreign bonds valued in domestic money $S^*.es$ – where the * denotes, as usual, a foreign variable valued in foreign money units and es is the spot exchange rate defined as the domestic price of foreign money – and bank loans, L. It follows that individuals' wealth WP can be defined as follows:

$$WP = BP + D + S^*.es - L \tag{5.1}$$

Following De Grauwe (1982) the asset demand schedules have the form

$$\begin{array}{rcllllll}
BP & = & BP(i_D^-, & & , i_D^* + \overset{-}{E}e - e, & & , \overset{+}{W}P) & (5.2)\\
D & = & D(i_D^+ & , i^- & , i_D^* + \overset{-}{E}e - e, & & , \overset{+}{W}P) & (5.3)\\
L & = & L(& , i^-, & & , i^* + \overset{+}{E}e - e, & \overset{+}{W}P) & (5.4)\\
S^*.es & = & S^*(i_D^- & , i^- & , i_D^* + \overset{+}{E}e - e, & i^* + \overset{+}{E}e - e, & \overset{+}{W}P) & (5.5)\\
\hline
\text{Column sum restrictions} & & 0 & 0 & 0 & 0 & 1 &
\end{array}$$

All variables are defined in Table 5.1. Ee denotes the expected logarithm of the spot rate for $t+1$ conditional on information up to $t-1$.

TABLE 5.1 *List of variables used in Chapter 5.*

A	= borrowing from monetary authorities
b	= A/D: domestic borrowing ratio
B	= monetary base
BC	= bank credit
BP	= Currency or base money held by the public
D	= sight deposits
e	= logarithm of the spot exchange rate
es	= spot exchange rate
i	= interest rate on loans
i_D	= interest rate on deposits
k	= currency deposit ratio
L	= bank loans
M	= money stock
ρ	= reserve requirement ratio
S	= stock of government bonds
S^b	= stock of bonds held by banks
S^p	= stock of bonds held by non-banks
WP	= private wealth

* indicates foreign variables

The signs of the partial derivatives of the functions are indicated above the respective variables by a '$-$' or a '$+$'. Column sum restrictions indicated below the dashed line tell us that wealth must be held and that changes in other arguments affect quantities demanded such that $dBP + dD + d(S^*.es) - dL = 0$. These are well-known features of Tobin-inspired financial models. Equations (5.2)–(5.5) are written in such a way as to imply additional constraints; for example the effect of i and $i^* + Ee - e$ on BP is zero.

Banks in our economy operate with balance sheet

$$\rho D + L = D \tag{5.6}$$

where ρ denotes the reserve requirement ratio and ρD = required reserves. In a world of certainty and perfect competition banks maximise

$$D[(1-\rho)i - i_D] - [\text{Cost function depending on } D] \tag{5.7}$$

with first-order condition

$$i = \frac{i_D + \phi}{1 - \rho} \tag{5.8}$$

where ϕ is the marginal cost, other than i_D, to supply an additional domestic-currency unit of deposits. ϕ can be either constant or rising. For simplicity we set $\phi = 0$ and replace i_D in (5.2)–(5.5) with $(1-\rho)i$ and in so doing we can reduce the arguments inside the asset demand functions to i, $i^* + Ee - e$ and WP, as shown in (5.2a)–(5.5a) below.[2]

$$BP = BP(\overset{-}{i}, i^* + E\overset{-}{e} - e, \overset{+}{W}P) \tag{5.2a}$$

$$D = D(\overset{+}{i}, i^* + E\overset{-}{e} - e, \overset{+}{W}P) \tag{5.3a}$$

$$L = L(\overset{-}{i}, i^* + E\overset{+}{e} - e, \overset{+}{W}P) \tag{5.4a}$$

$$S^*.es = S^*(\overset{-}{i}, i^* + E\overset{+}{e} - e, \overset{+}{W}P) \tag{5.5a}$$

with constraints on partial derivatives

$$BP_j + D_j - L_j + S^*_j \begin{cases} = 0 & j = 1, 2 \\ = 1 & j = 3 \end{cases}$$

where j indicates the number of the variable with respect to which the derivative is taken.

Next define the money stock

$$M = BP + D \tag{5.9}$$

The demand for money is obtained by adding (5.3a) to (5.2a); that is,

$$M = M^d(\overset{-}{i}, i^* + \overset{-}{E}e - e, \overset{+}{W}P) \tag{5.10}$$

The complete system of asset demand functions consists of (5.4a), (5.5a) and (5.10); one of these functions can be eliminated in the light of the fact that the definition of wealth permits one asset quantity to be determined implicity. In the analysis that follows the demand for foreign assets will be dropped. Wealth, we recall, is $BP + D + S^*.es - L$, whereas $L = (1 - \rho)D$ through the banks' balance sheet. Combining the two statements and defining the monetary base as

$$B = BP + \rho D \tag{5.11}$$

it is straightforward to see that $WP = S^*.es + B$.

Supply Behaviour

The essential, and often misunderstood, point about the supply of money and bank credit is that is *not* independent of the way individuals allocate their wealth between currency and bank deposits; or, stated in more general terms, supply behaviour is related to demand behaviour. As Saving (1977, p. 294) notes:

> This dependence stems from the fact that bank money is a reserve money and the banking system's principal competition for reserves is the non-bank public. The public in attaining its desired level of currency, for a fixed level of the monetary base and reserve ratio, determines the quantity of demand deposits supplied. Thus, an industry money supply schedule, i.e. the relation between the sum of currency and demand deposits supplied and the deposit rate, cannot be derived since the demand for currency is a function of the deposit rate and in turn affects the supply of demand deposits. It is, however, possible to derive a money supply schedule of the form usually used in macro-economics models, i.e. a locus of monetary sector equilibria.

The macro-type supply of money mentioned by Saving is derived by using the banks' balance-sheet identity $L = D(1 - \rho)$, the definitions of the money stock (5.9) and the monetary base (5.11) and postulating that individuals maintain a ratio k of currency to bank deposits:

$$BP = kD \tag{5.12}$$

From this the supply of money can be written in the familiar multiplier form:[3]

$$M = \frac{1+k}{k+\rho} B \tag{5.13}$$

Noting that $L = M - B$, the supply of bank credit becomes:

$$L = \frac{1-\rho}{k+\rho} B \tag{5.14}$$

It should be noted that the supply of money is not a mirror image of the supply of credit, a point often emphasised by Brunner and Meltzer (see especially Brunner and Meltzer (1968)). An increase in the reserve requirement ratio raises the supply of money relative to the supply of credit; similarly for an increase in k.

For analytical purposes we find it convenient to express (5.13) and (5.14) in functional form

$$M = M^s(\overset{+}{i},\ \overset{-}{i^* + Ee - e},\ \overset{-}{\rho},\ \overset{+}{B}) \tag{5.13a}$$

$$L = L^s(\overset{+}{i},\ \overset{-}{i^* + Ee - e},\ \overset{-}{\rho},\ \overset{+}{B}) \tag{5.14a}$$

The signs of the partial derivatives M^s_2 and L^s_2 were assigned a negative value based on the 'reasonable' assumption that an increase in $i^* + Ee - e$ lowers bank deposits more than currency, that is, it raises k. In addition, changes in the reserve requirement ratio have a larger impact on L^s than on M^s, whereas changes in the monetary base have a larger impact on M^s than on L^s.

Equilibrium Behaviour

Our financial economy, to repeat, has three asset demand schedules, one wealth constraint and two supply schedules. The wealth constraint makes one demand schedule redundant, in our case the demand for foreign assets. In equilibrium the system can be written as:

$$L(\overset{-}{i},\ \overset{+}{i^* + Ee - e},\ \overset{+}{B + S^*.es}) - L^s(\overset{+}{i},\ \overset{-}{i^* + Ee - e},\ \overset{-}{\rho},\ \overset{+}{B}) = 0 \tag{5.15}$$

$$-M^d(\overset{-}{i},\ \overset{-}{i^* + Ee - e},\ \overset{+}{B + S^*.es}) + M^s(\overset{+}{i},\ \overset{-}{i^* + Ee - e},\ \overset{-}{\rho},\ \overset{+}{B}) = 0 \tag{5.16}$$

and solves for i and $e(e)$, given the values of i^*, Ee (or Ees), B, S^* and ρ.

Comparison with Perfect Substitutability Assumption

The two equilibrium equations (5.15) and (5.16) are shown in Figure 5.1 in the i/es plane. MM refers to the money market and LL to the credit market. It is postulated that the domestic interest rate is approximately determined in the credit market and the exchange rate in the money market. This means that i has a comparative advantage relative to es in restoring conditions of equilibrium in the LL market while the opposite is true for the MM market.

Figure 5.1 is drawn to reflect this set of assumptions. An increase in i creates an excess supply of money; the domestic currency must depreciate (es rises) to restore equilibrium. The relative steepness of the MM curve reflects the view that es is the 'fast' variable of this market. An increase in i creates also an excess supply of credit; the domestic currency must appreciate (es falls) to restore equilibrium. This is so because the appreciation of the domestic currency makes foreign borrowing expensive, thereby inducing residents to increase their domestic borrowing. The comparative advantage of i shows up in a flat LL line, suggesting that it takes a larger change in es than in i to bring back equilibrium in the market for credit.

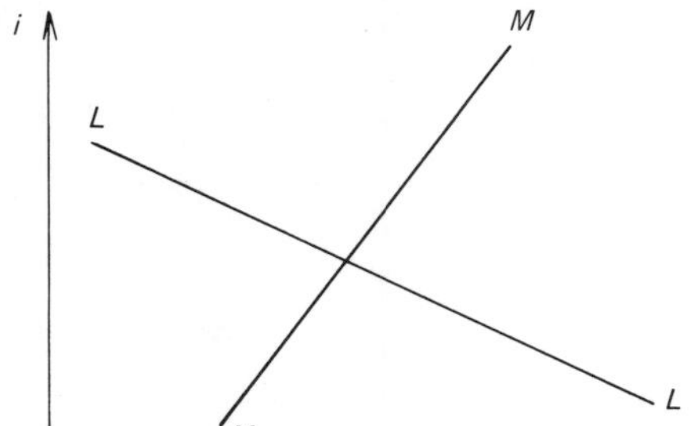

FIGURE 5.1 *The money and credit markets*

When domestic and foreign assets are perfect substitutes the portfolio-balance approach collapses into a monetarist model.[4] This is easily seen by imposing equality of yields across assets with different currency denominations:

$$i = i^* + Ee - e \tag{5.17}$$

Equation (5.17) replaces (5.15) and the money market determines the spot exchange rate. The specific results of this solution are well-known and need not be repeated here.[5]

Comparative Statics

We rewrite (5.15)–(5.16) in the differential form:[6]

$$\begin{bmatrix} a_{11} & a_{12} \\ a_{21} & a_{22} \end{bmatrix} \begin{bmatrix} di \\ des \end{bmatrix} = \begin{bmatrix} a_{1B}dB + a_{1i^*}(di^* + dEe) + a_{1\rho}d_\rho + a_{1S^*}dS^* \\ a_{2B}dB + a_{2i^*}(di^* + dEe) + a_{2\rho}d\rho + a_{2S^*}dS^* \end{bmatrix} \tag{5.18}$$

Where

$$a_{11} = L_1 - L_1^s < 0$$

$$a_{12} = \left(\frac{-L_2 + L_2^s}{es}\right) + L_3 S^* < 0 \qquad \text{by constraint}$$

$$a_{21} = M_1^s - M_1^d > 0$$

$$a_{22} = \left(\frac{-M_2^s + M_2^d}{es}\right) - M_3^d S^* < 0 \qquad \text{by constraint}$$

$$a_{1B} = L_4^s - L_3 > 0 \qquad \text{by constraint}$$

$$a_{2B} = M_3^d - M_4^s < 0 \qquad \text{by constraint}$$

$$a_{1i^*} = L_2^s - L_2 < 0$$

$$a_{2i^*} = M_2^d - M_2^s < 0 \qquad \text{by constraint}$$

$$a_{1\rho} = L_3^s < 0$$

$$a_{2\rho} = -M_3^s > 0$$

$$a_{1S^*} = -L_3(es) < 0$$

$$a_{2S^*} = M_3^d(es) > 0$$

Constraints on the relative order of magnitudes were imposed whenever the sign of the '*a*s' was ambiguous. To illustrate, a_{12} is negative on the assumption that the effect of the expected foreign yield on the credit market exceeds the impact on the same market of a change in wealth occurring because the spot exchange rate has changed. This constraint, as well as others, becomes an integral part of the hypothesis. In addition, stability conditions require that:

$$a_{11} + a_{22} < 0$$

and

$$\Delta = a_{11}a_{22} - a_{12}a_{21} > 0$$

which are automatically satisfied.

Table 5.2 summarises the results of the comparative statics. Five out of ten multipliers have ambiguous signs unless, again, additional constraints are imposed. The source of the ambiguities and the assumptions made to resolve them are best illustrated by reference to graphs. We begin with an increase in the monetary base which creates an excess supply in both the money and credit markets. See Figure 5.2.

TABLE 5.2 *Multipliers of the financial economy*

	Endogenous	
	i	*es*
Exogenous		
B	$\frac{a_{1B}a_{22} - a_{2B}a_{12}}{\Delta} < 0$	$\frac{a_{11}a_{2B} - a_{21}a_{1B}}{\Delta} > 0$ provided $a_{11}a_{2B} > \lvert a_{21}a_{1B}\rvert$
*i**, *Ee*	$\frac{a_{1i^*}a_{22} - a_{2i^*}a_{12}}{\Delta} > 0$ provided $a_{1i^*}a_{22} > a_{2i^*}a_{12}$	$\frac{a_{11}a_{2i^*} - a_{21}a_{1i^*}}{\Delta} > 0$
ρ	$\frac{a_{1\rho}.a_{22} - a_{2\rho}a_{12}}{\Delta} > 0$	$\frac{a_{11}a_{2\rho} - a_{21}a_{1\rho}}{\Delta} < 0$ provided $\lvert a_{11}a_{2\rho}\rvert > \lvert a_{21}a_{1\rho}\rvert$
*S**	$\frac{a_{1S^*}a_{22} - a_{2S^*}a_{12}}{\Delta} > 0$	$\frac{a_{11}a_{2S^*} - a_{21}a_{1S^*}}{\Delta} < 0$ provided $\lvert a_{11}a_{2S^*}\rvert > \lvert a_{21}a_{1S^*}\rvert$

As a result the *MM*-line shifts downwards, that is, we need a decline in the interest rate (for a given exchange rate) in order to eliminate the excess supply of money. The *LL*-curve also shifts downwards for the same reason. The effect on the loan rate is unambiguous. The exchange rate may or may not increase. Given our assumption that the loan rate

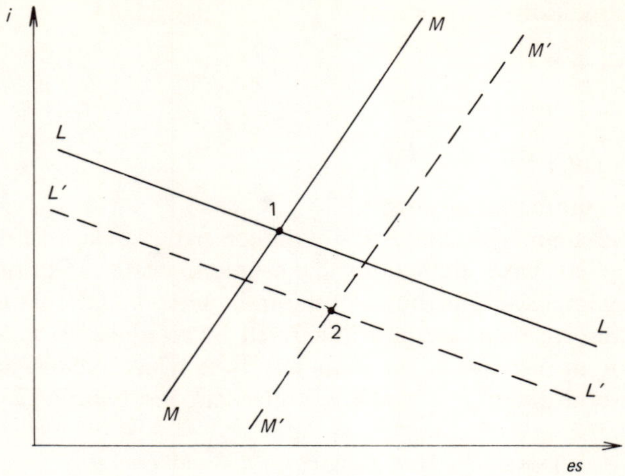

FIGURE 5.2 *Increase in the monetary base*

has a comparative advantage in eliminating the disequilibrium in the loan market it follows that the downward movement of the *LL*-curve is smaller than the downward movement of the *MM*-curve. This assumption ensures that the exchange rate increases after an increase in the money base.

A rise in the foreign interest rate (i^*) has the same effect as a rise in the expected future spot rate (*Ee*): both generate an excess supply of money and an excess demand for domestic bank loans. (See Figure 5.3.) As a result the *MM*-line shifts to the right, that is, in order to eliminate the excess supply of money the spot exchange rate must increase for any given level of the loan rate.[7] Because of the increase in i^* (or in *Ee*) the *LL*-line also shifts to the right, and upwards. This means that in order to eliminate the excess demand for loans the domestic loan rate must increase. The net effect of these two shifts is to increase the exchange rate. The effect on the loan rate is ambiguous. However, we can again invoke our assumption that the exchange rate has a comparative advantage in equilibrating the money market. In that case we know that the rightward shift of the *MM*-curve is smaller than the rightward shift of the *LL*-curve, that is, one needs a smaller increase in the exchange rate to eliminate the disequilibrium in the money market, than one needs to eliminate the disequilibrium in the credit market. Given this assumption the domestic loan rate increases unambiguously.

The effects of an increase in reserve requirements (ρ) are shown in

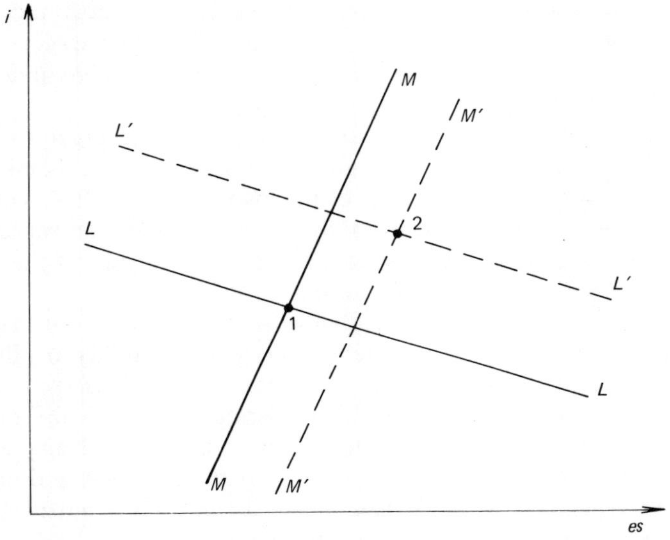

FIGURE 5.3 *Increase in the foreign interest rate or expected depreciation of the domestic currency*

Figure 5.4. A higher reserve requirement produces excess demand for loans as banks reduce the supply of loans. In order to maintain credit market equilibrium the loan rate must increase. Graphically, the *LL*-curve shifts upwards. In the money market we also have excess demand.

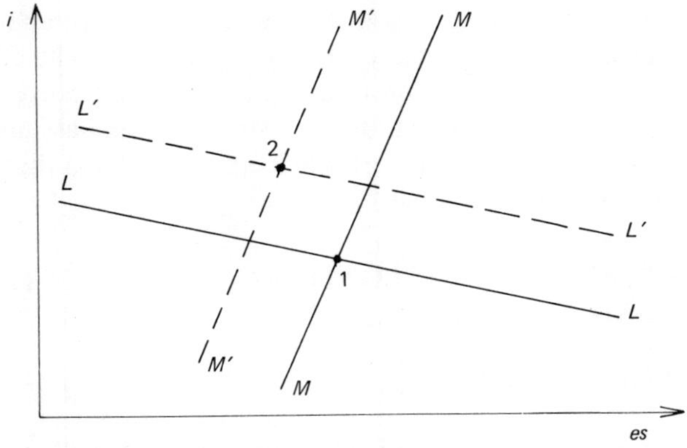

FIGURE 5.4 *Increase in reserve requirements*

This results from the fact that banks now compete for cash to comply with the higher reserve requirement. In order to eliminate excess demand in the money market the interest rate must increase: the *MM*-curve shifts upwards.

As a result of these shifts the loan rate increases unambiguously. The effect on the exchange rate is ambiguous. Using the same assumption about the comparative advantage of the loan rate to eliminate equilibrium in the loan market, we arrive at the conclusion that the upward shift of the *LL*-curve is small compared with the upward shift of the *MM*-curve, so that the exchange rate declines.

It is important to point out here that when domestic and foreign assets are perfect substitutes, reserve requirements lose their ability to influence the domestic interest rate and the exchange rate. Since reserve requirements are a form of tax on banking operations it raises the margin between the loan rate and the deposit rate. Residents, being totally indifferent between domestic and foreign loans and between domestic and foreign deposits, will shift their demand completely to outside banks not subject to reserve requirements. Thus in a world of perfect substitutability, reserve requirements cannot be used as an instrument of monetary control, even in a flexible exchange rate system. Monetary authorities will have to rely on 'Anglo-Saxon' instruments of monetary control such as open market operations.

A final comparative static exercise concerns the effect of an exogenous change in the stock of domestically-held foreign bonds (S^*). Such a change will in general come about as a result of shocks in the current account. We suppose here that the stock of foreign bonds held by residents increases (because of a current account surplus). The effects are shown in Figure 5.5. The increase in S^* increases wealth and leads to excess demand in both the credit and money markets. The effects are qualitatively the same as in the previous comparative statics exercise. The *LL* and *MM*-curves shift upwards. Invoking the same assumption as before we conclude that the interest rate increases and that the domestic currency appreciates (*es* declines).

III OUTSIDE DOMESTIC BONDS AND INTERVENTIONS IN THE EXCHANGE MARKET

Outside Domestic Bonds

The simplest way to introduce 'outside' domestic bonds into the model is to make their yield the same as the interest rate on loans; that is, perfect

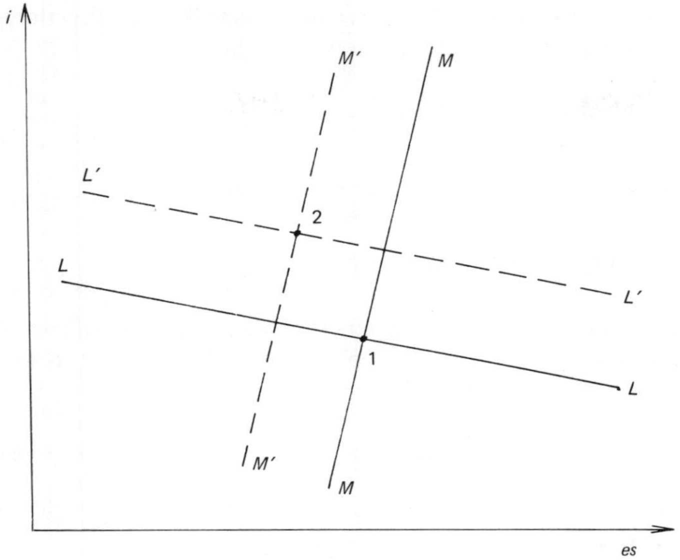

FIGURE 5.5 *Increase in the stock of domestically-held foreign bonds*

substitutability. This assumption will be relaxed later. Equation (5.19) defines the equilibrium condition in the market for bonds which are claims on government with a fixed price and a variable coupon equal to the rate of interest i:

$$S = S^p + S^b \tag{5.19}$$

S denotes the stock net of what is held by the monetary authorities, S^p the quantity demanded and held by the public and S^b the quantity demanded and held by banks.

Next, let us define bank credit BC = bank loans + S^b. In equilibrium:

$$L^s + S^b = L + S - S^p \tag{5.20}$$

where the left-hand side of (5.20) denotes the banks' supply of bank credit and the right-hand side the public's demand for bank credit.[8] The functional specification of the left-hand side of (5.20) is the same as (5.14a), that is:

$$L^s + S^b = BC(\overset{+}{i}, \overset{-}{i^* + Ee - e}, \overset{-}{\rho}, \overset{+}{B}) \tag{5.21}$$

To derive the functional relationship of the right-hand side of (5.20) we need first to reconsider the structure of the asset demand functions. With perfect substitutability between loans and bonds:

$$M = M^d(\overset{-}{i},\ i^* + \overset{-}{Ee} - e,\ B + \overset{+}{S} + S^*es) \tag{5.22}$$

$$-S^p + L = v(\overset{-}{i},\ i^* + \overset{+}{Ee} - e,\ B + \overset{+}{S} + S^*es) \tag{5.23}$$

$$S^*es = S^*(\overset{-}{i},\ i^* + \overset{+}{Ee} - e,\ B + \overset{+}{S} + S^*es) \tag{5.24}$$

where wealth now includes the stock of outside bonds, and v is the net indebtedness of the public.[9] Replacing (5.21) and (5.23) in (5.20) we express the bank credit market:

$$v(\overset{-}{i},\ i^* + \overset{+}{Ee} - e,\ B + \overset{+}{S} + S^*es) + S - BC(\overset{+}{i},\ i^* + \overset{-}{Ee} - e,\ \overset{-}{\rho},\ \overset{+}{B}) = 0 \tag{5.25}$$

and the money market

$$M^s(\overset{+}{i},\ i^* + \overset{-}{Ee} - e,\ \overset{-}{\rho},\ \overset{+}{B}) - M^d(\overset{-}{i},\ i^* + \overset{-}{Ee} - e,\ B + \overset{+}{S} + S^*es) = 0 \tag{5.26}$$

We are now ready to trace the effect of movements in S on i and es. A positive change in S raises wealth and excess demand conditions develop in MM and LL.

A rising i tends to restore equilibrium in the two markets. But an appreciating currency, holding Ee constant, raises the expected foreign yield, reduces the excess demand for money, while raising the excess demand for credit. A depreciating currency, on the other hand, reduces excess demand in LL, while raising it in MM. The concomitant occurrence of a higher i and a higher es is consistent with equilibrium when the credit market responds more forcefully than the money market to a change in S. This is the situation depicted in Figure 5.6. Analytically,

$$\frac{di}{dS} = \frac{a_{1S}a_{22} - a_{2S}a_{12}}{\Delta} > 0$$

$$\frac{des}{dS} = \frac{a_{11}a_{2S} - a_{21}a_{1S}}{\Delta} \gtrless 0$$

$$a_{1S} = -(1 + v_3) < 0$$

$$a_{2S} = M_3^d > 0$$

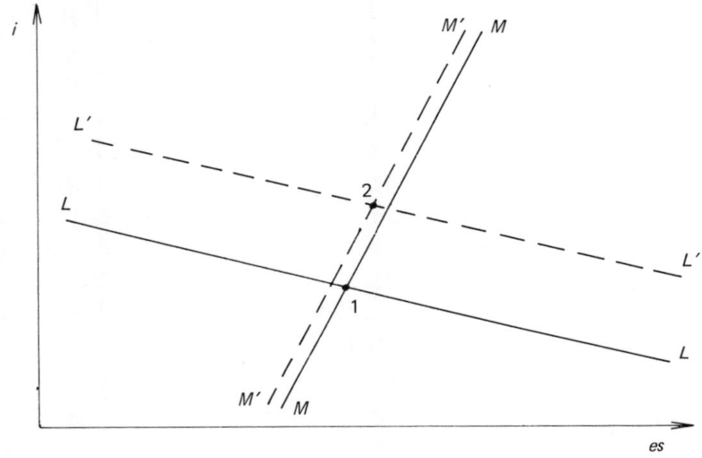

FIGURE 5.6 *Increase in the stock of domestic bonds*

Exchange Market Interventions

Consider now a sterilised intervention of the central authorities in the spot exchange market. The essential element of a sterilised intervention is that the monetary base does not change, for the authorities engage in two open market operations with opposite effects on *B*. More to the point,

$$dB = 0$$
$$dS + d(S^*es) = 0$$

Should the central bank be interested in forcing an appreciation of the domestic currency, it would sell foreign assets (destroy monetary base) and purchase domestic bonds (create monetary base). The impact on *i* and *es* of the two transactions can be stated formally under the simplifying assumption that $es = 1$ initially.[10]

$$\left.\frac{di}{dS^*}\right|_{(dS^* + dS = 0)} = \frac{a_{22}(a_{1S^*} - a_{1S}) + a_{12}(a_{2S} - a_{2S^*})}{\Delta} < 0$$

with

$$a_{1S^*} - a_{1S} = 1$$

and

$$a_{2S} - a_{2S^*} = 0$$

$$\left.\frac{des}{dS^*}\right|_{(dS^* + dS = 0)} = \frac{a_{11}(a_{2S^*} - a_{2S}) + a_{21}(a_{1S} - a_{1S^*})}{\Delta} < 0$$

It is hardly surprising to find that a central bank can force an appreciation of its currency by simultaneously selling foreign bonds and buying domestic bonds, in light of the fact that these assets are imperfectly substitutable for each other. Clearly as the degree of substitutability rises, the ability to influence *es* declines. When interest-rate parity holds at all points in time:

$$\left.\frac{di}{dS^*}\right|_{(dS^* + dS = 0)} = \left.\frac{des}{dS^*}\right|_{(dS^* + dS = 0)} = 0,$$

for there is one bond market in the world and sterilised interventions can only alter the distribution between bonds denominated in different monies, with no effect on *es*. But, as discussed in Chapter 4, there is evidence of imperfect substitution across assets and the difference between i and $(i^* + Ee - e)$ can theoretically be explained in terms of a time-varying risk premium. Interventions can affect *es* by altering this premium. The quantitative importance of this argument is an issue we will take up in Chapter 7.

Other Extensions

Two extensions to the model are considered. The first concerns relaxing the assumption of perfect substitutability between loans and bonds; the second involves modelling the domestic and foreign borrowing behaviour of banks. The first is treated in Brunner and Meltzer (1966) and Fratianni (1976) and the second in Fratianni (1976). Briefly, imperfect substitutability between loans and bonds requires that the bank credit market be decomposed into a market for loans and a market for bonds. The domestic interest rate i is replaced by a loan rate and a bond rate. The model acquires additional complexity but the main message does not change.

The second extension also implies that more structure be built around the basic framework. More specifically the banks' balance sheet would expand to include borrowing from the monetary authorities (A) and net foreign borrowing (A^*es)

$$\rho D + BC = D + A + A^*es \tag{5.27}$$

The demand schedules of A and A^*es would depend on the domestic interest rates, the expected foreign yield and the reserve requirement ratio. Letting $b = A/D$ (the domestic borrowing ratio), $b^* = A^*es/D$ (the foreign borrowing ratio), the supply of bank credit would become

$$BC = \frac{1 + b + b^* - \rho}{k + \rho} B \tag{5.28}$$

instead of the simpler equation (5.14).

The analysis of this section was carried out under the restriction of a parametrically-given expected rate of exchange. This restriction will be relaxed in the following section where we develop an internally consistent, or rational, solution for Ee.

IV THE RATIONAL EXPECTATIONS SOLUTION

We first write the reduced-form equation of e implied by our portfolio-balance model expressed in logarithmic linear form:

$$e_t = a_1 \underset{t-1}{E} e_{t+1} + \sum_{j=2}^{6} a_j x_t^j + u_t \tag{5.29}$$

where x_t^j is the natural logarithm of $B(j = 2)$, $i^*(j = 3)$, $\rho(j = 4)$, $S^*(j = 5)$ and $S(j = 6)$; and u_t is a stochastic term.

We assume that each exogenous variable of the financial model can be optimally forecast by considering only its first-period lagged value; that is, $x_t^j = \beta_j x_{t-1}^j + \varepsilon_t^j$ where β_j is a coefficient and ε_t^j a stochastic term. In addition, we denote by μ_t a martingale process that depends exclusively on the current and past values of the white-noise stochastic term u_t. A crucial property of the martingale is that μ_{t-1} is the value of the expectations of future values of μ conditional on information up to time $t-1$; more formally:

$$\underset{t-1}{E} \mu_{t+n} = \mu_{t-1} \qquad \text{for } n = 0, 1, 2, \ldots$$

As shown in the appendix to this chapter, the rational expectations solutions for e_t and e_{t+1}, are:

$$e_t = \frac{1}{a_1^{t-1}} \mu_{t-1} + \sum_{j=2}^{6} \frac{a_j \beta_j}{1 - a_1 \beta_j} x_{t-1}^j + \sum_{j=2}^{6} a_j \varepsilon_t^j + u_t \tag{5.30}$$

$$e_{t+1} = \frac{1}{a_1^t}\mu_t + \sum_{j=2}^{6} \frac{a_j(\beta_j)^2}{1-a_1\beta_j} x_{t-1}^j + \sum_{j=2}^{6}\left(\frac{a_j\beta_j}{1-a_1\beta}\right)\varepsilon_t^j$$

$$+ \sum_{j=2}^{6} a_j\varepsilon_{t+1}^j + u_{t+1} \tag{5.31}$$

Without loss of generality we can simplify these two solutions by reducing the number of exogenous variables to one; this permits us to rewrite (5.30) and (5.31) as:

$$e_t = \frac{1}{a_1^{t-1}}\mu_{t-1} + \frac{a_2\beta}{1-a_1\beta} x_{t-1} + a_2\varepsilon_t + u_t \tag{5.30a}$$

$$e_{t+1} = \frac{1}{a_1^t}\mu_t + \frac{a_2\beta^2}{1-a_1\beta} x_{t-1} + \left(\frac{a_2\beta}{1-a_1\beta}\right)\varepsilon_t + a_2\varepsilon_{t+1} + u_{t+1} \tag{5.31a}$$

The first term on the right-hand-side represents the homogeneous solution or bubble component; the rest the particular solution.[11] The solution is explosive when the coefficient of the expected spot rate, a_1, is less than unity unless $\mu_{t-1} = 0$.

The value of e changes over time, as can be seen by subtracting (5.30) from (5.31):

$$e_{t+1} - e_t = \frac{1}{a_1^t}\mu_t - \frac{1}{a_1^{t-1}}\mu_{t-1} + \frac{a_2\beta}{1-a_1\beta}(\beta-1)x_{t-1}$$

$$+ \frac{a_2}{1-a_1\beta}(a_1\beta+\beta-1) + a_2\varepsilon_{t+1} + u_{t+1} - u_t \tag{5.32}$$

Both the homogeneous and the particular solutions contribute to the time path of e. The particular solution drops out when the exogenous variable follows a random-walk processes, that is, $\beta = 1$.

Finally, we obtain the expected spot exchange rate Ee_{t+1} conditional on information up to $t-1$ by taking the conditional expectation of (5.31):

$$\underset{t-1}{E}\, e_{t+1} = \frac{1}{a_1^t}\mu_{t-1} + \frac{a_2\beta^2}{1-a_1\beta} x_{t-1} \tag{5.33}$$

and the expected change in the spot rate by taking the conditional expectations of (5.32):

$$\underset{t-1}{E}\,(e_{t+1} - e_t) = \left(\frac{1}{a_1^t} - \frac{1}{a_1^{t-1}}\right)\mu_{t-1} + \frac{a_2\beta}{1-a_1\beta}(\beta-1)x_{t-1} \tag{5.34}$$

It is instructive to compare (5.32) with the simple market efficiency hypothesis, discussed in Section III of Chapter 4, and with the evidence that most structural models do not outperform a random-walk process of the exchange rate.[12] According to the latter $e_{t+1} - e_t$ responds to unpredictable 'news'. The poor performance of the forward premium in tracking $e_{t+1} - e_t$ (cf. Table 4.4) provides corrobative evidence for this view. Equation (5.32), however, says that there is more than that: the particular solution captures systematic movements in the series, while 'news' is imbedded in μ_t, ε_{t+1}, ε_t, u_{t+1}, and u_t.

Assuming that a test based on (5.32) was successful in explaining a significant fraction of $e_{t+1} - e_t$, could we infer that the evidence is consistent with a risk premium? Not necessarily, because there is always the danger that a researcher has modelled the 'news' *ex post* with his data. To link $e_{t+1} - e_t$ with a risk premium one has to go beyond and provide direct evidence that the variable being the source of the risk is not captured by the forward premium.

V SUMMARY

This chapter has developed the theory of the financial economy. Having argued for imperfect substitutability between domestic and foreign assets in Chapter 4, we have chosen to model the financial economy according to portfolio-balance principles. Unlike existing models, ours has an explicit banking sector that permits us to analyse how the typical instruments of monetary control in European countries (for example, changes in reserve requirements, credit ceilings and discount rates) affect the equilibrium spot exchange rate. Furthermore, the expected rate of exchange is solved internally by the model according to the dictates of the rational expectations literature. We will apply this model in the next chapter in an empirical analysis of the financial markets in a number of European economies.

NOTES

1. The reader may want to consult Krueger (1983, pp. 81–90) for a more extensive treatment of these general issues and essential bibliographical references.
2. The sign of $D_1 = \frac{\partial D}{\partial i_D}(1-\rho) + \frac{\partial D}{\partial i}$ can be either positive or negative. Saving (1977) argues for $D_1 \geqslant 0$, a finding we accept.

3. The key references are Friedman and Schwartz (1963), Brunner and Meltzer (1964) and Cagan (1965).
4. See De Grauwe (1982), Section IV on this point.
5. For example, cf. Bilson (1978) and Frenkel (1978).
6. Notice that for ease of presentation in Sections II and III we express *es*, the level of the exchange rate, in terms of *Ee*, the expected value of its logarithm.
7. Note that we could have turned this around and stated that for a given exchange rate the interest rate must decline to eliminate excess supply.
8. For details see Fratianni (1976). The classical references concerning this approach are Brunner and Meltzer (1964 and 1968).
9. Since $WP = M + S^p + S^*es - L$, $L = D(1-\rho) - S^b$, $M = B + (1-\rho)D$ and $S = S^p + S^b$, it follows that $WP = B + S + S^*es$.
   In addition, the cross-equation constraints of (5.22)–(5.24) are $M_j^d + S_j^* - v_j \begin{cases} = 0 \text{ for } j = 1, 2 \\ = 1 \text{ for } j = 3 \end{cases}$
10. We are thus ignoring capital gains or losses attributable to the intervention.
11. Technique and terminology are those of Gourieroux, Laffont and Monfort (1982).
12. The reader should consult Meese and Rogoff (1983) as a good synthesis of this evidence.

APPENDIX: DERIVATION OF THE RATIONAL EXPECTATIONS SOLUTION

We begin by rewriting equation (5.29) of the text in the simplified notational form of considering only one exogenous variable in the model:

$$e_t = a_1 E_{t-1} e_{t+1} + a_2 x_t + u_t \tag{A.1}$$

The general solution is found, following Gourieroux–Laffont–Monfort (1982), by finding a particular solution to (A.1), and a general solution to the homogeneous part of (A.1) or the bubble component.

The particular solution can be found as follows, using the method of undetermined coefficients. Suppose:

$$e_t = \pi_0 x_t + \pi_1 x_{t-1} + \pi_2 u_t \tag{A.2}$$

then

$$e_{t+1} = \pi_0 x_{t+1} + \pi_1 x_t + \pi_2 u_{t+1} \tag{A.3}$$

To give analytical substance to the solution we assume the following process for the exogenous variable:

$$x_t = \beta x_{t-1} + \varepsilon_t \tag{A.4}$$

then

$$E_{t-1} x_t = \beta x_{t-1} \tag{A.5}$$

and

$$E_{t-1} x_{t+1} = \beta^2 x_{t-1} \tag{A.6}$$

Hence:

$$E_{t-1}e_{t+1} = (\pi_0\beta^2 + \pi_1\beta)x_{t-1} \tag{A.7}$$

and substituting into (A.1):

$$e_t = a_1(\pi_0\beta^2 + \pi_1\beta)x_{t-1} + a_2x_t + u_t \tag{A.8}$$

which implies, given (A.2), that:

$$\pi_0 = a_2$$

$$\pi_1 = a_1(\pi_0\beta^2 + \pi_1\beta) \qquad \text{or} \qquad \pi_1 = \frac{a_1a_2\beta^2}{1-a_1\beta}$$

$$\pi_2 = 1$$

Hence the particular solution:

$$e_t = a_2x_t + \frac{a_1a_2\beta^2}{1-a_1\beta}x_{t-1} + u_t$$

$$= a_2\beta x_{t-1} + \frac{a_1a_2\beta^2}{1-a_1\beta}x_{t-1} + a_2\varepsilon_t + u_t$$

or

$$e_t = \frac{a_2\beta}{1-a_1\beta}x_{t-1} + a_2\varepsilon_t + u_t \tag{A.9}$$

To find the bubble component, add the component r_t to the solution found previously. For the new formula to be a solution of (A.1), we must have:

$$r_t = a_1E_{t-1}r_{t+1} \tag{A.10}$$

For this to be true we must have:

$$r_t = \frac{1}{a_1^{t-1}}\mu_{t-1} \tag{A.11}$$

where μ_t is a martingale, that is,

$$E_{t-1}\mu_{t+i} = \mu_{t-1} \quad \forall\, i \geqslant 0$$

Then the general solution of (A.1) is the sum of the particular solution and the bubble component:

$$e_t = \frac{1}{a_1^{t-1}}\mu_{t-1} + \frac{a_2\beta}{1-a_1\beta}x_{t-1} + a_2\varepsilon_t + u_t \tag{A.12}$$

Similarly we find the solution for e_{t+1}:

$$e_{t+1} = \frac{1}{a_1^t}\mu_t + \frac{a_2\beta^2}{1-a_1\beta}x_{t-1} + \left(\frac{a_2\beta}{1-a_1\beta}\right)\varepsilon_t + a_2\varepsilon_{t+1} + u_{t+1} \tag{A.13}$$

6 Modelling the Financial Markets: Empirical Findings

I INTRODUCTION

The theoretical analysis of the last chapter will now be employed to estimate the structure of the financial markets. Portfolio-balance models are specified and estimated for six European economies: Germany, France, Italy, the Netherlands, Belgium and the United Kingdom. The financial sector of the last-named country has so many institutional characteristics, as well as specific data requirements, that we found it necessary to treat it separately. In fact, the UK model is presented in Section VI. For the other five countries we employ, instead, a common framework, discussed in Section II. Section III tackles the problems of exchange rate modelling and exchange rate expectations; Section IV, estimation methods; Section V, the findings for the five European countries and Section VII the simulation and tracking performance of the models.

It should be noted that throughout this chapter real income, the price level, and the current account balance are taken as given. The real sector of Chapters 2 and 3 dealt with the determination of manufacturing output and prices. Since a large fraction of gross domestic product is not explained, it is not possible to integrate the real and financial sectors without explicitly endogenising agricultural output, services and other industrial activities, a task beyond the scope of this work. Furthermore, an expected inflation variable of the extrapolative-forecast type is employed in this chapter, in contrast with the rational expectations solution of Chapters 2 and 3. Although a complete integration of the real and financial sector would be a natural and interesting extension of this work, this is not carried out here.

II EMPIRICAL SPECIFICATIONS

The empirical specification of country models is based on the theoretical model of Chapter 5. A number of modifications are made to enrich the empirical analysis and to take into consideration specific institutional characteristics and data limitations.

The Demand for Monetary Assets by the Non-bank Public

Three domestic monetary assets are held by the non-bank public, which, using the notation of Table 6.1, are: base money (*BP*), sight deposits (*D*) and time deposits (*T*). The disaggregation of deposits into two components[1] was made necessary to obtain correct and significant interest rate effects.[2]

The demand for each monetary asset is a function of permanent and transitory income, interest rates and expected inflation. Permanent income (*YPR*) is a proxy for wealth and is measured as a weighted average of past real income with geometrically declining weights *à la* Friedman. As widely used,[3] this scale variable takes account of human and non-human wealth and is a major determinant of the demand for money. The transitory income variable (*YTR*) is the ratio of current real income to permanent real income. The use of this variable can be justified by two separate arguments. The first is that it represents a proxy for the rate of return on wealth, as suggested in Korteweg and Van Loo (1977).[4] The variable would then have a negative effect on the demand for monetary assets. The second argument, following Darby (1972), suggests that transitory income receipts imply larger holdings of liquid assets since they imply larger savings according to the traditional permanent income theory of consumption. Then this variable would have a positive effect on the demand for monetary assets. To the extent that it includes both effects the variable may have a positive or negative coefficient.

Two domestic interest rates are included in the equations: the three-month time deposit rate (*IT*) and the yield on government bonds (*IS*). Since the interest rate on sight deposits is usually zero or very low and varies little, it has not been introduced in the empirical analysis.

In open economies a foreign interest rate has to be included as an argument of the demand for monetary assets. In some studies, such as Arango and Nadiri (1981), the foreign interest rate and the expected exchange rate variation are introduced separately.[5] In agreement with the theory of Chapter 5, our foreign interest rate is adjusted for expected

TABLE 6.1 *List of variables used in the financial model*

A	Advances by the Central Bank
B	Money base
BE	Excess reserves
BF	International reserves of the Central Bank
BP	Base money held by the public
BR	Required reserves
BRR	Required reserve ratio
BTR	Treasury component of the monetary base
CAB	Current account balance
D	Demand deposits
es	Spot exchange rate (domestic currency per dollar), with e denoting its natural logarithm
ef	Forward exchange rate (three months), with f denoting its natural logarithm
FP	Forward premium
FR	Free reserves
IA	Discount rate*
IEA	Bank credit interest rate, calculated as a weighted sum of IS and IL**
IEC	Covered Eurodollar rate (three-month deposits) = $IEU + FP$
IEU	3-months Eurodollar deposit rate
IL	Loan rate*
IS	Bond rate*
IT	Time deposit rate*
K	Capital flow. If $K > 0 \rightarrow$ capital inflow
KP	Capital flow of the non-bank public
L	Bank loans
NFB	Net foreign assets of the banks
NFP	Net foreign assets of the public
OAB	Other assets of the banks
OB	Other assets of the Central Bank
OK	Other capital flow
P	Consumer price index (CPI, base year 1975)
π	Expected rate of inflation
S_i	Seasonal dummies (i = 1, 2, 3)
S	Total stock of government bonds
SB	Bond holdings of banks
SD	Savings deposits
SP	Bonds in hands of the public
T	Time deposits
YC	Current income
YPR	Permanent income
YTR	Transitory income $\left[= \left(\frac{YC}{P}\right) \Big/ YPR\right]$

* There is a change in notation with respect to Chapter 5. Here we do not use subscripts while all letters are capitalised e.g., i_S in Chapter 5 is equivalent to IS in Chapter 6.

** This corresponds to i of Chapter 5.

exchange rate variations. The foreign rate is the three-month Eurodollar deposit rate. The issue of exchange rate expectations modelling is taken up in Section III.

Finally, the expected rate of inflation is an additional explanatory variable, and is measured by a weighted average of past inflation rates. The measurement procedure is conceptually equivalent to that of permanent income.

In general, the behavioural equations of the non-bank public are a combination of log-linear and semi-log-linear forms. All quantity variables are transformed into natural logarithms, while interest rates, exchange rate changes and seasonal dummies are expressed in levels. This is a commonly-used functional form of the demand for assets by the public. It would have been more efficient to estimate these equations as a proportion of wealth, but the unavailability of wealth data argued practically against this approach. Three seasonal dummy variables appear in all equations.

The Demand for Bonds and Bank Loans by the Non-bank Public

The demand schedules for government bonds (*SP*) and for bank loans (*L*) have a specification similar to those of monetary assets: the same explanatory variables are included. On this point two general remarks need to be made. First, for all countries the stock of government bonds held by the public (*SP*) is calculated by subtracting from the total stock of bonds (*S*) that portion held by the banks (*SB*). Therefore *SP* includes domestic government bonds held by foreigners. This error in the measurement of *SP* makes it difficult to estimate correctly a demand for government bonds by the public.

Second, the two equations for *SP* and *L* are empirically estimated, in most cases, in inverted form, that is, with the own interest rate being the dependent variable: *IS* for government bonds, and *IL* for bank loans. This approach was made necessary to obtain 'well-behaved' simulations of the model. The two interest rates are determined endogenoulsy by equilibrium conditions of the bond and bank loan markets. When *IS* and *IL* are solved implicitly through the equilibrium conditions the model simulates nonsensical results. In fact, it turns out that small residual errors in the stock variables *SP* or *L* imply large relative errors in terms of the interest rate variables.[6] Therefore we estimate these demand equations in inverted form to overcome these difficulties. This issue is further taken up in Section V.

Wealth Constraints for the Non-bank Public

As discussed in Chapter 5, the wealth constraint implies the redundancy of one asset demand equation for the non-bank public, in our case the demand for foreign assets. With the exception of the United Kingdom, there are no reliable data on total or financial wealth. Consequently, the wealth constraint could not be imposed explicitly in the model. Furthermore, we have no reliable data on total holdings of foreign assets. Therefore, we estimate all asset demand schedules and assume that the model is part of a larger model where other financial and non-financial assets play the role of residual or redundant assets. Foreign assets show up as flow demand equation in capital flows sections of the model.

Banks Behavioural Equations

In the model banks supply deposits (demand, time, savings) and loans. In addition they hold government bonds (SB), reserves at the Central Bank, net foreign assets (NFB), and other assets (OAB) which are exogenous in the model. The balance sheet of the banks can be written:

$$D+T+A = BR+BE+L+SB+NFB+OAB \tag{6.1}$$

where the meaning of the variables are defined in Table 6.1.

On the asset side required reserves (BR) are determined by the required reserve ratio and deposits. The portfolio behaviour of the banks is determined through equations for the demand for government bonds (SB), net foreign assets (NFB), and free reserves (FR).

On the liabilities side only the behavioural equation for borrowing from the Central Bank (A) is specified. This allows the determination of excess reserves from the identity:

$$BE = FR + A.$$

The supply of deposits and the supply of bank credit (L) are obtained following the procedure outlined in Chapter 5, that is, using the balance-sheet constraint. These supply schedules can be expressed in terms of multipliers.

Since in the empirical analysis we distinguish between demand and time deposits, an additional interest rate is introduced: an interest rate i_D on demand deposits, and i_T (IT) on time deposits. Since for most European countries rates on sight deposits are zero or very low, we do not introduce them in the model. The interest rate on time deposits is the basic deposit rate. As shown in equation (5.8) of Chapter 5, under competitive behaviour, the time deposit rate is related to the yield on earnings assets of the banks:

$$i_T = i(1-\rho) - \phi \tag{6.2}$$

Given the slow movement in *IT*, we use an estimated version of this equation allowing for adjustment lags between the two rates:

$$IT = \alpha + \beta\, IEA(1 - BRR) + \gamma IT_{-1} \tag{6.3}$$

For some countries an additional variable is introduced to account for the effect of the rate of interest on foreign assets (*IEC*).

The behavioural equations of the banking sector are specified in ratio form. The variables *A*, *FR* and *NFB* are expressed as ratios of total deposits $(D+T)$, whereas *SB* is expressed as a ratio of total banks domestic earnings assets $(SB+L)$. Each ratio is a function of various interest rates and the required reserve ratio. Seasonal dummy variables are also included when found statistically significant.

The Central Bank

A simplified balance sheet of the Central Bank or monetary authorities is as follows:

$$BTR + BF + A + OB = BP + BR + \mathrm{BE} \tag{6.4}$$

The monetary base in the hands of the public is demand-determined. It includes currency and coins, and for countries such as Belgium, France and Italy, it includes also postal deposits. Required reserves are determined by the required reserve ratio and deposits.

Different institutional and policy arrangements exist in various countries concerning the determination of excess reserves and banks' borrowing from the Central Bank. This particular aspect motivates in part the different specifications used for the United Kingdom (for more details see Section VI). For the other countries there is a common specification. We assume that the monetary authorities fix the discount rate (*IA*), and satisfy the demand for reserves by the banks; hence *BE* and *A* are demand-determined. This specification may be somewhat suspect for countries such as France, where credit controls and rationing by the Central Bank are a dominant feature. But this disadvantage is offset by the benefit of adopting a common framework.

The treasury base (*BTR*), that is, the cumulative government deficit financed by the Central Bank, is an exogenous variable determined by fiscal policy and open market operations of the Central Bank. The stock of international reserves (BF) depends on the exchange rate regime and intervention policies of the Central Bank in the foreign exchange market. Alternative arrangements and policies are the subject of Chapter 7. Finally, for simulation purposes, we select other unspecified assets (OB) to be the slack variable in the balance sheet of the Central Bank.

Balance of Payments and Capital Flows

The balance of payments (BOP) identity used in the model is written as:

$$CAB = \Delta BF + \Delta NFB - KP - OK \tag{6.5}$$

where a positive value of a capital flow variable indicates an inflow.

In general data on changes in the net foreign asset position of the banks obtained from their balance sheets are inconsistent with those obtained from balance-of-payments statistics. We use ΔNFB obtained from the balance sheets as a measure of bank-related capital flows.

Using total capital flows (K), short- and long-term, from balance-of-payments statistics, we compute capital flows generated by the non-bank public through the identity:

$$KP = K + \Delta NFB \tag{6.6}$$

Variable K, in fact, includes capital movements attributable to the non-bank public, as well as errors in recording capital movements by the banking sector. The residual item (OK) includes all other transactions (direct investment, government transactions . . .); this is taken to be exogenous.

Attempts to estimate capital flow equations for KP are based on portfolio behaviour of the non-bank public. The basic equation is:

$$NFP = f(YPR, CAB, IT, IEU, Ee - e) \tag{6.7}$$

The current-account balance (CAB) is included to account for trade credit and lags in payments. Ee is the expected value of the natural logarithm of the exchange rate. The capital flow equation is obtained from (6.7):

$$KP = -\Delta NFP = f'(\Delta YPR, CAB, CAB_{-1}, \Delta IT, \Delta IEU, \Delta Ee - \Delta e) \tag{6.8}$$

The balance-of-payments identity 'determines' the change in international reserves or the exchange rate, according to the exchange rate regime. In the fixed exchange rate case, the identity 'determines' the change in international reserves. However in a floating or managed floating regime, international reserves are either fixed or determined by a policy reaction function of the monetary authorities. The balance-of-payments identity in this case 'determines' the exchange rate.

III MODELLING SPOT EXCHANGE RATES AND EXPECTATIONS

In this section we address the two issues of the determination of spot exchange rates, and the modelling of the expectations of exchange rates which are the part of the expected foreign yield variable included in the asset demand equations.

Spot Exchange Rate Determination

Conditional on the expected future exchange rate and other exogenous variables, the financial model determines the spot exchange rate along with interest rates. In the theoretical analysis of Chapter 5, demand schedules for foreign assets and liabilities were dropped through the wealth constraint, and the money market equilibrium condition was used to 'determine' the spot exchange rate. In the empirical model, we follow a somewhat different approach, one based on the idea that the exchange rate adjusts so as to equilibrate the balance of payments, through changes in the demand for foreign assets and liabilities. Hence the balance-of-payments equilibrium condition 'determines' the spot exchange rate. On the other hand, the money market equilibrium condition is not used explicitly. The asset demand equations for money generate monetary stocks, but the equilibrium condition is ignored.

With the current account balance (CAB) and direct investment and government capital transactions (OK) exogenous, the exchange rate adjusts to make the demand schedules for foreign assets and liabilities by banks and the non-bank public compatible with balance-of-payments equilibrium.

Our approach is similar to that of the Multicountry Model of the Federal Reserve Board,[7] and the World Economic Model of the Economic Planning Agency of Japan.[8] In particular, it is close to the Board version called 'Inverted Capital Approach'.[9] In principle, the banks' demand for net foreign assets:

$$\frac{NFB}{D+T} = a_0 + a_1(IEU + Ee - e) + a_2 IT \tag{6.9}$$

the capital flow equation (6.8) and the equilibrium condition (6.5) can solve for the spot exchange rate. Since this solution often leads to a very erratic behaviour of the exchange rate, we adopt the technique of estimating demand schedules for net foreign assets in inverted form.[10] With stock data being available only for banks assets, we invert equation (6.9) while estimating equation (6.8) directly and using (6.5) to determine NFB.

On inversion of (6.9) we obtain an equation for the spot exchange rate:

$$e = \frac{a_0}{a_1} + IEU + Ee + \frac{a_2}{a_1} IT - \frac{1}{a_1}\left(\frac{NFB}{D+T}\right)$$

or

$$e = a_0' + a_1' \, IEU + a_1'' Ee + a_2' IT + a_3' \left(\frac{NFB}{D+T}\right) \tag{6.10}$$

Under condition of imperfect substitution between domestic and foreign assets equation (6.10) reduces to the interest rate parity condition with:

$$a_o' = 0, a_1' = a_1'' = 1, a_2' = -1, a_3' = 0.$$

Under conditions of imperfect substitution we will have $a_3' < 0$ and the other parameters different from those implied by interest rate parity. In empirical estimation we allow the coefficients of IEU and Ee to take different values.

Exchange Rate Expectations

The expected foreign yield consists of two components: the yield on the foreign asset, i^*, and the expected capital gain or loss in being long on foreign currency, $\underset{t-1}{E} e_{t+1} - e_t$. There is no conceptual or empirical difficulty concerning i^*. The three-month Eurodollar rate (IEU) is a good approximation of i^* given the importance of the Eurocurrency market and the potentially high substitutability between Eurodollar deposits and many of the domestic assets included in our financial model. The expected capital gain or loss component is a difficult variable to deal with because it involves the unobserved $\underset{t-1}{E}\, e_{t+1}$. Three alternatives were considered. First, as indicated in Chapter 5, most exchange rate models do not seem to outperform the random-walk process:

$$e_{t+1} = e_t + u_{t+1}^{RW} \tag{6.11}$$

where u_{t+1}^{RW} = error term.

The implication of (6.11) is that the relevant expected foreign yield is the uncovered Eurodollar rate of interest. The second alternative is to take the forward premium as the best available forecast for $\underset{t-1}{E}\, e_{t+1} - e$. This hypothesis was discussed in Chapter 4 under the simple market efficiency label:

$$e_{t+1} - e_t = \alpha + \beta(f_t - e_t) + u_{t+1}^{ME} \tag{6.12}$$

As Table 4.4 illustrates, the evidence is not too favourable towards (6.12), although it is much better for its level form – see Levich (1983):

$$e_{t+1} = \alpha' + \beta'(f_t) + u_{t+1}^{ME'} \tag{6.13}$$

Regardless of whether (6.12) or (6.13) is the appropriate form to test the simple market efficiency hypothesis, it is an accepted fact that the forward premium explains a very small fraction of the variance of $e_{t+1} - e_t$. These results corroborate the view that the exchange rate can best be described by equation (6.11). It follows that the covered interest rate, $i_t^* + f_t - e_t$, may do somewhat better than the uncovered rate, i^*, but not that much better. These two series are shown in Figure 6.1, with i^* proxied by the three-month Eurodollar rate and $f_t - e_t$ being the premium of the dollar with respect to the Deutsch mark.

The final alternative is the rational expectations solution of the exchange rate developed in Section IV of Chapter 5. The key equations are (5.30a) and (5.31a). It behoves us to rewrite the first of the two equations in the testable form:

$$\Delta_4 e_t = A(L)\Delta_4 X_{t-1} + \beta\Delta_4 e_{t-1} + er_1 \tag{6.14}$$

where $A(L)$ = polynominal in the lag operator L
X = vector of exogenous variables
er_1 = error term.

The expected value of e_t conditional on information up to time $t-1$ is:

$$\underset{t-1}{E}\, e_t = e_{t-4} + \hat{A}(L)\Delta_4 X_{t-1} + \hat{\beta}\Delta_4 e_{t-1} \tag{6.15}$$

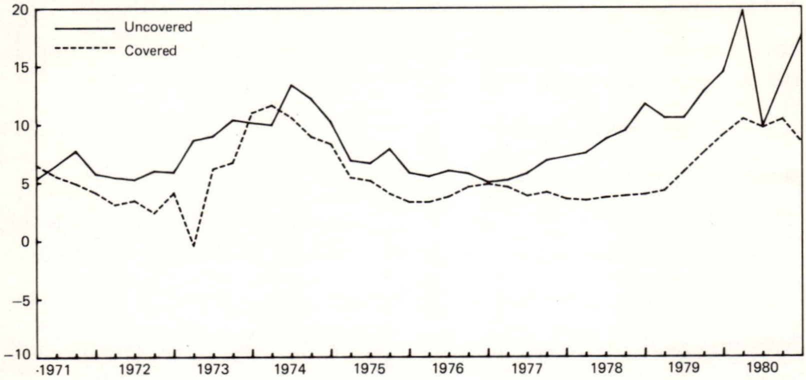

FIGURE 6.1 *Covered with respect to the DM and uncovered Eurodollar rate (per cent)*

where the ^ denotes estimated values.

Let X be governed by the following empirical model:

$$\Delta_4 X_t = C(L)\Delta_4 X_{t-1} + er_2 \tag{6.16}$$

Using (6.14), (6.15) and (6.16) we can deduce:

$$\underset{t-1}{E}\ e_{t+1} = \underset{t-1}{E}\ \{\underset{t}{E}\ e_{t+1}\}$$

$$= \underset{t-1}{E}\ \{e_{t-3} + \hat{A}(L)\Delta_4 X_t + \hat{\beta} e_t - \hat{\beta} e_{t-4}\}$$

using (6.15) with information up to t

$$\begin{aligned}\underset{t-1}{E}\ e_{t+1} &= e_{t-3} + \hat{A}(L)[\hat{C}(L)\Delta_4 X_{t-1}] - \hat{\beta} e_{t-4} + \hat{\beta}[e_{t-4} \\ &\quad + \hat{A}(L)\Delta_4 X_{t-1} + \hat{\beta}\Delta_4 e_{t-1}] \\ &= e_{t-3} + \hat{A}(L)[\hat{C}(L) + \hat{\beta}]\ \Delta_4 X_{t-1} + \hat{\beta}^2 \Delta_4 e_{t-1}\end{aligned} \tag{6.17}$$

In other words, given a solution for $e_t - e_{t-4}$ and well-defined processes of the underlying exogenous variables, the value of $\underset{t-1}{E}\ e_{t+1}$ is computed according to (6.17). The latter is the rational expectations solution obtained from an 'idealised' reduced-form equation of the financial model. The shortcoming of this procedure is that there are a large – potentially infinite – number of models consistent with the estimated reduced form. The 'proper' way is to generate $\underset{t-1}{E}\ e_{t+1}$ from the structure itself of the financial economy. For the time being it suffices to say that the reduced-form approach of (6.14)–(6.16) is an economical way to assess the relative merit of quantifying $\underset{t-1}{E}\ e_{t+1} - e_t$ in a 'rational' manner as opposed to models (6.11) or (6.12).

In sum the three alternatives are the random-walk hypothesis (uncovered interest rate), the simple market efficiency hypothesis (covered interest rate) and rational expectations $(i^* + \widehat{\underset{t-1}{E}\ e_{t+1}} - e_t)$.

Figures 6.2 and 6.3 compare $(e_{t+1} - e_t)$ with $(f_t - e_t)$ and $\widehat{\underset{t-1}{E}\ e_{t+1}} - e_t$ computed according to (6.14)–(6.17) for Germany and the United Kingdom.[11] It is immediately clear that the tracking power implied by our procedure (6.14)–(6.17) is significantly superior to that of the forward premium. From these results one should not deduce that an investor can systematically make money by following our 'rule'. The more modest claim we are making is that we have been able to model *ex-post* 'news'. The superiority of the rule must be established on the much tougher grounds of relative predictability outside the sample period. For this reason the in-sample predictability was deemed to be secondary to the criterion of the sensitivity of the structure of the financial economy to the three ways of modelling $\underset{t-1}{E}\ e_{t+1} - e_t$.

All our equations were estimated using alternatively $i_t^* + \underset{t-1}{E}\ e_{t+1} - e_t$,

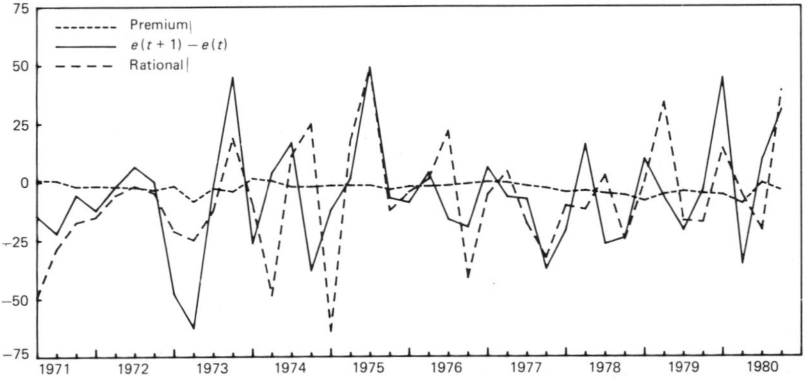

FIGURE 6.2 *Exchange rate expectations: Germany (annual percentage changes)*

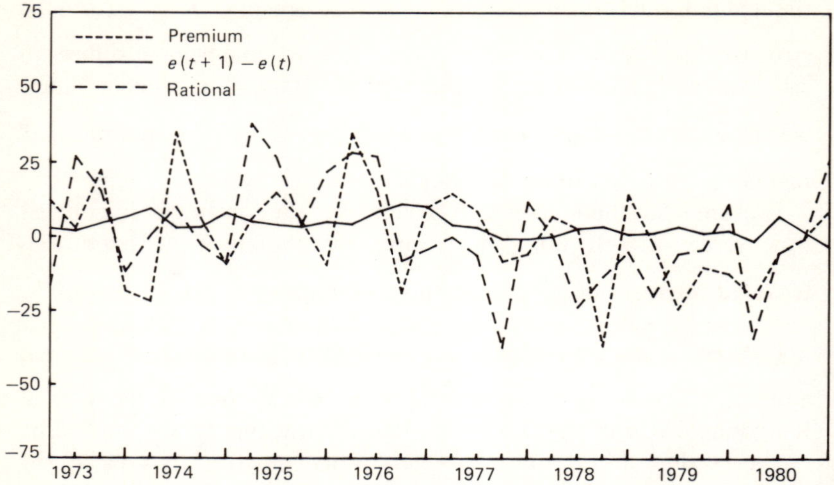

FIGURE 6.3 *Exchange rate expectations: the United Kingdom (annual percentage changes)*

$i_t^* + f_t - e_t$, and i^*. The best results were obtained with the covered rate, where 'best' is understood in terms of achieving minimum variance of the regression and correctly signed coefficients. The uncovered rate had a slight advantage over the rational expectations solution.

In the empirical work reported later the forward premium is used as a proxy for expected changes in the exchange rate since it yields the most satisfactory results. This can be regarded as a first step in a multiple step estimation procedure, where these estimates can be used to generate model-consistent exchange rate expectations. These next values can be used to obtain a second step estimate of the model parameters, and so on until convergence. However, for the purposes of this study we limit ourselves to this first step.

In model simulations (see the next chapter), the forward rate is replaced by the forecast or solution value of the exchange rate generated by the model for the next period.

IV ESTIMATION PROBLEMS AND METHODS

The specification of Section II was estimated using quarterly data from the early 1960s to the end of 1980. Because of data availability, different sample periods were employed for each country or for different equations relating to one country. This section deals with general issues of estimation to facilitate the presentation and understanding of the empirical findings of Section V. The Appendix Data Tables A.1 to A.6 provide a complete description of data sources and definitions.

Constraints on parameters

The large number of theoretically relevant explanatory variables and the strong correlation among these variables make it impossible to be comprehensive in estimating behavioural equations. Some constraints, thus, have to be imposed on parameters. There are three types of constraints.

First, *a priori* zero constraints are imposed on the parameters of some variables. For instance, the loan rate (IL) is usually not introduced in the demand for monetary assets equations. Similarly, variables that are believed *a priori* to be irrelevant are ignored in a given equation. Second, parameters found to be statistically not different from zero in the initial specification search process are also eliminated. Third, after preliminary testing, coefficients of different variables, in particular interest rates, appeared to be quantitatively equivalent. For these an equality constraint was imposed and shows up with variables appearing in sum or difference form.

This approach on parameter restrictions poses the problem of consistency across equations given the balance sheet and wealth constraints. The Brainard–Tobin (1968) framework for modelling portfolio behaviour, further developed by Ladenson (1971), implies in principle that all rates of returns on assets should be included in each equation. But this approach is impossible empirically because of the colinearity among rates of return when the number of assets exceeds two or three. Therefore, when imposing constraints on interest rate parameters, it is assumed that the residual equation in the system takes up the slack to impose consistency. In our study the residual assets are physical and equity capital for the non-bank private sector, and bank loans for the banks. It is quite possible that some of the implied effects on the residual assets are 'unrealistic'.

Lags and Adjustment

A lagged endogenous variable is included in all equations of the non-bank public behaviour. This assumes a common geometric lag structure on all explanatory variables which is justified in terms of a partial adjustment mechanism.

A first issue with this type of specification is the slow speed of adjustment it tends to generate. However, when account is taken of lags in the formation of the expected income variable, speeds of adjustment rise, at least for narrow money.[12] The speed of adjustment may be lower for time deposits and other than monetary assets. This study will shed some light on this issue.

A second problem with this specification is related to the aforementioned issue of consistency with balance sheet and wealth constraints. As shown particularly by Ladenson (1971) the demand for a given financial asset in a system of asset demand equations is a function of all rates of return, wealth and lagged wealth, and lagged values of all the financial assets. Wealth constraints and partial adjustment imply that not only the own-lagged values are to be included, but also those of all other assets. In a study for Australia, Hunt and Volker (1981) have shown that such a consistent specification yields speeds of adjustment that are higher than usually found, and eliminates the serial correlation in the errors that is typical in demand-for-money equations. We did not make a complete attempt to include all lagged asset variables in each equation. Tests with two or three lagged variables in some asset demands did not show any significant improvement in most cases. Therefore this approach was not pursued further; we followed instead the traditional single-equation method.

The same approach is employed in the specification of the behavioural equations of banks, where the partial adjustment mechanism applies to the relevant ratios. More on this will be said in Section V.

Method of Estimation

All equations are estimated using the 'two-stage least squares' procedure, with the model's exogenous variables playing the role of instruments. Because the model contains a large number of lagged endogenous variables, we have restricted the instruments in each equation to those that appear directly in the equation.

The UK model of Section VI was estimated with a 'three-stage least squares' procedure that appears to be more efficient than the 'two-stage least squares' technique. It did not seem useful to implement a full-information estimation technique for the five countries for which the wealth constraint could not be imposed and some equations had to be estimated in inverted form.

An additional problem is the existence of serial correlation in the residuals of many of the estimated equations, in particular the interest rate equations and the banks' behavioural equations. This is apparent from the reported values of the *DW* or Durbin's *h*-statistic in the tables. We have not used techniques to correct for serial correction in the residuals. Not being interested in forecasting but rather in simulation, we could ignore serial correlation and concentrate on the basic structure of interest. In addition, correction for serial correlation leads in many cases to less plausible estimates. In sum, we rely on 'two-stage least squares' estimation.

V ESTIMATION RESULTS FOR FIVE COUNTRIES

In this section we present and discuss the results of the estimation of the financial models for five countries; those of the United Kingdom are in Section VI. The estimated equations are shown in Appendix Tables 6.A to 6.E to this chapter. Table 6.F contains definitions and identities for each country.

We will discuss the empirical results by type of equations, a procedure that facilitates comparison across countries. But before doing so, a few country characteristics are pointed out.

Specific Country Characteristics

A number of country-specific characteristics in each model need to be highlighted. In the German model an equation for saving deposits is added even though there is no separate interest rate. This is a major liability of the banks. A second characteristic of the German model is the exclusion of the free reserves (*FR*) equation. In fact, excess reserves (*BE*) are very small and vary little, a fact suggesting a negligible role of *BE* in the portfolio behaviour of banks. Therefore they are treated exogenously, making free reserves approximately equal to the negative of advances from the Central Bank. The same treatment holds for the French model.

In the Dutch model we employ two interest rates for time deposits. The first is the interest rate on ordinary saving deposits at banks (*IT*).

The second is the rate of interest on call money (*ITT*). Korteweg and Van Loo (1977) argue that *ITT* is more relevant than *IT* as the rate of interest for time deposits. *ITT* is found to be most significant in the asset demand equations of the non-bank public, whereas *IT* in the capital flow equation and the demand for government bonds (the *IS* equation).

We do not submit exchange rate equations for Belgium and the Netherlands, since these two countries have more often than not pegged their exchange rate to the Deutsch mark. In other words, the Belgian franc and the Dutch guilder currency price of the dollar is given by the DM/dollar rate. For both countries there is an equation for *NFB*; the balance-of-payments condition determines international reserves.

Finally, the capital flows of the French and Italian non-bank public are assumed exogenous: it proved difficult to estimate satisfactory equations for *KP*. This is not particularly surprising in view of the extensive use of foreign exchange controls in France and Italy. It follows that quantity adjustments through capital movements cannot take place in the models of these two countries.

Demand for Monetary Assets by the Non-bank Public

In the demand equations for monetary assets we find a strong effect for permanent income. On the other hand, transitory income appears significantly only in the demand deposit equations (with the exception of France). There are strong interest rate effects, with at least one domestic interest rate in each equation. The foreign rate is also a significant factor of the demand for sight and time deposits across countries.

Estimates of the coefficients, expressed in terms of elasticities, are shown in Table 6.2. The reader can see that the elasticities with respect to permanent income are in general low for base money, and much larger for demand and time deposits. Indeed for the latter the long-run elasticities are always higher than unity, and in many cases reach 2 or more. The interest rate elasticities of time deposits are much higher than of base money or sight deposits. Particularly strong are the elasticities of demand deposits with respect to the own rate, (*IT*), the bond rate (*IS*) and the foreign rate (*IEC*). Finally, the adjustment coefficients are greater than 0.5 in most cases, indicating a low speed of adjustment towards equilibrium. The adjustment speed tends to be faster for time than sight deposits.

TABLE 6.2 *Short-term (S) and long-term (L) elasticities in the demand for monetary assets*

Assets variables	*Germany*		*France*		*Italy*		*Belgium*		*Netherlands*	
	S	*L*	*S*	*L*	*S*	*L*	*S*	*L*	*S*	*L*
Demand for base money (BP)										
YPR	0.255	1.027	0.113	0.235	0.295	1.175	0.020	0.080	0.042	0.229
IT	−0.013	−0.062	—	—	−0.134	−0.535	−0.026	−0.107	−0.004	−0.025
IEC	—	—	—	—	—	—	—	—	—	—
IS	−0.019	−0.087	−0.103	−0.216	—	—	−0.020	−0.083	—	—
π	−0.030	−0.138	−0.080	−0.167	0.026	0.104	—	—	−0.031	−0.173
Adjustment coefficient	0.781	—	0.521	—	0.749	—	0.750	—	0.817	—
Demand deposits (D)										
YPR	1.172	1.562	0.263	1.077	0.140	2.295	0.611	1.455	0.649	1.316
IT	−0.037	−0.049	−0.035	−0.143	−0.014	−0.244	−0.016	−0.039	−0.041	−0.083
IEC	−0.037	−0.050	−0.057	−0.233	−0.048	−0.797	−0.016	−0.040	−0.056	−0.114
IS	—	—	—	—	—	—	—	—	—	—
π	−0.058	−0.077	—	—	—	—	—	—	—	—
Adjustment coefficient	0.250	—	0.756	—	0.939	—	0.580	—	0.507	—
Time deposits (T)										
YPR	0.499	1.750	0.386	3.860	0.229	1.055	0.067	2.481	0.314	1.670
IT	0.154	0.540	0.080	0.800	0.197	0.911	—	—	0.054	0.291
IEC	−0.088	−0.309	−0.026	−0.260	−0.031	−0.145	−0.031	−1.151	—	—
IS	—	—	−0.030	−0.300	−0.292	−1.348	—	—	−0.088	−0.471
π	−0.088	−0.311	−0.118	−1.180	—	—	—	—	—	—
Adjustment coefficient	0.715	—	0.900	—	0.783	—	0.793	—	0.812	—

NOTES 1. The figures are derived from Tables 6.A to 6.E.
2. Elasticities with respect to interest rates are computed at the mean value of the variable for the period 1971(I)–1980(IV).

Interest Rate Equations

Generally there are three interest rate equations in each country model: the inverted demand schedules for bank loans and for government bonds and the equation for *IT*. As pointed out above, the estimation in inverted form of *IL* and *IS* proved necessary to obtain satisfactory simulation results. But even so we encountered difficulties in obtaining correctly signed and significant coefficients. Let us illustrate the nature of the problem by considering a typical demand for bank loans:

$$\log \frac{L}{P} = b_0 + b_1 \log YPR + b_2 IT + b_3 IEC + \delta IL + \lambda \log \left(\frac{L}{P}\right)_{-1} \tag{6.18}$$

with inverted form:

$$IL = -\frac{b_o}{\delta} - \frac{b_1}{\delta} \log YPR - \frac{b_2}{\delta} IT - \frac{b_3}{\delta} IEC + \frac{1}{\delta} \log \frac{L}{P} - \frac{\lambda}{\delta} \log \left(\frac{L}{P}\right)_{-1} \tag{6.19}$$

In many cases, direct estimation of (6.18) yields a satisfactory fit, correct and statistically significant signs. But this comes at the expense of unrealistic behaviour of the interest rate variable when the model is simulated. On the other hand, direct estimation of (6.19) often yields unsatisfactory results in terms of correct signs and parameter significance. Therefore, we had to impose *a priori* values for some parameters, particularly for λ, the adjustment coefficient. In general the imposed value was consistent with that obtained from direct estimation of (6.18). The most commonly-used value for λ is 0.9. Sometimes, a value for b_1 was also imposed, as in the case of the *IS* equation for France.

An additional problem is that the interest rate equations exhibit strong serial correlation in the residuals. Attempts to correct for serial correlation – by including a lagged endogenous variable or by other techniques – produced undesirable changes in the structure of the equation. Thus, we often retain equations exhibiting strong serial correlation when the performance of the equation is satisfactory in terms of signs of coefficients and their significance.[13] In a few cases a lagged endogenous variable is included as an explanatory variable.

In most *IL* and *IS* equations the time deposit rate and the foreign covered rate are significant determinants and the quantity variables have correct signs with respect to the loan and the bond rate.[14]

Despite the fact that equations for *IL* and *IS* in the form of (6.19) are derived from (6.18) one cannot use the estimates so obtained to calculate elasticities of the demand for loans and for bonds with respect to the various variables. Such a procedure would yield implausible results. It is best to think of the inverted equations as interest rate equations that describe the response of *IL* and *IS* to movements in the various explanatory variables.

The equation for *IT* is specified in (6.3). The estimates of that equation for Germany and Italy show a unitary long-run response of the time deposit rate to changes in the interest rate of the alternative earning assets, as defined by equation (6.2). This response is only about 0.5 for France and Belgium, indicating that there are strong regulatory effects in the determination of the time deposit rate. For the Netherlands the time deposit rate *IT* has a very low response to a change in the interest rates on the earnings assets of the banks, while the interest rate on call money *ITT* responds more quickly and strongly to *IEA* and *IEC*.

Banks Behavioural Equations

The asset demand equations for the banks are estimated in ratio form. Each equation includes interest rate variables and a lagged endogenous variables. The lagged adjustment coefficient poses the most difficult problem in the estimation of these equations. In many cases the coefficient is around unity, in turn swamping all interest rate effects. Occasionally, we had to fix *a priori* the values of this parameter, as in the case for the *A* and *FR* equations of Italy and the *SB* equation of France.[15] In fact the problem is most acute in the demand for government bonds. The parameter of the lagged endogenous is always very large. It reaches unity for Germany, leading to non-significant or very low interest rate effects. This seems to indicate strong rigidities in the behaviour of the banks with respect to their holdings of government bonds, and the existence of regulatory constraints not accounted for by our simplified equations. In any case, the estimated equations show that interest rates play an important part in the portfolio decisions of banks: the elasticities, shown in Table 6.3, are fairly large across countries.

The demand schedules for Central Bank advances show significant interest rate elasticities, except for France. The low French values are consistent with the application of quantitative limits at the discount window. For the other countries, the elasticities with respect to the discount rate are between 1 and 2 in the short run and between 2 and 5 in

TABLE 6.3 *Short-term (S) and long-term (L) elasticities of banks' demand for assets*

Assets variables	*Germany* S	*Germany* L	*France* S	*France* L	*Italy* S	*Italy* L	*Belgium* S	*Belgium* L	*Netherlands* S	*Netherlands* L
Advances from Central Bank (A)										
IA	−1.105	−3.811	−0.083	−0.129	−0.949	−1.898	−2.668	−4.987	−3.001	−3.001
IS	—	—	—	—	—	—	—	—	—	—
IL	2.282	7.871	0.103	0.160	—	—	—	—	—	—
IEA	—	—	—	—	2.483	4.967	2.678	5.006	4.459	4.459
IEC	1.310	4.517	0.083	0.129	0.259	0.519	0.679	1.269	0.295	0.295
BRR	—	—	—	—	—	—	—	—	0.014	0.014
Adjustment coefficient	0.710	—	0.360	—	<u>0.5</u>	—	0.465	—	<u>0.0</u>	—
Free reserves (FR)										
IA	—	—	—	—	6.745	11.242	4.049	8.003	10.571	10.571
IS	—	—	—	—	—	—	—	—	—	—
IL	—	—	—	—	—	—	—	—	—	—
IEA	—	—	—	—	−4.193	−6.988	−4.873	−9.641	−17.930	−17.930
IEC	—	—	—	—	−4.356	−7.261	−0.610	−1.206	—	—
BRR	—	—	—	—	—	—	—	—	−0.228	−0.228
Adjustment coefficient	—	—	—	—	<u>0.4</u>	—	0.494	—	<u>0.0</u>	—
Government bonds (SB)										
IS	0.026	—	0.750	2.500	0.267	3.077	−0.048	−0.951	0.011	1.437
IL	—	—	−0.826	−2.750	−0.044	−0.511	—	—	—	—
IEC	—	—	−0.874	−2.910	−0.129	−1.487	−0.004	−0.082	−0.010	−1.250
Adjustment coefficient	1.015	—	0.700	—	0.913	—	0.949	—	0.992	—
Net foreign assets (NFB)										
IT	—	—	—	—	—	—	—	—	−0.842	−7.321
IEC	—	—	—	—	—	—	0.189	2.560	0.722	6.278
IEA	—	—	—	—	—	—	−0.408	−5.526	—	—
Adjustment coefficient	—	—	—	—	—	—	0.926	—	0.885	—

NOTES 1. See notes on Table 6.2
2. Underlined coefficients have been constrained.

the long run. The elasticity with respect to interest rates on domestic earnings assets is also very large. It lies between 2 and 5 in the short run and 5 or more in the long run. It should be noted that for the Netherlands we did not find evidence of adjustment lags, that is, the short-run and long-run effects are the same. The foreign covered rate elasticities are significant but much lower than those with respect to rates on domestic earnings assets.

Equations for free reserves are estimated for Italy, Belgium and the Netherlands, but not for Germany and France. The domestic interest rate elasticities are very large, and generally exceed 4 in the short run and 7 in the long run. The foreign rate effect is strongest in Italy, low for Belgium and zero for the Netherlands.

The demand schedules for net foreign assets are estimated in direct form for Belgium and the Netherlands. For the other three countries they are inverted and estimated as exchange rate equations and discussed below. The Belgian and Dutch elasticities with respect to both domestic and foreign interest rates are smaller than unity in the short run but much higher in the long run.

Finally, the demand for government bonds, the most difficult to estimate, yields somewhat lower elasticities than other assets, except for France. In general, the own rate effect is strongest; the foreign rate is significant in most cases.

Capital Flows

Capital-flow equations – cf. (6.8) – are estimated for Germany, Belgium and the Netherlands. The French and Italian *KP* is assumed exogenous. The estimated equations are all consistent with *a priori* expectations. Both the domestic and the foreign interest rates are significant determinants of capital movements. Permanent income enters the equations multiplied by interest rates, and separately also for Belgium. In general, the effect of the domestic rate is equal to or stronger than the foreign rate. The current account variable, proxying for the impact of trade credits, has an effect in Germany and the Netherlands. Trade credits are almost totally offset after one quarter in the German case.

Exchange Rates

The equation for the spot exchange rate (6.10) is employed for Germany, France and Italy. In all instances the forward rate is the strongest 'determinant' of the spot rate, with a coefficient not significantly different from unity. The domestic time deposit rate has a negative impact, with a coefficient higher than unity for Germany and Italy. For these two countries the Eurodollar rate has a coefficient significantly smaller than unity, while the net foreign asset variable has a strong impact. Estimation of equation (6.10) for France yielded a coefficient for net foreign assets that is negative but not significantly different from zero. This variable was dropped, and the equation that is used in the model is not different from an interest rate parity condition. This is consistent with tests on *IRP* of Table 4.3.

In sum, the evidence suggests significant departures from interest rate parity and the existence of non-negligible risk premiums for two countries, Germany and Italy, but not so for France.

VI THE FINANCIAL MODEL OF THE UNITED KINGDOM*

The reason for dealing with the United Kingdom separately is that, although the model shares with the others the same spirit, it differs both in structure and institutional detail.

The major institutional difference built into the UK model is the absence of any framework for quantitative or monetary base control. Interest rates are technically the instruments of control; consequently, both money and bonds are demand-determined in the short term. The monetary base, including that held by the banking sector is also considered to be demand-determined. Furthermore, there is no direct link between the change in international reserves and the monetary aggregates. The link can be made from the government sector balance sheet via a government reaction.[16] Another important difference is that advances from the Central Bank to the banking sector (a negligible proportion of the total portfolio) is taken as exogenous to the model.

The main instruments of monetary control, to be found in the government Green paper on 'monetary control', are fiscal policy,[17] gilt-edged financing, short-term interest rates and quantitative controls. The instrument which we concentrate, and that which is assumed to be a control variable in model simulation, is the short-term rate of interest.

---

* The financial model of the United Kingdom was developed by Kent Matthews and John Thompson of the University of Liverpool. For more details see Matthews and Thompson (1982).

Short-term interest rate control is achieved through the issue of treasury bills and the Minimum Lending Rate (*MLR*), originally linked to the treasury bill rate but an administered rate after 1978 and now abolished. The technique involves issuing a quantity of treasury bills in excess of the funds available to the markets as estimated by the authorities. Consequently, the discount houses are forced 'into the bank' to borrow funds, so that, provided the market is kept short of funds, the Bank of England can relieve this shortage at the structure of interest rates desired. In other words, the supply of monetary base becomes infinitely elastic at the rate of interest desired by the authorities. Alterations in the rate of interest can be engineered by variations in *MLR* and the support price.

In sum, the main method of controlling the growth of the money supply is to change rates of interest rather than bring about changes in the size of the monetary base. Nevertheless, it is true that interest rates are varied according to the state of the monetary aggregates. Given the latter, therefore, the interest rate structure is also a means of achieving quantitative targets. Monetary policy is in all likelihood a compromise between achieving a desired interest rate structure and a targeted quantity of money.

Private Sector Portfolio

Unlike the structure of the private sector portfolio behaviour of the other European countries which implicitly assumes a simultaneous determination of asset demand schedules, the UK structure imposes a recursive determination. The reason for this is twofold. First, the proposed structure satisfies the private sectors' balance sheet which is imposed according to available data constraints without recourse to complicated 'adding up' conditions of the Brainard–Tobin (1968) kind, and second for ease of empirical estimation.

Previous empirical studies have focused on aspects of the private sector rather than the non-bank private sector (*NBPS*) as a whole. The Clearing Banks were studied by Parkin, Gray and Barrett (1970), White (1975), and Bewley (1981). Households were investigated by Barrett, Gray and Parkin (1975) and discount houses by Parkin (1970). The main conclusion of these studies is that interest rates are important in influencing portfolio decisions. In summarising the empirical work Parkin and Copplestone (1978) conclude that interest elasticities tended to be low in the personal non-financial sector and high in the competitive discount market, and that the insensitivity of the banks' response to interest rate changes is explained by the extent of government regulation.

We propose an alternative approach to financial model-building and private sector asset-acquisition. We suggest that the non-bank private sector decision to accumulate assets is part of a nesting process, in which closely related assets are nested at different levels so as to represent a multilevel series of sequential decisions.[18] At its highest level the decision to accumulate financial assets is part of the non-bank private sectors' consumption-saving decision. Given the history of financial net worth and the current flow addition to it, the next decision in the sequence of decisions is at the second level where the *NBPS* allocates its financial net worth (*NWP*) between net domestic assets (*NDA*) and net foreign assets (*NFP*). Given the level of net domestic assets it then proceeds to the third level in the sequence of decisions and allocates between its gross domestic assets (*GDA*) and its liabilities to the banking sector (*L*). In this way the non-bank private sector proceeds in successive stages to a level in the nesting hierarchy as low as is feasible. Therefore, given its level of gross domestic assets, the *NBPS* then decides how much to allocate to liquid assets (broad money M_2) and how much to illiquid financial assets (broadly bonds *SP*). Within its broad holding of money it can then go to a lower level in the decision hierarchy and decide its allocation between narrow money (M_1) and time deposits (*T*) and finally it can then decide within M_1 how much to allocate to notes and coin (*BP*) and how much to demand deposits (*D*).

The hierarchy of decisions, shown graphically in Figure 6.4, is in principle responsive to the degree of substitution between the respective nested assets. However institutional and theoretical considerations also come to play. For instance, one would not think that notes and coins are more substitutable for bonds than for sight deposits.

Figure 6.4 describes the 'utility tree' implied by the *NBPS* utility function in the sense of Strotz (1957). The utility function we employ is the 'nested' *CES* first proposed by Sato (1967) which has the additional advantage of powerfully simplifying the analytical and estimation problems.[19]

The effects of the independent variables on the asset ratios, except for the key terms representing substitution effects, are largely ambiguous. Traditionally one would expect inflation to act on nominal assets as a tax reducing the holding of such assets. It would seem likely that its negative impact would be stronger on non-interest-bearing assets than

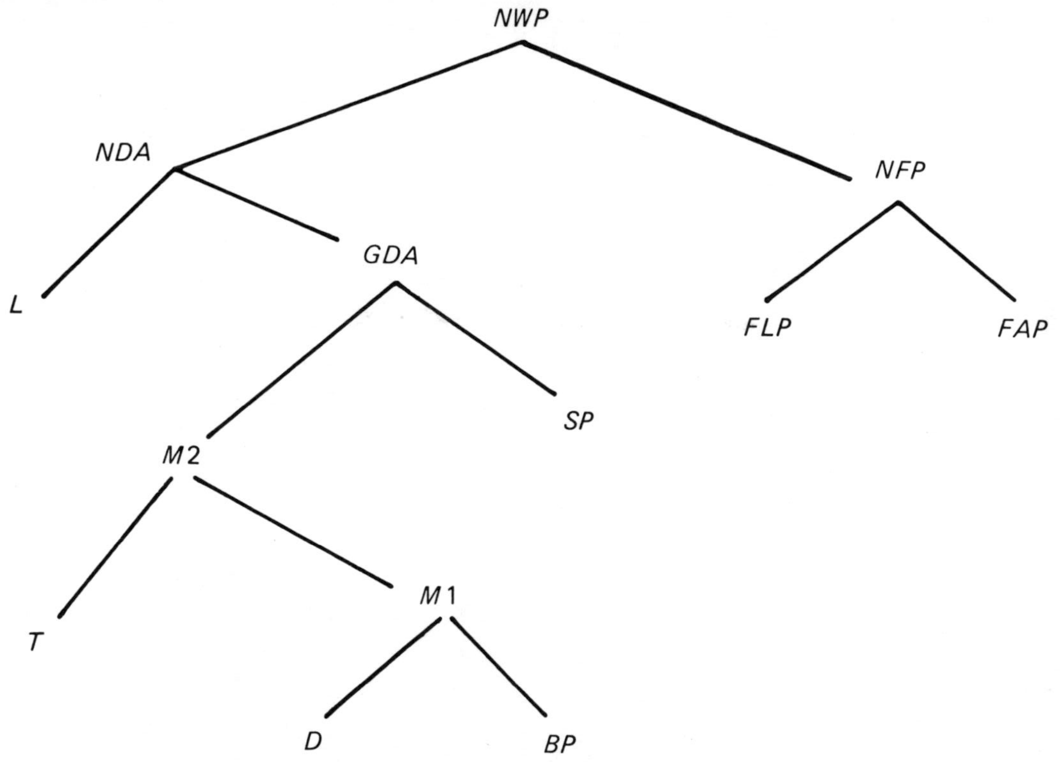

FIGURE 6.4 *Decision tree of the non-bank private sector*

on interest-bearing ones, but we are not dogmatic on this. We would expect bank lending to rise with expected inflation as inflation compensates the debtor and penalises the saver. Real net worth would have a positive impact on all assets. It is by no means clear, however, that the elasticity of asset demand with respect to net worth will always be unity. We allow for the possibility for the *NBPS* to reflect varying preferences of relative asset holdings as wealth increases. A rise in the foreign covered rate of interest would be expected to divert asset holdings from domestic to foreign sources. Similarly, a rise in the foreign rate of interest also increases the cost of borrowing from abroad and, consequently, increases the demand for domestic bank credit. A rise in expected or permanent income would in all likelihood raise the demand for all assets and credit, but it is not all clear what impact this variable would have on asset ratios.[20]

It is also by no means clear that expected inflation should affect notes and coins any differently from demand deposits, but we consider the likelihood of it reducing the ratio of M_1 to time deposits since it is likely to impinge upon a relatively weak interest-bearing asset harder than upon a full interest-bearing asset. Since expected inflation affects assets negatively and the demand for bank credit positively, a rise in expected inflation should unequivocally raise the ratio of bank credit to gross domestic assets. A rise in the foreign covered rate should have positive impacts on the cash-demand deposit ratio and the M_1-time deposit ratio, reflecting our assumption that demand deposits are a closer substitute for foreign assets than notes and coins, and time deposits are a closer substitute for foreign assets than demand deposits. Similarly, a rise in the foreign covered rate should raise the cost of foreign borrowing and reduce the level of domestic assets holdings, consequently raising the bank credit-gross domestic asset ratio. Expected income would be likely to have a negative impact on the cash-demand deposit ratio and the M_1-time deposit ratio. This reflects our assumption and the evidence of much empirical work that suggests a higher income elasticity on time deposits than M_1 and a higher income elasticity on sight deposits than cash.

Estimating the resulting desired asset ratios in log-linear form,[21] and assuming quadratic adjustment costs, our preferred results are presented in Table 6.G in the Appendix to this Chapter. Data for the level of bank lending to the private sector in foreign currency was available only since 1972(IV). This element was correspondingly netted out of total bank lending to the private sector in domestic currency, and added on to the private sectors' net foreign asset position. The consequence of this was that estimation of the asset functions could only be conducted for the period 1973(I) onwards.

Since balance sheet data for the private sector were readily available, a system estimation was considered most appropriate. In most cases there were substantial gains in efficiency in using 'three stage least squares' over 2*SLS*, but in some cases the use of the former estimation produced serial correlation in the residuals. Early experimentation with the currency-deposit ratio function suggested that the deposit rate and the covered foreign rate should be summed together to provide a tighter fit. The positive sign on the joint interest rates suggests that sight deposits are a closer substitute for both foreign assets and time deposits than currency, a wholly plausible result, given the known insensitivity of currency demand to interest rate movements. The negative impact of expected income suggests again the wholly plausible result that sight deposits have a higher income elasticity of demand than currency. The speed of adjustment is moderately rapid with 50 per cent of the adjustment occurring in the first quarter, an expected result in light of the highly liquid nature of the dependent variable.

Even adjusting for first-order serial correlation the estimates emerge as fairly robust. Turning to the ratio of M_1 to time deposits, again the results are fairly well determined, and yet again it was found that the summing of the foreign covered rate to the deposits rate produced the best results. Here the foreign covered rate does not behave in the expected direction. A rise in the foreign interest rate decreases the demand for M_1 relative to time deposits, a startling result given the universally-held assumption that time deposits are more substitutable than demand deposits for Eurocurrency deposits.[22] Constraining the foreign rate to produce a positive sign only worsened the estimates by producing an unstable lagged dependent coefficient. We present the result as a curiosity. Expected inflation comes in with a positive sign which says that this variable has a stronger impact on time deposits than on narrow money, a fairly surprising result.[23] The speed of adjustment is also disappointingly slow for such a liquid variable, between 10 and 15 per cent in the first quarter. Turning to the ratio of broad money to bonds, it turned out that the short rate proved to be a better variable in estimating the elasticity of substitution between the two variables than the long rate. The effect of the foreign rate is positive and from this we may infer that bonds are a better substitute for foreign assets than broad money. The negative effect of net worth confirms the presumption that the more illiquid an asset becomes the higher its elasticity with respect to financial wealth.

In the case of the bank lending to gross domestic assets the long rate of interest proved to be a better indicator of the return on the composite asset of gross domestic assets. The sign on the difference between the loan rate and the consol rate was of the expected direction,[24] but inflation expectations were consistently of the wrong sign and not statistically significant at 5 per cent. Consequently, this variable was excluded in subsequent estimation. The foreign covered rate acts as a proxy for the cost of borrowing from abroad, and therefore has the correct impact on the ratio of loans to assets.

The ratio of net foreign assets to net domestic assets was the least problematic. The key variable – the difference between the foreign covered rate and the domestic bond rate (consols) – had consistently the correct sign and statistically significant, suggesting strong substitution effects. The magnitude of the coefficient on the expected income term is surprisingly large, suggesting that the income elasticity of demand for domestic assets overwhelms the income elasticity of demand for net foreign assets. Speed of adjustment is also fairly rapid, indicating a curious asymmetry regarding the adjustment of net foreign assets *vis-à-vis* adjustment of elements of domestic assets within net domestic assets as a whole.

Strong substitution effects emerge for net foreign assets relative to net domestic assets and for broad money (M_2) relative to bonds. The long-run elasticity of substitution between broad money and bonds is 16.6 and the elasticity of substitution between narrow money (M_1) and time deposits is 4.8. This suggests a powerful degree of substitutability between time deposits and public-sector debt. The elasticity of substitution between domestic and foreign assets (net) is 20.2 implying that foreign bonds are a good substitute for domestic assets. The most surprising result to note here is that, although bonds can be regarded as a better substitute for foreign assets than broad money, narrow money is a better substitute than time deposits. This suggests that both sight deposits and bonds are closer substitutes with foreign assets than time deposits; a curious result which we have already noted is at variance with findings for the other countries.

An alternative interpretation is to assume that the changes in the covered Eurodollar rate has a speculative impact on the ratio of M_2 to bonds. Since the rise in the covered rate, following a rise in the uncovered rate, necessarily implies some form of intervention, the change in the Eurodollar rate can be interpreted as a signal that domestic rates would follow the same course in sympathy. This makes bonds relatively more risky than money and consequently indicate a gearing of the portfolio towards money and away from bonds.

The Banking Sector

The general strategy adopted in estimating the banking sector was to assume that the authorities attempted to fix the treasury bill rate by their daily intervention in the money markets. Given this rate (that is, it is treated as exogenous to the banking sector) the banks demand a quantity of base assets which is met by the authorities. Similarly, the banks demand public sector debt given the various rates of interest. Consequently, the quantity of both the monetary base and government debt held by the banking sector is demand-determined. This strategy requires the Public Sector Borrowing Requirement (*PSBR*) to be specified in the following manner:

$PSBR =$	Bond sales	+ Foreign exchange market intervention	$+\Delta(BP + BE)$	+ Government intervention in the domestic money markets

Bond sales include all forms of public sector debt to the non-bank private sector and banks. Government intervention in the domestic money markets is the slack variable which ensures that total demand for monetary base and public sector debt is satisfied, given that the treasury bill rate of interest is influenced by the authorities and given the size of the *PSBR*. The banks are assumed to have some control over their supply of sterling loans and time deposits. The model incorporates the supply of these items through equations specifying the rate of interest on sterling loans and interest-bearing deposits.

To summarise, holdings of money base (*BE*), government bonds (*SB*), total lending to domestic sector (*L*) and overseas (*LO*), time deposits, and net foreign currency assets (*NFB*) are treated as choice assets. Sight deposits (*D*) are demand-determined, that is, treated as being perfectly elastic in supply and other sterling liabilities (*OSL*) advances from the Central Bank (*A*) and special deposits (*DS*) are assumed to be exogenous.[25] The banks' supply of loans as a ratio to total liabilities is hypothesised to be a function of own and cross rates of interest. The representative cross rate of interest was taken to be the exogenous treasury bill rate.

For purposes of estimation the supply-of-loans function was inverted to obtain the loan rate of interest.[26] The rationale underlying such a specification is that banks set the loan rate in light of the short-term rate of interest fixed by the authorities and the proportion of their portfolio held in the form of bank loans.

Similar to the specifications of the banks' supply of loans, the supply of time deposits, expressed as a ratio of total liabilities, is hypothesised to be a function of the own rate of interest and of yields on assets held against deposits. Again this function was inverted to obtain the deposit rate for purposes of estimation.[27] The rationale underlying this specification is that banks set the rate of interest on time deposits according to the returns on the assets held against deposits and the ratio of time deposits to total liabilities. Note that this approach assumes that banks offer an infinitely elastic supply of sight deposits. The demand for public sector debt by the banks relative to its loan portfolio is expected to vary positively with respect to the interest rate on bonds (consols) and the loan rate, whilst the demand for base money relative to total deposits is expected to vary negatively to the treasury bill rate. The empirical results are in Table 6.G in the Appendix to this Chapter.

Both the loan-rate and deposit-rate functions performed satisfactorily. Since the loan rate and the covered Eurodollar rate were expected to influence the deposit rate in the same direction, and given the problem of multicolinearity, the sum of the two interest rates produced superior results. Again, the banks' bonds-to-liabilities ratio function performed satisfactorily with the inclusion of a lagged dependent variable, but had to be adjusted for first-order serial correlation. The banks' base–deposit ratio function proved to be the weakest in estimation.[28] Two reasons may perhaps be advanced for our difficulties. First official intervention occurs on a daily basis, whereas the estimation is based on the selection of quarter ends. Second, the introdution of competition and credit control may have meant that the banking system took some time to learn how the system worked, resulting in unstable time-varying parameters. Although the sign on the treasury bill rate conformed with our *a priori* expectations, the estimate was not statistically significant. The function was retained for simulation purposes but we emphasise that this aspect of the model requires cautious interpretation.

VII SIMULATION AND TRACKING PERFORMANCE

Model Simulation

The models developed in this chapter are used in the next chapters to study various issues in monetary and exchange rate policies. In simulation experiments the country models include the estimated equations, definitions and identities listed in Appendix Table 6.F at the end of this Chapter.

For each country the full model includes about ten behavioural equations, and ten definitions and identities. The model solves essentially for interest rates (loan, bond and time deposit rates) and a number of monetary aggregates. In addition it solves for the expected appreciation of the exchange rate, or in our empirical implementation, for the forward premium; in turn, it solves for the spot exchange rate given the expected future rate or the forward rate. One further restriction is therefore needed to solve the model. This restriction is provided by the imposition of the rational expectations constraint (or perfect foresight in our case) together with a terminal value condition for the expected or forward rate.[29] In using this solution technique the forward rate is replaced by the expected future rate that is consistent with the model solution for next period, with a boundary or terminal condition imposed *a priori*. This condition is fairly restrictive, whereas a proper rational expectations solution would have required that the solution for period t be obtained using expected solutions for the exchange rate conditional on forecasts of the exogenous variables for all future periods. The procedure would be repeated for period $t+1$ with an updating of the forecasts given additional information about period t.[30] However, this complete procedure is not followed here.

The solution for the spot rate is obtained from the estimated inverted equations for the demand for net foreign assets of the banks for Germany, France and Italy. In the model for the UK, the spot rate is solved by inverting the equation for the ratio of net foreign assets to net domestic assets held by the private sector. The net foreign asset position of the private sector is then derived from the identity for the current account (CAB), where:

$$CAB = BF + \Delta NFP + \Delta NFB + OTHER$$

and $OTHER$ refers to a composite variable which includes all other items necessary to close the identity. One of the problems associated with the above identity is that the values of ΔNFP and ΔNFB, derived from the statistics for net worth, also incorporate valuation effects due to exchange rate changes. An attempt to model the valuation effect based on the discrepancy between ΔNFP and ΔNFB and the identified capital flows of the two sectors concerned proved to be unsuccessful largely because of the erratic movement of the discrepancy. Consequently, the problem of valuation effects was ignored in the model.

Tracking Performance of the Financial Models

The tracking performance of the estimated models within sample was evaluated through dynamic simulations for the period 1971(I)–1980(IV): over a ten-year period for France, Italy, Belgium, the Netherlands, an eight-year period for the United Kingdom (1973(I)–1980(IV)), and a four-year period for Germany (1977(I)–1980(IV)). The shorter period for the UK is in sympathy with the estimation period. The German dynamic simulations for the complete period 1971–80 yielded very unsatisfactory results, particularly for the years 1973–74. These two years witnessed strong controls on financial markets, particularly bearing on capital flows, possibly being responsible for strong deviations of the model results from actual experience. Therefore, we limit our attention to the shorter period indicated.

Simulations were carried out using the complete models under the hypothesis of an exogenous forward rate, that is, non-rational expectations. The spot exchange rate is endogenous for Germany, Italy, France and the UK, and exogenous for Belgium and the Netherlands.

Summary statistics bearing on the performance of the models are given in Table 6.H. Three statistics are shown: the 'root mean squared error' as a percentage of the mean value of the variable during the period, the correlated coefficient between actual and simulated values, and Theil's inequality coefficients. The general picture that emerges is that the models track fairly well the non-banks asset variables, but less satisfactorily banks' behaviour. Large errors are recorded in advances from the Central Bank, net foreign assets and holdings of bonds. On the other hand, the models seem to track interest rates and exchange rates plausibly well.

NOTES

1. For Germany a major component of the banks' balance sheet is considered separately: saving deposits consisting of time deposits of four years and longer, bank savings bonds and saving deposits. See Appendix for exact definitions.
2. Laidler (1980) notes that research, including Goldfeld (1973), shows that there is strong evidence in favour of separating M_1 from time deposits.
3. For instance consult Darby (1972) and Arango and Nadiri (1981).
4. If income (Y) is the current yield on wealth (W), then the rate of return is $d = (Y/Y^*) \cdot (Y^*/W)$, where Y^* is permanent or expected income. If the ratio of permanent income to wealth is approximately constant, the ratio Y/Y^* (or YTR) is a proxy for the rate of return on wealth. This would apply more specifically to human wealth.

5. The coefficients are not significantly different in most cases.
6. Interest rates may even become negative.
7. This approach is presented in a number of papers. Cf. for example Hooper *et al.* (1983) Hooper *et al.* (1982) and Haas *et al.* (1980).
8. See for instance Amano (1983).
9. See Hooper *et al.* (1982, 1983).
10. The problem is similar to that of solving for interest rates from credit market equilibrium conditions. This problem with the exchange rate was found to be critical by the Federal Reserve Staff also in the context of the Multicountry Model. Cf. Hooper *et al.* (1982, 1983).
11. The vector of exogenous variables differed from country to country. For Germany it included world prices of manufactured goods, oil prices, the US money supply, the Treasury component of the monetary base, the stock of domestic government bonds, the cumulative current account balance and the Eurodollar interest rate. For the UK the set of exogenous variables was restricted to the oil price, the US money stock, the Treasury component of the monetary base and the stock of government securities. The current values of the change in the exogenous variables were forecast with VAR models of the type used in Chapter 3. OLS regressions applied to (6.14) yielded relatively high R^2: 0.77 for Germany (0.65 the adjusted R^2) and 0.83 for the UK (0.80 the adjusted R^2). The predicted values of $E_{t-1}e_{t+1} - e_t$ obtained by subtracting (6.15) from (6.17) were then compared with the forward premium in explaining $e_{t+1} - e_t$. The Theil's coefficients of inequality, reported below, suggest that our procedure tracks the one-period ahead change in the log of the spot rate much better than the forward premium:

	Theil's inequality coefficient
Germany	
Rational expectations	0.49
Forward premium	0.84
UK	
Rational expectations	0.52
Forward premium	0.79

12. Al-Khouri and Nsouli (1978), in a six-country study, find that the speeds of adjustment are relatively high, except for broad money in the case of Germany and the United Kingdom.
13. Under the usual caveats about the biases in the standard errors of the parameters.
14. Permanent income has the wrong sign in the equation for *IS* for Italy and the Netherlands.
15. Attempts to estimate such equations in difference form are not successful either, and search procedures for the values of the adjustment parameter yield a corner solution of a unit value.
16. See Coghlan (1980) Chapter 10.
17. HMSO Green Paper 1980 'Monetary Control' Cmnd. 7858.

18. See Matthews and Minford (1980) for an analytical construction and application of this method to both financial and commodity assets for post-war Britain.
19. An earlier study not dealing with the nesting implications but examining the substitutability of money to near-money was done by Chetty (1969).
20. A negative sign would indicate that the denomination has a higher income elasticity than the numerator.
21. For a complete derivation of the asset demand functions see Matthews and Thompson (1982).
22. This is also contrary to findings for the other European countries. Refer to Table 6.3 where elasticities for the foreign rate are larger for time than demand deposits, except for the Netherlands.
23. This is also contrary to results for Germany and France in Table 6.3.
24. The sign on IL and IS is strictly ambiguous.

    Note that if $\frac{\partial L}{\partial IL} < 0$ *a priori* and $g = \frac{L}{NDA + L} = f(IL - IS)$

    where $GDA = NDA + L$

    $$\frac{\partial g}{\partial IL} = \frac{\partial L}{\partial IL}\left\{\frac{1}{NDA+L}\right\} - \frac{L}{(NDA+L)^2}\frac{\partial L}{\partial IL} = \frac{1}{NDA+L}(1-g)\frac{\partial L}{\partial IL}$$

    $$\frac{\partial g}{\partial IL} \lesseqgtr 0 \text{ if } g \lesseqgtr 1$$

    Similarly if $\frac{\partial GDA}{\partial IS} > 0$ *a priori*, then $\frac{\partial g}{\partial IS} = \frac{1}{NDA+L}\{1-g\}\frac{\partial L}{\partial IS}$

    and since $\frac{\partial GDA}{\partial IS} = \frac{\partial L}{\partial IS}$ from the identity

    then $\frac{\partial g}{\partial IS} \gtrless 0$ if $g \lesseqgtr 1$
25. See notes to Table 6.G for definitions of these variables.
26. The approach is similar to that followed by Melitz and Sterdyniak (1979). Note that for the other European countries it is the demand for loans that is inverted.
27. This is similar to equation (6.3) used for the other models.
28. Despite the confident assertion by one researcher on the effect of having estimated a well-defined and well-behaved function of banks' demand for cash reserves relative to deposit liabilities. See Howard (1982).
29. See Fair (1980) and Minford, Matthews and Marwaha (1980).
30. For such a complete procedure see Fair and Taylor (1983).

APPENDIX TABLES

Tables 6.A to 6.E report the estimated equations of the financial models of Germany, France, Italy, the Netherlands and Belgium. The tables contain the following information:

1. the sample period for the equation, the dependent variable and the explanatory variables;
2. the t-ratio for each coefficient, in parentheses. The absence of a t-ratio indicates that the parameter value has been imposed *a priori*;
3. the standard error of regression (SE) and the mean of the dependent variable (μ);
4. the Durbin–Watson Statistic (DW) and the h-statistic if the equation includes a lagged dependent variable (h). The notation (–) indicates that the h-statistic could not be calculated;
5. seasonal dummies are not reported in the tables.

TABLE 6.A *The German financial model*

Period of estimation	*Dependent variable*	*Explanatory variables*: *C*	*log YPR*	*log YTR*	*Interest rates*	*Lagged dependent*	*SE* μ	*DW* *(h)*
Demand for monetary assets								
1968(I)–1980(IV)	$\log\left(\frac{BP}{p}\right)$	0.708 (2.69)	0.255 (2.58)		$-0.0024(IT+IS)-0.0064\pi$ (4.43) (1.87)	0.781 (9.48)	0.012 10.89	 (0.08)
1968(I)–1980(IV)	$\log\left(\frac{D}{P}\right)$	0.750 (3.71)	1.172 (5.43)	0.519 (2.49)	$-0.0066(IT+IEC)-0.0123\pi$ (5.32) (3.27)	0.250 (1.88)	0.019 11.58	 (1.27)
1968(I)–1980(IV)	$\log\left(\frac{T}{P}\right)$	−0.083 (0.16)	0.499 (2.91)		$0.0272IT-0.0155IEC-0.0187\pi$ (3.53) (3.08) (2.69)	0.715 (6.51)	0.050 11.52	 (0.58)
1968(I)–1980(IV)	$\log\left(\frac{SD}{P}\right)$	0.369 (6.67)	0.264 (4.27)		$-0.0036IT-0.0028IS$ (3.81) (1.33)	0.837 (24.88)	0.006 13.00	 (1.69)
Interest rate equations								
1968(I)–1980(IV)	*IL*	$0.302\log YPR-0.107\left(\log\frac{L}{P}-0.9\log\left(\frac{L}{P}\right)_{-1}\right)+0.400\,IT$ (0.59) (0.04) (10.37) $+0.093\,IEC+0.524\,IL_{-1}$ (3.28) (13.22)					0.289 9.76	
1968(I)–1980(IV)	*IS*	$31.35-4.789\log YPR+4.217\left(\log\frac{SP}{P}-0.9\log\left(\frac{SP}{P}\right)_{-1}\right)$ (4.14) (3.00) (1.12) $+0.534\,IT+0.485\,\pi$ (11.25) (5.61)					0.621 7.83	1.34
1968(I)–1980(IV)	*IT*	$-2.056+0.536\,IEA(1-BRR)+0.546\,IT_{-1}$ (1.88) (2.47) (3.41)					0.858 5.45	0.73 (–)

Banks' behaviour				
1968(I)–1980(IV)	$\frac{A}{D+T+SD}$	$\underset{(0.27)}{0.0014} - \underset{(1.59)}{0.00066}(IA - IL - IEC) + \underset{(7.85)}{0.710}\left(\frac{A}{D+T+SD}\right)_{-1}$	0.0081 0.029	(2.69)
	FR	$FR = BE - A$		
1968(I)–1980(IV)	$\frac{SB}{L+SB}$	$\underset{(0.78)}{-0.0079} + \underset{(0.99)}{0.00067}\,IS + \underset{(33.83)}{1.015}\left(\frac{SB}{L+SB}\right)_{-1}$	0.004 0.192	(3.11)
Capital flows and exchange rate				
1970(I)–1980(IV)	KP	$\underset{(1.27)}{1016.56} + \underset{(1.55)}{1.362}\,\Delta[(IT - IEC)\,YPR] - \underset{(2.52)}{0.515}\,CAB + \underset{(1.65)}{0.374}\,CAB_{-1}$	4880.0 1021.3	2.43
1971(I)–1980(IV)	e	$\underset{(0.67)}{0.0042} + \underset{(6.73)}{0.877}\,\frac{IEU}{400} + \underset{(221.51)}{1.014}\,f - \underset{(7.22)}{1.365}\,\frac{IT}{400} - \underset{(3.98)}{0.250}\left(\frac{NFB}{D+T+SD}\right)$	0.0035 0.896	1.57

TABLE 6.B *The French financial model*

Period of estimation	*Dependent variable*	*C*	*log YPR*	*log YTR*	*Interest rates*	*Lagged dependent*	*SE* / μ	*DW* / (h)
Demand for monetary assets								
1964(I)–1980(IV)	$\log\left(\frac{BP}{P}\right)$	5.279 (4.37)	0.113 (1.91)	−0.274 (1.77)	$-0.010\ IS - 0.010\ \pi$ (1.81) (2.25)	0.521 (4.62)	0.028 11.97	(−3.54)
1964(I)–1980(IV)	$\log\left(\frac{D}{P}\right)$	1.632 (2.85)	0.263 (3.40)		$-0.0063\ (IT + IEC)$ (3.92)	0.756 (10.27)	0.028 12.22	(0.36)
1964(I)–1980(IV)	$\log\left(\frac{T}{P}\right)$	−0.867 (2.03)	0.386 (2.28)		$-0.0029\ (IS + IEC) + 0.014\ IT$ (2.71) (1.78) $-0.014\ \pi$ (3.51)	0.900 (20.09)	0.022 12.12	(1.41)

Interest rate equations				
1964(I)–1980(IV)	IL	$\underset{(1.38)}{-9.470}+\underset{(1.57)}{2.926}\,\log\,YPR-\underset{(0.66)}{2.390}\left(\log\frac{L}{P}-0.85\log\left(\frac{L}{P}\right)_{-1}\right)$ $+\underset{(1.91)}{0.474}IT+\underset{(9.98)}{0.488}IEC+\underset{(1.74)}{0.180}\,\pi$	0.831 9.64	0.89
1964(I)–1980(IV)	IS	$\underset{(1.85)}{0.114}\left(\log\frac{SP}{P}-0.6\log\left(\frac{SP}{P}\right)_{-1}-0.4\log YPR\right)+\underset{(4.16)}{0.120}IEC+\underset{(1.72)}{0.100}\pi$ $+\underset{(9.85)}{0.796}IS_{-1}$	0.396 8.81	(1.48)
1964(I)–1980(IV)	IT	$\underset{(0.47)}{0.062}+\underset{(3.04)}{0.078}\,IEC\,(1-BRR)+\underset{(17.27)}{0.843}\,IT_{-1}$	0.285 4.742	(0.71)
Banks' behaviour				
1971(IV)–1980(IV)	$\frac{A}{D+T}$	$\underset{(3.40)}{0.045}-\underset{(1.19)}{0.001}\,(IA-IL-IEC)+\underset{(5.26)}{0.915}\,BRR+\underset{(3.04)}{0.360}\left(\frac{A}{D+T}\right)_{-1}$	0.016 0.135	(2.48)
	FR	$FR=BE-A$		
1964(I)–1980(IV)	$\frac{SB}{L+SB}$	$\underset{(5.55)}{0.025}+\underset{(1.03)}{0.0015}\,(IS-IL)-\underset{(3.68)}{0.0020}\,IEC+\underline{0.7}\left(\frac{SB}{L+SB}\right)_{-1}$	0.010 0.011	(–)
Capital flows and exchange rate				
1971(IV)–1980(IV)	e	$\underset{(0.80)}{-0.027}+\underset{(45.97)}{1.011}\left(\frac{IEU}{400}+f-\frac{IT}{400}\right)$	0.007 1.518	1.61
	KP	Exogenous		

TABLE 6.C *The Italian financial model*

Period of estimation	*Dependent variable*	*Explanatory variables* *C*	*log YPR*	*log YTR*	*Interest rates*	*Lagged dependent*	*SE* / μ	*DW* / *(h)*
Demand for monetary assets								
1965(I)–1980(IV)	$\log\left(\frac{BP}{P}\right)$	−0.781 (2.78)	0.295 (4.36)	0.200 (1.59)	$-0.0153IT + 0.0023\pi$ (4.17) (1.36)	0.749 (12.98)	0.017 9.97	 (3.55)
1965(I)–1980(IV)	$\log\left(\frac{D}{P}\right)$	−0.870 (0.88)	0.140 (1.05)	0.365 (2.50)	$-0.0017IT - 0.0034IEC$ (0.34) (3.45)	0.939 (18.22)	0.021 10.59	 (1.62)
1965(I)–1980(IV)	$\log\left(\frac{T}{P}\right)$	−0.259 (0.91)	0.229 (2.58)	0.151 (0.81)	$0.0225(IT - IS) - 0.0022IEC$ (2.57) (2.76)	0.783 (10.05)	0.023 10.51	 (2.18)
Interest rates								
1965(I)–1980(IV)	IL	$7.722 - 0.130\log(YPR) - 4.480\log\left(\frac{L}{P} - 0.9\left(\frac{L}{P}\right)_{-1}\right) + 0.301IT + 0.282IEC$ (0.41) (0.07) (0.98) (5.62) (5.62) $+0.166\pi + 0.317IL_{-1}$ (1.41) (2.52)					1.284 11.95	 (−)
1965(I)–1980(IV)	IS	$-23.915 + 2.198\log(YPR) + 3.226\log\left(\frac{SP}{P} - 0.9\left(\frac{SP}{P}\right)_{-1}\right) + 0.564IT + 0.108IEC$ (1.95) (2.08) (2.38) (4.93) (2.90)					0.818 9.84	1.36
1965(I)–1980(IV)	IT	$-0.546 + 0.265IEA(1 - BRR) + 0.718IT_{-1}$ (2.87) (6.08) (14.53)					0.522 7.01	 (−0.86)

Banks' behaviour				
1965(I)–1980(IV)	$\frac{A}{D+T}$	$\underset{(9.61)}{0.030} - \underset{(3.60)}{0.0023}\,IA + \underset{(1.57)}{0.00041}\,(IEA+IEC) + \underline{0.5}\left(\frac{A}{D+T}\right)_{-1}$	0.008 0.017	(–)
1965(I)–1980(IV)	$\frac{FR}{D+T}$	$-\underset{(0.56)}{0.0026} - \underset{(2.09)}{0.0008}\,(IEA+IEC) + \underset{(2.03)}{0.0019}\,IA + \underline{0.4}\left(\frac{FR}{D+T}\right)_{-1}$	0.011 –0.0023	(–)
1965(I)–1980(IV)	$\frac{SB}{L+SB}$	$-\underset{(1.84)}{0.017} + \underset{(2.19)}{0.0060}\,IS - \underset{(1.09)}{0.0023}\,IL - \underset{(1.05)}{0.0008}\,IEC + \underset{(17.92)}{0.913}\left(\frac{SB}{L+SB}\right)_{-1}$	0.015 0.215	(–0.74)
Capital flows and exchange rate				
1971(I)–1980(IV)	e	$\underset{(0.57)}{0.2329} - \underset{(1.34)}{1.819}\,\frac{IT}{400} + \underset{(0.13)}{0.045}\left(\frac{IEU}{400}\right) + \underset{(14.83)}{0.965}\,f - \underset{(2.61)}{0.852}\,\frac{NFB}{D+T}$	0.013 6.580	0.95
	KP	Exogenous		

TABLE 6.D *The Dutch financial model*

Period of estimation	Dependent Variable	Explanatory variables: C	log YPR	log YTR	Interest rates	Lagged dependent	SE / μ	DW / (h)
Demand for monetary assets								
1963(I)–1980(IV)	$\log\left(\frac{BP}{P}\right)$	1.562 (2.36)	0.042 (1.74)		$-0.00089\ ITT - 0.0044\pi$ (0.52) (1.70)	0.817 (10.80)	0.020 / 9.59	(−4.23)
1963(I)–1980(IV)	$\log\left(\frac{D}{P}\right)$	1.692 (6.29)	0.649 (6.80)	0.637 (5.35)	$-0.0079\ (ITT + IEC)$ (6.17)	0.507 (7.19)	0.026 / 10.12	(0.0)
1963(I)–1980(IV)	$\log\left(\frac{T}{P}\right)$	0.413 (2.85)	0.314 (3.08)		$0.0105\ (ITT - IS)$ (2.92)	0.812 (4.51)	0.026 / 10.72	(0.69)
Interest rates equations								
1963(I)–1980(IV)	IL	$-3.771 + 5.117 \log YPR - 17.66 \left(\log\frac{L}{P} - 0.9 \log\left(\frac{L}{P}\right)_{-1}\right) + 0.770\ IEC$ (1.13) (2.17) (1.67) (11.21)					1.157 / 7.91	1.40
1963(I)–1980(IV)	IS	$-18.690 + 1.374 \log YPR - 10.880 \left(\log\frac{SP}{P} - 0.9 \log\left(\frac{SP}{P}\right)_{-1}\right) + 0.926\ IT$ (3.58) (2.52) (2.43) (3.50) $+ 0.390\ IS_{-1}$ (2.85)					0.490 / 7.45	(−)
1963(I)–1980(IV)	IT	$0.410 + 0.029\ (IEA + IEC)(1 - BRR) + 0.812\ IT_{-1}$ (3.40) (6.27) (23.98)					0.142 / 4.27	(0.13)
1963(I)–1980(IV)	ITT	$-0.967 + 0.287\ IEA\ (1 - BRR) + 0.533\ IEC\ (1 - BRR)$ (1.03) (1.05) (2.36)					1.649 / 4.70	2.31

Banks' behaviour				
1963(I)–1980(IV)	$\frac{A}{D+T}$	$-0.0088 - 0.0065\,IA + 0.0074\,IEA + 0.0006\,IEC + 0.162\,BRR$ (1.80) (3.22) (3.45) (0.64) (1.17)	0.006 0.010	1.36
1963(I)–1980(IV)	$\frac{FR}{D+T}$	$0.0351 + 0.0105\,IA - 0.0130\,IEA - 1.114\,BRR$ (4.84) (2.94) (4.10) (4.68)	0.011 −0.001	1.60
1963(I)–1980(IV)	$\frac{SB}{L+SB}$	$-0.0068 + 0.00028\,(IS - IEC) - 0.992\left(\frac{SB}{L+SB}\right)_{-1}$ (1.92) (0.45) (94.37)	0.007 0.290	(0.55)
1963(I)–1980(IV)	$\frac{NFB}{D+T}$	$0.0084 + 0.0047\,IEC - 0.0075\,ITT + 0.885\left(\frac{NFB}{D+T}\right)_{-1}$ (1.00) (2.04) (2.79) (14.96)	0.021 0.047	(−0.19)
Capital flows				
1963(I)–1980(IV)	KP	$-561.0 - 0.757\,\Delta(IEC \times YPR) + 10.641\,\Delta(IT \times YPR) - 0.242\,CAB$ (3.02) (1.00) (2.19) (2.41) $+0.309\,KP_{-1}$ (2.32)	681.6 −185.3	(–)

TABLE 6.E *The Belgian financial model*

Period of estimation	*Dependent variable*	*Explanatory variables* *C*	*log YPR*	*log YTR*	*Interest rates*	*Lagged dependent*	*SE* μ	*DW* (*h*)
Demand for monetary assets								
1963(I)–1980(IV)	$\log\left(\frac{BP}{P}\right)$	1.358 (3.75)	0.020 (1.73)	0.105 (1.81)	$-0.0031\ (IT+IS)$ (5.28)	0.750 (12.44)	0.012 5.86	 (−1.77)
1963(I)–1980(IV)	$\log\left(\frac{D}{P}\right)$	−2.278 (3.90)	0.611 (4.08)	0.328 (2.98)	$-0.0019\ (IT+IEC)$ (2.57)	0.580 (5.71)	0.025 5.43	 (−1.07)
1963(I)–1980(IV)	$\log\left(\frac{T}{P}\right)$	−0.322 (0.45)	0.067 (0.50)	0.198 (1.75)	$-0.0035\ IEC$ (3.33)	0.973 (17.92)	0.022 5.52	 (−1.14)
Interest rates equations								
1963(I)–1980(IV)	*IL*	$\underset{(1.50)}{-11.924}+\underset{(2.04)}{2.718}\log YPR-\underset{(2.00)}{9.285}\left(\log\frac{L}{P}-0.9\left(\frac{L}{P}\right)_{-1}\right)+\underset{(13.49)}{0.408}\,(IT+IEC)$					1.17 8.84	1.28
1963(I)–1980(IV)	*IS*	$\underset{(2.22)}{2.843}-\underset{(2.56)}{0.516}\log YPR+\underset{(1.13)}{1.269}\left(\log\frac{SP}{P}-0.9\log\left(\frac{SP}{P}\right)_{-1}\right)+\underset{(5.14)}{0.074}\,IT$ $+\underset{(17.18)}{0.958}\,IS_{-1}$					0.200 6.21	 (2.06)
1963(I)–1980(IV)	*IT*	$\underset{(2.54)}{-1.584}+\underset{(5.53)}{0.496}\,IEC(1-BRR)+\underset{(2.74)}{0.527}\,IEA\,(1-BRR)+\underset{(1.39)}{0.129}\,IT_{-1}$					0.950 7.18	 (5.15)

Banks' behaviour				
1963(I)–1980(IV)	$\frac{A}{D+T}$	$-0.006 - 0.018\, IA + 0.015\, IEA + 0.0038\, IEC + 0.465 \left(\frac{A}{D+T}\right)_{-1}$ (0.38) (2.60) (2.00) (2.05) (4.44)	0.020 0.046	 (0.45)
1963(I)–1980(IV)	$\frac{FR}{D+T}$	$0.038 + 0.020\,(IA - IEA) - 0.0025\, IEC + 0.494 \left(\frac{FR}{D+T}\right)_{-1}$ (2.61) (2.67) (2.53) (4.33)	0.021 −0.023	 (−3.84)
1963(I)–1980(IV)	$\frac{SB}{L+SB}$	$-0.011 + 0.0027\, IS - 0.0005\, IEC + 0.949 \left(\frac{SB}{L+SB}\right)_{-1}$ (0.52) (1.32) (0.83) (26.05)	0.009 0.402	 (−1.02)
(1963(I)–1980(IV)	$\frac{NFB}{D+T}$	$0.026 + 0.0050\, IEC - 0.0108\, IEA + 0.926 \left(\frac{NFB}{D+T}\right)_{-1}$ (2.52) (2.74) (3.45) (15.07)	0.018 −0.216	 (0.06)
Capital flows				
1963(I)–1980(IV)	KP	$6.092 + 0.0009\,\Delta(IT \times YPR) - 0.0002\,\Delta(IEC \times YPR) - 0.187\,\Delta YPR$ (1.99) (2.09) (2.31) (1.55)	7.529 −0.570	2.11

TABLE 6.F *Definitions and identities used in the models for Germany, France, Italy, the Netherlands and Belgium*

1. Balance sheet of the banks ('determines' L).

   $D+T+A = L+SB+NFB+BR+BE+OAB$

   (For Germany add SD to left-hand side).

2. Balance of payments ('determines' BF or NFB according to exchange rate regime).

   $CAB = \Delta NFB - KP - OK + \Delta BF$

3. Bond market equilibrium

   $S = SP + SB$

4. Required reserves

   $BR = BRR\,(D+T)$

   For Germany:

   $BR = BRR \times BRK \times (S+T+SD)$

   where BRK is an adjustment factor to account for the fact that only a fraction (about 70 percent on the average) of domestic liabilities of banks are subject to reserve requirements.

5. Excess reserves

   $BE = FR + A$

   For France and Germany BE is exogenous, and the equation 'determines' FR.

6. Monetary base

   $B = BR + BE + BP$

7. Other assets of Central Bank (residual item)

   $OB = B - BTR - BF - A$

8. Bank credit interest rate

   $$IEA = \frac{(IL \times L) + (IS \times SB)}{L+SB}$$

9. Forward premium

   $$FP = \frac{EF - ES}{ES} \times 400$$

10. Foreign covered rate

    $IEC = IEU + FP$

TABLE 6.G *The UK financial model (Method of estimation: 'three-stage least squares')*

Period of estimation	*Dependent variable*	*Explanatory variables*											*SE*	*DW*
		C	$(IT+IEC)$	$(IT-ILA)$	$(IL-IS)$	$(IEC-IS)$	IEC	π	$log(YPR)$	$log\left(\frac{NWP}{P}\right)$	*time*	*Lagged dependent*	μ	(h)
Asset demands by the non-bank private sector														
1973(I)– 1980(IV)	$\log\left(\frac{BP}{D}\right)$	9.912 (1.37)	0.215 (6.77)						−0.605 (1.48)	−0.111 (1.15)	0.0021 (1.10)	0.596 (2.09)	0.0148 −0.7426	(−)*
1973(I)– 1980(IV)	$\log\left(\frac{M_1}{T}\right)$	1.686 (1.33)	−0.690 (4.74)					0.4644 (1.72)		−0.159 (1.42)	0.0024 (1.61)	0.8554 (9.50)	0.0344 −0.0164	(1.10)
1973(I)– 1980(IV)	$\log\left(\frac{M_2}{SP}\right)$	5.413 (5.10)		13.472 (2.55)			1.754 (8.44)			−0.442 (4.80)	−0.0151 (8.34)	0.1867 (1.76)	0.0294 −0.0234	(0.7)
1973(I)– 1980(IV)	$\log\left(\frac{L}{M_2+SP}\right)$	−2.72 (2.45)			−0.700 (1.59)		1.057 (6.56)			0.2114 (2.07)	0.001 (0.63)	0.753 (7.46)	0.0181 −1.0114	(0.34)
1973(I)– 1980(IV)	$\log\left(\frac{NFP}{M_2+SP-L}\right)$	153.66 (2.89)			13.719 (4.55)				−15.483 (2.89)		0.0304 (1.88)	0.321 (1.93)	0.2124 −2.3943	(2.83)

TABLE 6.G *Continued*

Period of estimation	*Dependent variable*	*Explanatory variables*							*SE*	*DW*
		Constant	IA	$(IL+IEC)$	$(IS-IL)$	$\frac{(L+LO)}{(liabilities)}$	$\frac{T}{(liabilities)}$	*Lagged dependent*	μ	
Banks' behaviour										
1973(I)–1980(IV)	IL	−0.0652 (2.29)	0.8772 (23.64)			0.1134 (2.71)			0.0049 0.1157	1.74
1973(I)–1980(IV)	IT	0.1823 (1.13)		0.5294 (17.04)			−0.088 (1.60)		0.0077 0.1190	1.77*
1973(I)–1980(IV)	$\log \frac{SB}{L+LO}$	−0.5499 (2.70)			1.520 (2.30)			0.5476 (3.70)	0.077 −1.337	−0.62*
1973(I)–1980(IV)	$\log BE/(D+T)$	−3.3065 (23.6)	−0.3387 (0.4)						0.0846	2.69*

NOTES
1. *indicates that the equation was corrected for serial correlation
2. Variables used in the UK model not defined in Table 6.1
   ILA: local authorities rate (short-rate)
   NWP: net worth of private sector
   RES and $RESID$ are residual items in the respective balance sheets
   LO: Lending in sterling to overseas
   OSL: Other sterling liabilities
   DS: Special deposits of banks at the Bank of England
3. Definitions and Identities
   $M_1 = BP + D$
   $M_2 = M_1 + T$
   $NFB = D + T + A + OSL - BE - (L + LO) - DS - SB - RES$
   $SP = NWP - M_2 - NFP - RESID + L$

TABLE 6.H *Within-sample tracking performance of financial models*

	Germany			*France*			*Italy*			*United Kingdom*			*Netherlands*			*Belgium*		
Variables	*RMSE/ μ*	*r*	*U*	*RMSE/ μ*	*r*	*U*	*RMSE/ μ*	*r*	*U*	*RMSE/ μ*	*r*	*U*	*RMSE/ μ*	*r*	*U*	*RMSE/ μ*	*r*	*U*
BP	0.03	0.96	0.017	0.06	0.99	0.030	0.06	0.99	0.026	0.005	0.99	0.002	0.03	0.99	0.014	0.01	0.99	0.007
D	0.04	0.94	0.02	0.30	0.99	0.170	0.10	0.98	0.046	0.005	0.99	0.003	0.03	0.99	0.015	0.03	0.99	0.017
T	0.05	0.99	0.028	0.07	0.99	0.032	0.08	0.99	0.034	0.001	0.99	0.003	0.06	0.99	0.029	0.03	0.99	0.015
M_2	0.023	0.99	0.014	0.08	0.99	0.039	0.06	0.99	0.024	0.050	0.99	0.002	0.04	0.99	0.017	0.01	0.99	0.008
SP	0.10	0.94	0.044	0.21	0.93	0.112	0.25	0.98	0.086	0.002	0.99	0.001	0.06	0.99	0.030	0.04	0.99	0.017
A	0.33	0.76	0.12	0.19	0.86	0.097	0.42	0.57	0.181	—	—	—	0.73	0.67	0.277	0.67	0.58	0.279
FR	−0.35	0.77	0.12	—	—	—	(*)	−0.016	0.675	0.015	0.99	0.007	(*)	0.54	0.443	(*)	0.55	0.368
NFB	—	—	—	—	—	—	(*)	0.96	0.136	0.154	0.92	0.071	1.29	0.67	0.650	(*)	0.91	0.126
SB	0.094	0.98	0.018	1.33	0.82	0.357	0.24	0.96	0.101	0.009	0.99	0.005	0.19	0.95	0.080	0.09	0.97	0.040
IL	0.25	0.74	0.095	0.11	0.73	0.058	0.19	0.80	0.093	0.007	0.99	0.004	0.14	0.85	0.071	0.15	0.88	0.072
IS	0.22	0.27	0.095	0.21	0.87	0.115	0.12	0.89	0.057		Exogenous		0.10	0.67	0.050	0.017	0.81	0.046
IT	0.51	0.78	0.15	0.15	0.49	0.075	0.16	0.89	0.079	0.018	0.99	0.009	0.07	0.59	0.037	0.16	0.91	0.076
es	0.01	0.99	0.005	0.007	0.99	0.003	0.016	0.99	0.008	0.070	0.99	0.004	—	—	—	—	—	—

Notes *RMSE/μ*: 'Root mean squared error'/mean of variable
r: correlation coefficient between actual and simulated values
U: Theil's inequality coefficient
(*): not reproduced as mean was too close to zero

Part III
Exchange Rate and Monetary Policies and World Financial Interdependence

7 Policy Choices under Different Exchange Rate Regimes

I INTRODUCTION

In this chapter the behaviour of the financial model, described in the previous chapter, is analysed under different exogenous disturbances. All disturbances are of the unexpected kind and can thus be considered as 'news'. It is well known from the rational expectations literature that only expected disturbances are already reflected in prices, exchange rates, and interest rates.

The disturbances under consideration are domestic price and foreign interest rate disturbances. We restrict ourselves to these two shocks because the number of simulation results increases rapidly. The main points of the analysis will be illustrated with simulations from two countries only, France and Germany. The inclusion of results for the four other countries would complicate unnecessarily the presentation in light of the similarity of model structures.

We first analyse the model under a freely floating exchange rate. This allows us to identify some problems concerning this arrangement and to discuss to what extent official management of the exchange rate can deal with these problems. This, in turn, will lead us to an assessment of the effectiveness of foreign exchange market intervention.

II THE MODEL UNDER FREE FLOATING

We analyse consecutively the effect of an unanticipated price disturbance and an unanticipated (foreign) interest rate shock. The simulation design involves comparing the value of the endogenous variables obtained when the model is shocked with the values of the endogenous variables of the control solution. All simulations are done under the hypothesis of rational expectations. Since these simulations are non-stochastic and exogenous variables are set equal to their actual values, the rational expectations solution becomes one of perfect foresight. To obtain a unique solution we impose a terminal condition on the path of the exchange rate (see Fair, 1979).

The models are simulated for the period 1977(I) to 1980(IV). The terminal condition is set for the last quarter of 1980. The choice of terminal date may affect the results. However, since the period simulation is sufficiently long (16 quarters), the results should not be too sensitive, at least for the first two years.[1] As will be seen below, the pattern of results from the first two years is not significantly modified by looking at the four-year period. The terminal value for the exchange rate is set in accordance with the type of disturbance analysed, as explained below.

Domestic Price Shock

Assume that the domestic price level increases by 10 per cent. The origin of this price shock is not spelled out here. It could result, for example, from a cost–push phenomenon. We assume that in the long run purchasing power parity holds: a 10 per cent increase in the price level is expected to lead to a 10 per cent increase in the exchange rate in the terminal date. The results of this 10 per cent unexpected, yet permanent, increase in the domestic price level are shown in Figures 7.1 to 7.3. Figure 7.1 shows the time-path of the dollar exchange rate for Germany and

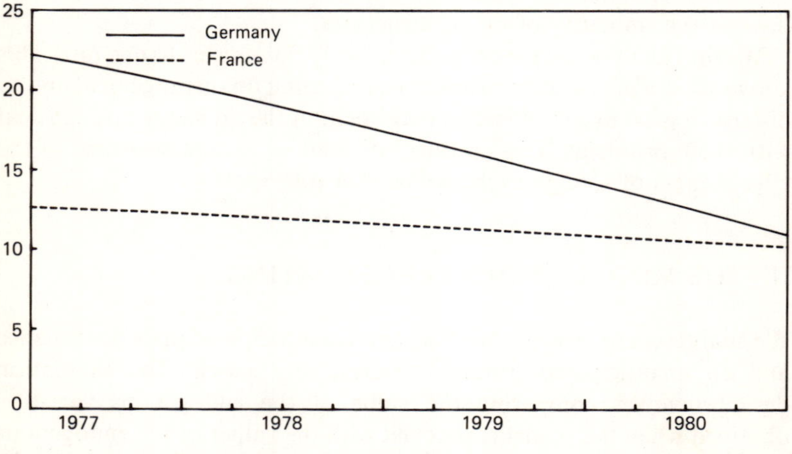

FIGURE 7.1 *Change in dollar exchange rate after* 10 *per cent price shock* (*annual percentage changes*)

France. The exchange rate initially overshoots its long-run value. This overshooting is more pronounced in Germany than in France, in turn suggesting that when these two countries peg their exchange rates, intervention is necessary in the DM/FF market.

Figures 7.2 and 7.3 show the time-path of the money base and of the money stock M_2 in these two countries, following the domestic price level increases. It is noteworthy that in both countries the monetary aggregates tend to increase substantially. The explanation of this result is as follows: after the initial overshooting, the exchange rate tends to appreciate towards its long-run value. Thus, during the whole period *after* the initial disturbance the FF and DM are expected to appreciate relative to the dollar. This produces a forward premium on the FF and the DM which tends to reduce the loan interest rate. The net effect is to raise the demand for domestic bank loans, setting in motion a process of credit expansion, that is fuelled by a passive central bank. This means that by keeping the instruments of monetary control (discount rate, reserve requirements and open market operations) unchanged during this simulation exercise the monetary authorities automatically accomodate the initial price shock with a large increase in the monetary aggregates.

Automatic monetary accomodation follows directly from the initial overshooting of the exchange rate. To avoid this automaticity some form

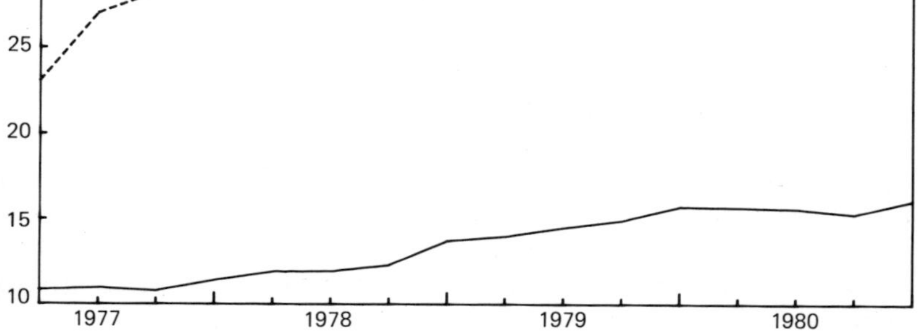

FIGURE 7.2 *Change in money base after* 10 *per cent price increase (in billions of national currency)*

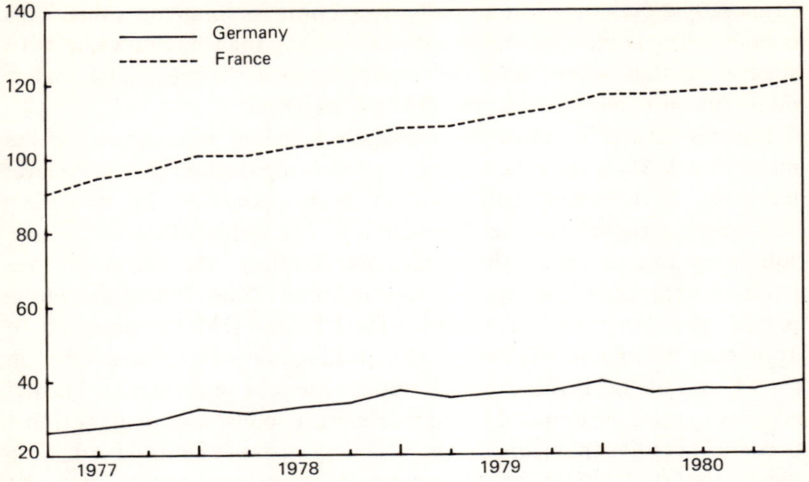

FIGURE 7.3 *Change in M_2 after* 10 *per cent price increase* (*in billions of national currency*)

of control of the domestic monetary aggregates is necessary. Lacking this, the automatic monetary accomodation inherent in the financial system of these countries may easily generate further price increases and may lead to 'vicious circle' effects (See Basevi and De Grauwe, 1977; Bilson, 1979b).

In the next section we ask the question 'how useful can intervention in the foreign exchange markets be in reducing automatic monetary accomodation?'

A Foreign Interest Rate Shock

The second unanticipated shock takes the form of an increase of 1 per cent in the Eurodollar interest rate. We make a distinction here between a permanent interest rate shock and a temporary one. In the former case the interest rate increase is maintained throughout the simulation period. This shock also increases the terminal value of the dollar exchange rate. In the case of a temporary increase of the dollar interest rate we allow it to increase during four quarters, after which it returns to its control value. In this case the terminal value of the exchange rate is kept unchanged (that is, it is equal to the terminal value of the control solution).

The results of these two disturbances are shown in Figures 7.4 and 7.5. It can be seen that a permanent increase in the foreign interest rate has a considerable effect on the dollar exchange rate. In addition, the dollar exchange rate tends to overshoot substantially its long-run value, which has increased by approximately 1 per cent.

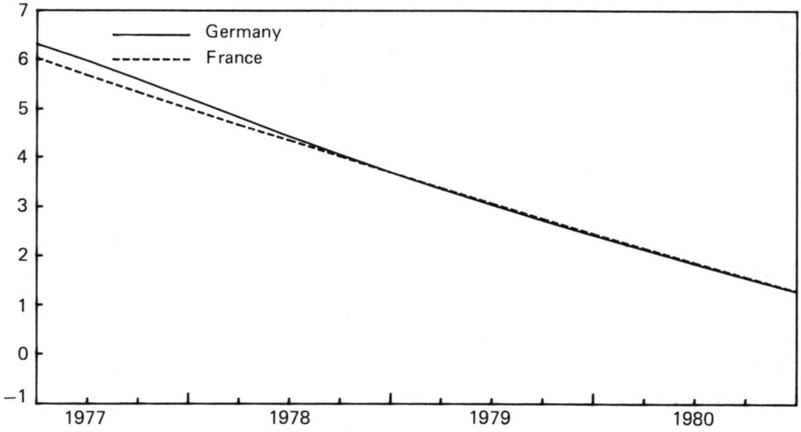

FIGURE 7.4 *Change in dollar exchange rate after permanent increase of Eurodollar interest rate (annual percentage changes)*

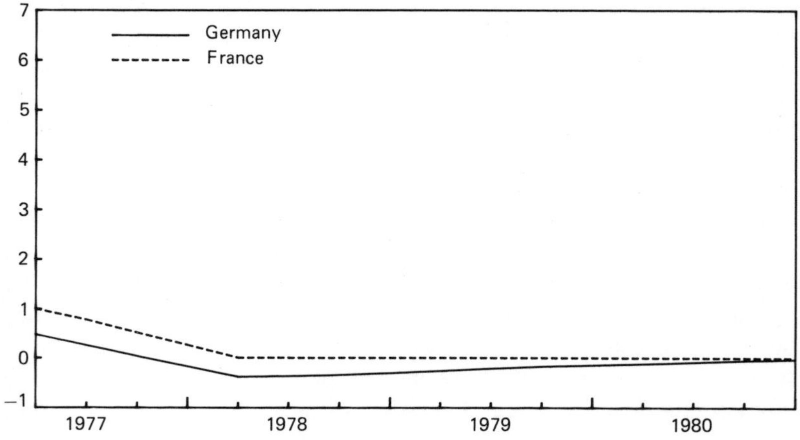

FIGURE 7.5 *Change in dollar exchange rate after temporary increase in Eurodollar interest rate (annual percentage changes)*

When the foreign interest rate increase is perceived to be temporary there are minimal effects on the dollar exchange rate. The same foreign interest rate shock occurring today can have substantially different effects on the exchange rates depending on whether it is perceived to be permanent or temporary. The general importance of distinguishing temporary from permanent stocks has been underscored by Brunner, Cukierman and Meltzer (1980). This feature also explains why the observed relation between interest rates and exchange rates has been very unpredictable since the advent of floating, a feature that has puzzled many observers.

In the next section we analyse the question of how, and to what extent, intervention in the exchange market can be used to mitigate the effects of foreign interest rate disturbances on the exchange rate.

III THE EFFECTIVENESS OF INTERVENTION IN THE EXCHANGE MARKET

As a result of the large official interventions in the foreign exchange markets since 1973 there has been renewed interest in assessing the effectiveness of these intervention policies: this is done, among others, by Artus (1976), Quirk (1977), Tosini (1977), Genberg (1981), and Branson (1982). There is agreement that a large part of official interventions follows a 'leaning against the wind' strategy; and that non-sterilised interventions are effective in influencing the exchange rate. Controversy continues to exist, however, about the effectiveness of sterilised intervention.[2] A study by Obstfeld (1982) on German intervention policies concludes that sterilised invervention policies are relatively powerless in changing the time path of the exchange rate. Using a different methodology, Wonnacott (1983) and Mayer and Taguchi (1983) arrive at a different conclusion.

As is usual in this debate a distinction is made between sterilised and non-sterilised intervention. Sterilised interventions have no effect on the domestic money base, that is, sales (purchases) of foreign exchange, which tend to reduce (increase) the domestic money base, are offset by opposite interventions in the domestic money market so that the money base is unaffected by foreign exchange market interventions. Non-sterilised interventions affect the money base: when the authorities sell (buy) foreign exchange the domestic money base declines (increases).

As indicated earlier, the empirical evidence suggests that most intervention policies have been of the 'leaning against the wind' type. In the simulations performed here we assume that the authorities follow such a rule, which can be specified as follows:

$$\Delta BF_t = -\varepsilon \Delta es_t \tag{7.1}$$

where BF_t is the stock of international reserves held by the central bank in period t; es_t is the spot exchange rate in period t; $\varepsilon \geqslant 0$, is the parameter indicating the degree of 'leaning against the wind'. Thus when the exchange rate increases, the authorities sell foreign exchange so that BF_t declines.

Again, we assume rational expectations (perfect foresight in our case) throughout. This implies that economic agents know the intervention rules used by the monetary authorities. Although it may seem extreme, the rational expectations assumption is essential in evaluating the effectiveness of foreign exchange market interventions. It allows us to ensure that economic agents take the known intervention rule into account when they set their expectations about the future exchange rate.

The Effectiveness of Sterilised Intervention

Here we concentrate on the effectiveness of *sterilised* intervention. We do so by analysing again the effect of a domestic price level and a foreign interest rate shock. The monetary authorities intervene in the market according to intervention rule (7.1).[3] We compare these simulation results with the ones obtained under free floating. The free floating benchmark allows us to assess how effective are these intervention policies.

Figures 7.6 and 7.7 show the time path of the exchange rate with and without intervention, following an (unanticipated but permanent) increase of 10 per cent in the domestic price level. In the French model we find that sterilised intervention has no perceptible influence on the dollar exchange rate. In the German model sterilised intervention appears to have a significant effect on the time path of the exchange rate; but to achieve this the amount of intervention must be substantial. During the first period the German authorities sell approximately DM9bn. Thus, it can be said that this kind of sterilised intervention, in the face of a permanent price shock, is relatively ineffective because it requires intervention in amounts too large to have a significant effect on the exchange rate. In addition, these intervention activities in the foreign exchange market do very little to reduce the automatic monetary accomodation of the domestic price level disturbance. This point is illustrated in Figures 7.8 and 7.9, which show the time path of M_2 under

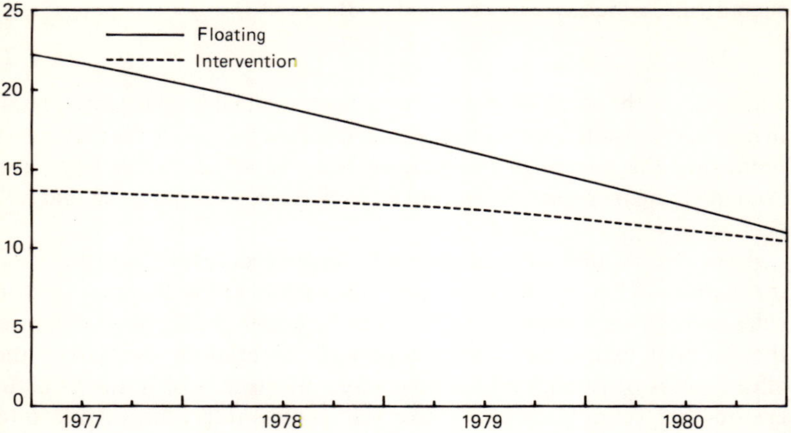

FIGURE 7.6 *Change in dollar/DM rate after* 10 *per cent price increase (annual percentage changes)*

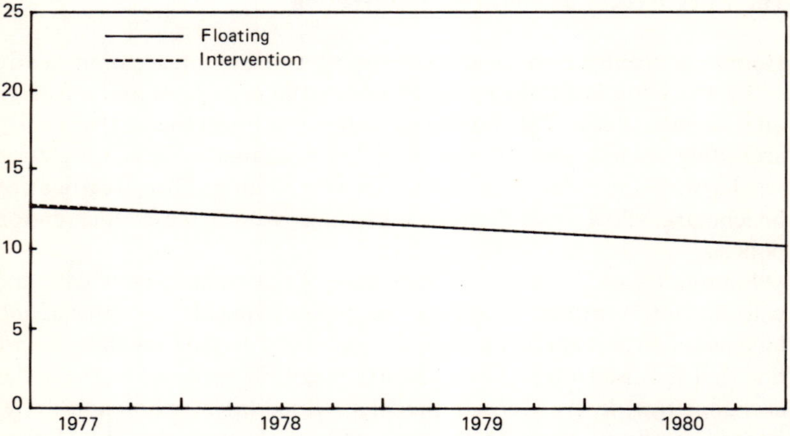

FIGURE 7.7 *Change in dollar/FF rate after* 10 *per cent price increase (annual percentage changes)*

the alternative regimes of sterilised intervention and perfect floating. It can be seen that in the case of Germany the automatic monetary accomodation is barely reduced when the monetary authorities intervene in the foreign exchange market. In the case of France, the intervention policies produce no effect whatsoever.

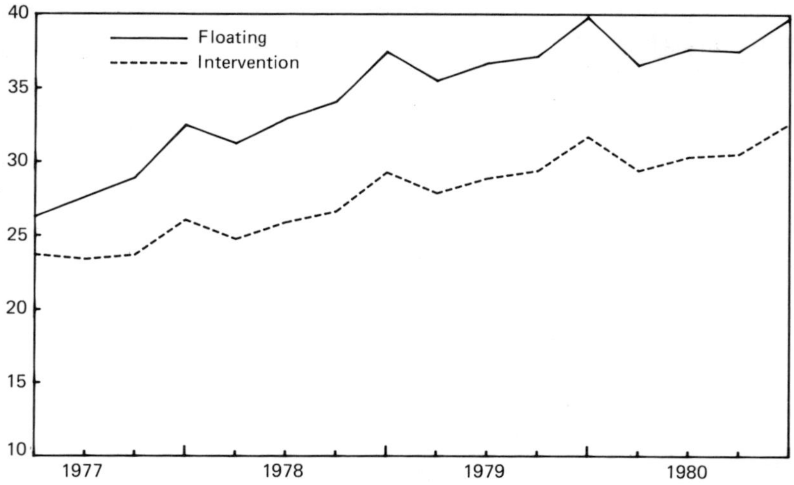

FIGURE 7.8 *Change in M_2 after* 10 *per cent price increase* (*Germany*), *in billions DM*

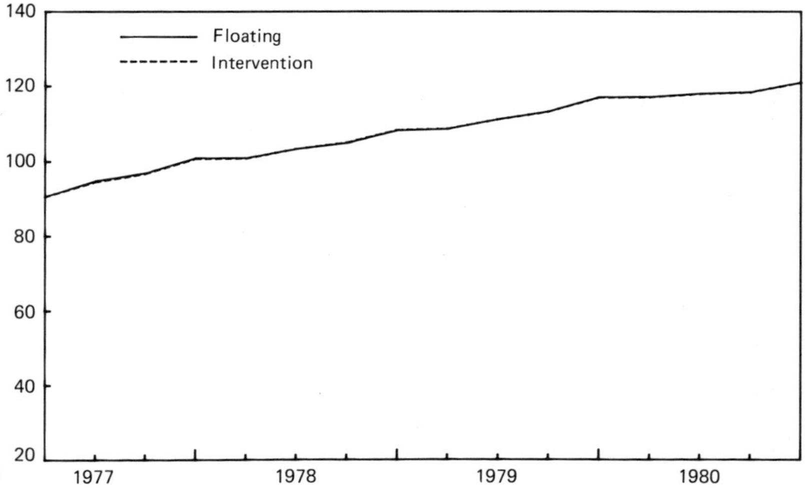

FIGURE 7.9 *Change in M_2 after* 10 *per cent price increase* (*France*), *in billions FF*

The difference between the results for Germany and France can be explained by the different exchange rate equations for the two countries. The equation for Germany implies departures from interest rate parity, and the existence of risk premium leaving room for effective intervention. The equation for France, however, is an interest rate parity condition which implies the ineffectiveness of intervention policies.[4]

Additional evidence on the effectiveness of sterilised intervention policies is obtained from the simulations of interest rate shocks: Figures 7.10 and 7.11. There we compare the time paths of the exchange rate after a permanent 1 per cent increase in the Eurodollar rate,

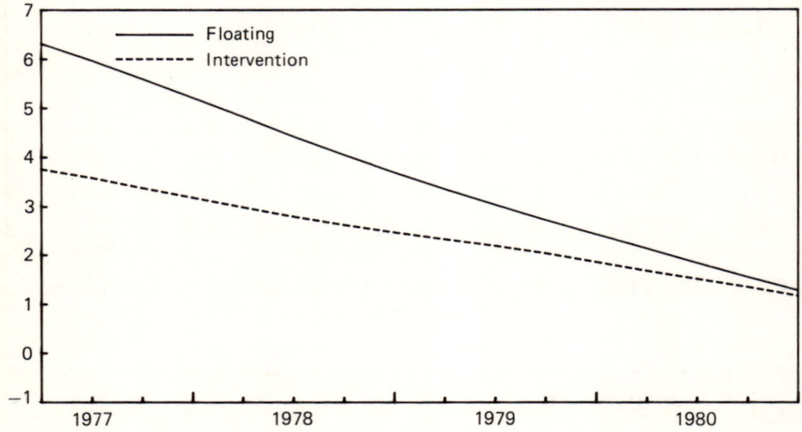

FIGURE 7.10 *Change in dollar/DM rate after 1 per cent increase in Eurodollar rate (annual percentage changes)*

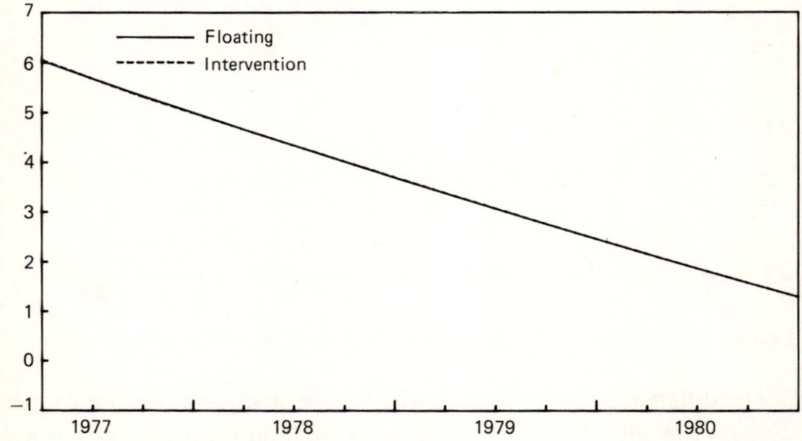

FIGURE 7.11 *Change in dollar/FF rate after 1 per cent increase in Eurodollar interest rate (annual percentage changes)*

alternatively under pure floating and under a regime of sterilised intervention. The simulations were run by imposing the same terminal condition on the two exchange rate regimes. This is an important assumption because it implies that economic agents consider the *long-run* effectiveness of the intervention policy to be zero, that is, the exchange rate converges to the same value under pure floating and under sterilised interventions. We return to this issue when we ask the question of how non-sterilised intervention could affect the terminal condition.

From the results of Figures 7.10 and 7.11 one can draw the following conclusions. In Germany sterilised intervention appears to have a significant impact on the exchange rate. It reduces overshooting substantially. To achieve this the authorities have to sell DM 1.9bn worth of dollars in the first period. In later periods the authorities buy dollars back so that at the end of the simulation period the total loss of international reserves amounts to 0.6bn DM. In France sterilised intervention has no perceptible influence on the dollar/FF rate.

Let us take up the issue of how domestic interest rates and monetary aggregates are affected by interventions. As an example, we show the time path of the loan interest rate and M_2 in Germany, following the 1 per cent increase in the Eurodollar rate (see Figures 7.12 and 7.13). The assumptions are the same as those underlying Figure 7.10, namely, the authorities use sterilised interventions. The most striking result is that, despite

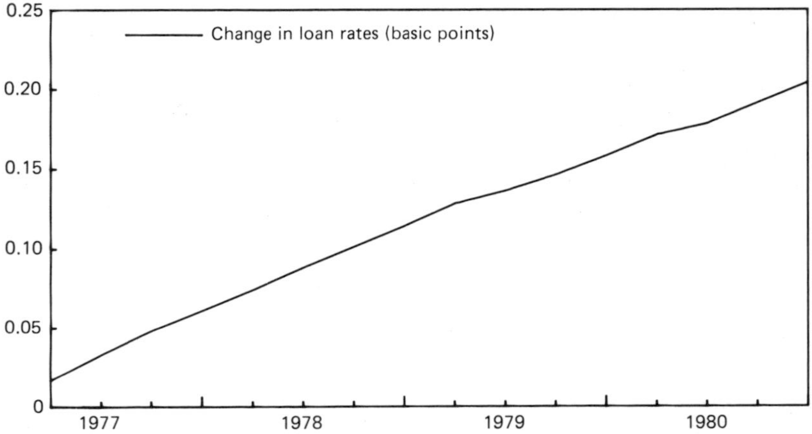

FIGURE 7.12 *Change in loan rate after* 1 *per cent increase in Eurodollar interest rate (Germany)*

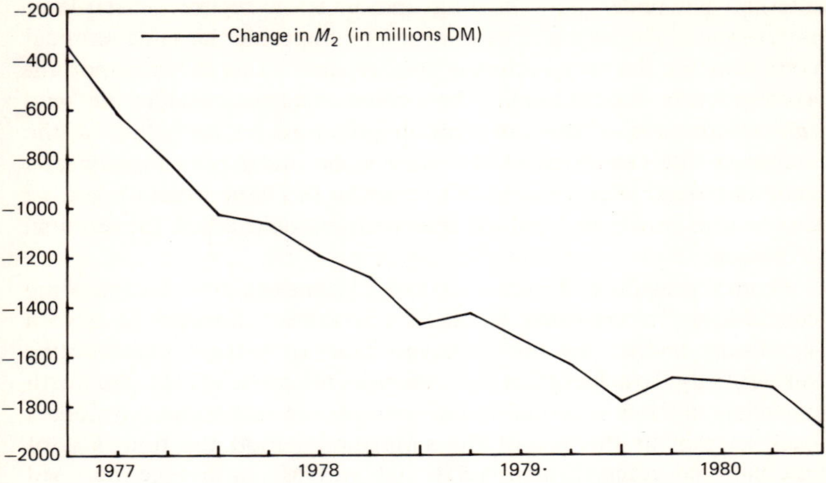

FIGURE 7.13 *Change in M_2 after* 1 *per cent increase in Eurodollar interest rate, (in millions of DM)*

full sterilisation, the German loan rate tends to increase and the money stock M_2 tends to decline. Recall that under pure floating the loan interest rate and the money stock were not affected by the increase in the Eurodollar interest rate.

These results can best be understood by going back to the time path of the exchange rates shown in Figure 7.10. By reducing the initial jump, the intervention policies alter the future path of the exchange rate. In particular, the rate of appreciation of the DM following the initial depreciation is reduced compared with the one obtained under pure floating. As a result, the *expected* rate of appreciation after the initial jump is smaller in the intervention regime than under floating. It also follows that the forward discount on the dollar is smaller in the former case; and the *covered* dollar interest rate is higher. But the covered dollar rate, through portfolio decisions, raises domestic interest rates, reduces bank credit and the money stock M_2.

In sum, although a sterilised intervention insulates the domestic money base from outside shocks, it does not insulate the money and credit markets. To insulate the domestic money and credit markets fully from changes in the dollar interest rate the monetary authorities would have to take corrective action by changing either the discount rate or the reserve requirement ratio.

On the Difference Between Sterilised and Non-sterilised Intervention

The question asked in this section concerns the difference between sterilised and non-sterilised intervention. We recall that a sterilised intervention does not affect the domestic money base, whereas non-sterilised intervention does. In the simulations reported here, sales (purchases) of foreign exchange by the Central Bank reduce (increase) currency in circulation, and therefore reduce (increase) the money base.

To begin with, we compare the time path of the exchange rate after a (temporary) increase in the dollar interest rate under both sterilised and non-sterilised intervention. We assume first that the terminal condition is the same in the two regimes. The results are shown in Figure 7.14. (We restrict ourselves to Germany). We find that the time path of the exchange rate is almost identical in both intervention regimes. There are two reasons for this result. First, by keeping the terminal condition unchanged we make the two types of intervention have the same long-run outcome. Second, the monetary authorities keep the discount rate, the reserve requirement and the other instruments of control unchanged. This tends to maintain the same structure of interest rates in the model.

Monetary authorities can do non-sterilised intervention by taking active policy measures. One such measure is an increase in the discount rate that will have a different impact on domestic monetary aggregates

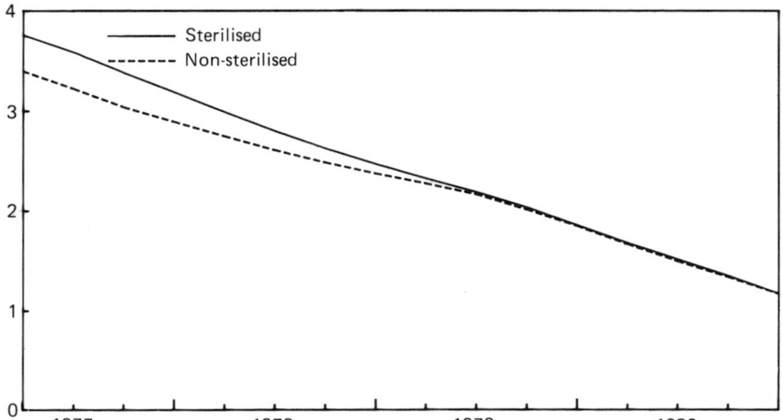

FIGURE 7.14 *Change in dollar/DM rate after* 1 *per cent increase in Eurodollar interest rate* (*sterilised and non-sterilised intervention*) (*annual percentage changes*)

and on the terminal value of the exchange rate. Therefore, one can no longer retain the assumption of equivalent terminal condition under different intervention regimes.

As an illustration, we simulated the two intervention regimes assuming that the terminal value of the exchange rate (the price of the dollar) is higher in the sterilised intervention regime than in the active non-sterilised intervention regime. The results are shown in Figure 7.15. The active non-sterilised intervention regime now appears to be more effective in limiting the effects of the increase in the dollar interest rate than the sterilised intervention regime. In addition, the amount of intervention involved in the former regime is relatively small. At the end of the simulation period the monetary authorities have restored their initial stock of international reserves, compared with a net loss of DM 0.6 bn in the sterilised intervention regime.

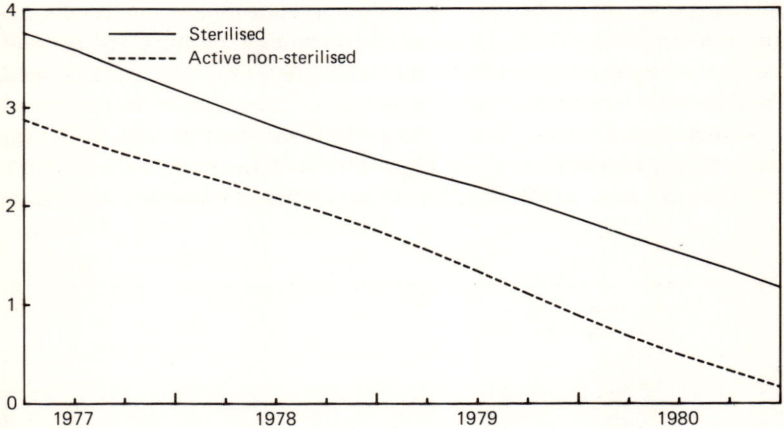

FIGURE 7.15 *Change in Dollar/DM rate after* 1 *per cent increase in Eurodollar interest rate* (*active non-sterilised intervention*) (*annual percentage changes*)

IV CONCLUSION

In this chapter we analysed issues concerning intervention policies in the foreign exchange market and monetary control. The framework of analysis was an econometric money and banking model of France and Germany which was subsequently simulated under different intervention regimes. The underlying assumption throughout all these simulations was perfect foresight. The main results can be summarised as follows.

First, when domestic price shocks occur the overshooting of the exchange rate sets in motion an automatic monetary accommodation. This leads to an increase in the monetary aggregates and a potential further increase in the price level. The monetary authorities can avoid monetary accommodation, inherent in the financial system of the two countries under consideration, by controlling domestic monetary aggregates. It appears thus that a system of flexible exchange rates increases the need to exert some control on domestic monetary aggregates. In this context we analysed the question whether sterilised intervention of the 'leaning against the wind' type could significantly alter the process of automatic monetary accommodation. We concluded that it could not, essentially because such an intervention policy has a relatively low effectiveness in controlling the exchange rate.

A second result is that sterilised intervention appears to alter the time path of the dollar exchange rate in the case of Germany. We did not find similar evidence for France. However, we also found that the German monetary authorities need to intervene quite heavily to obtain this result.

A third result is that non-sterilised intervention achieves a stronger impact on the exchange rate than sterilised intervention only if the monetary authorities take active policy measures, such as changing the discount rate. In addition, active non-sterilised intervention increases in effectiveness relative to sterilised intervention to the extent that it changes expectations. If it does not, the difference between sterilised and non-sterilised intervention is small.

A final result is that sterilised intervention policies insulate the domestic money base from outside shocks, but do not insulate the rest of the domestic money and credit markets. In particular, an increase in the foreign interest rate puts upward pressure on the domestic interest rates and a downward pressure on the money stock even under a regime of sterilised intervention.

NOTES

1. Fair and Taylor (1983) suggest iterating on different dates for the terminal condition until convergence. However, this procedure seems to be cumbersome and expensive.
2. For a survey see Mussa (1981) and Argy (1982).
3. The parameter ε was set at 0.5. Other values were experimented with. Although these change the intensity of the intervention activities, and thus the quantitative effects on the exchange rate, the results reported here are not changed in their essence.

4. Simulations with an alternative exchange rate equation for the exchange rate for France, where the net foreign assets for banks variable is included, with a negative but low value, yielded results not qualitatively different from those reported here.

8 Monetary Interdependence Within the European Monetary System

I INTRODUCTION

The large fluctuations of the dollar in the European exchange markets led to the creation of the European Monetary System (EMS) in 1979. The major objective of this system was to reduce the exchange rate volatility within Europe, without, however, returning to immutably fixed exchange rates.

The question raised in this chapter is 'how successful has the EMS been in fostering more exchange rate stability in Europe?' Since the institutional features of the EMS are not widely known, we start out by presenting the main characteristics of the system. Subsequently, we deal with the issue of whether or not the EMS has achieved the stated objective. Finally, we employ the econometric models of the EC-countries to ascertain how the new exchange rate arrangements have affected monetary relations within the EMS, in particular the role of official interventions in the exchange markets.

II MAIN FEATURES OF THE EMS[1]

The EMS is basically an agreement to maintain exchange rates of the participating currencies within a band of permissible fluctuations. However, the agreement does not rule out changes in the parities (central rates) around which these bands are defined. Central rates are defined in terms of an artificial currency, the European Currency Unit (ECU), and take the form of a matrix of bilateral rates. The band of permissible fluctuations is 2.25 per cent of the bilateral central rates (an exception is made for the Lira which can fluctuate within a band of 6 per cent).

When a currency reaches its limits against another EMS currency, the participating central banks have to intervene to keep the currencies within the band. Central rates can be adjusted, provided this is done after due consultation. In principle, intervention is to be made with EMS currencies; in practice, EMS central banks have used dollars on a large scale.[2]

A novel feature of the EMS is the artificial currency (ECU), defined as a basket of the participating EMS currencies.[3] In principle, the ECU is the regional (European) counterpart of the SDR. The ECU is used as an accounting measure to settle transactions among EMS central banks. An initial stock of ECUs was created when central banks agreed to deposit 20 per cent of their gold and dollar holdings with the European Monetary Co-operation Fund (in exchange for ECUs). With the valuation of gold linked to the gold price, the amount of ECUs in the books of the EMS central banks has fluctuated in relation to the market price of gold.

The ECU functions also as an 'indicator of divergence'. To the extent that the change in the ECU value of a currency represents an average change against other EMS currencies it can be used as a signal to indicate whether a currency's value is diverging from that of other participating currencies. The EMS agreement prescribes that when a currency's value deviates from its ECU central rate by more than 75 per cent of the allowed maximum spread, the authorities concerned are presumed to correct the situation. This feature was intended to provide more symmetry in the adjustment process than existed in the previous 'snake arrangement'. There is evidence that the ECU as an indicator of divergence has not achieved this objective.[4]

Finally, official interventions in the exchange markets are facilitated by a system of short-term credit lines, allowing central banks to borrow other countries' currencies in unlimited amounts. Other programs of financial assistance are in place but have not been used.

III THE EMS AND EXCHANGE RATE STABILITY

The theme of this section is whether or not the EMS has reduced exchange rate fluctuations in Europe. Measuring the impact of the EMS on exchange rate variability is a complicated matter. There are two reasons for this. First, it is difficult to disentangle the effect of a major change, like the launching of the EMS, on exchange rate variability from other major shocks which have occurred simultaneously. This problem is especially relevant because at the time the EMS was constituted the second oil-price shock occurred. The latter can be presumed to have affected exchange rates in a substantial way. A second problem relates to the way exchange rate changes are measured. It matters a great deal for the outcome whether one takes nominal or real exchange rate changes, bilateral or effective exchange rates. Despite these difficulties, the existing evidence allows us to draw some conclusions, albeit tentative.

A superficial perusal of the evidence makes the EMS appear a success. *Short-term* (daily, monthly) fluctuations of EMS currencies against each other have been substantially lower than short-term fluctuations of the EMS currencies against the dollar or against other non-EMS currencies.[5] This pattern has been less clear since 1981. Up to the middle of 1981 the average monthly changes of EMS currencies against each other amounted to approximately 0.5 per cent (except for the Lira). From the middle of 1981 to 1983 the monthly changes of the EMS currencies against each other have averaged more than 1 per cent. This is still far below the 3 per cent monthly variations of the dollar exchange rates. In sum, it is fair to say that the EMS has succeeded in reducing the risk concerning short-term changes in EMS bilateral exchange rates.

This conclusion, however, is only part of the story. What matters in most decisions about investment, output, export, and import is the exchange rate outlook beyond the very short horizon, as well as the behaviour of *real* exchange rate changes. Real exchange rates measure the exchange value of the currency adjusted for movements in the domestic and foreign price level. Changes in the real exchange rates measure whether currencies become cheaper or dearer in terms of goods and services, and thus are informative about the competitiveness of countries.

Evidence on changes in real exchange rates of the EMS currencies is provided in Table 8.1, which compares the yearly changes of the real exchange rates before and after 1979 for both EMS and non-EMS countries. The following observations can be made. First, there does not seem to be evidence that real exchange rates within the EMS have changed less (on a yearly basis) since 1979. On the contrary, the period immediately before the inauguration of the EMS seems to have experienced smaller real exchange rate changes. This is confirmed by Table 8.2, which reports the mean absolute change of real exchange rates during the four years before and after the establishment of EMS. On average real exchange rates were more variable (on a yearly basis) in the post-EMS than in the pre-EMS period. This phenomenon could be explained by the fact that the post-EMS period was characterised by large worldwide disturbances, such as the 1979–80 oil shock. Some support for this view comes from a comparison with the period 1973–4,

TABLE 8.1 *Real effective exchange rate changes (yearly) in per cent*

Country	*Pre-EMS*						*Post-EMS*			
	1973	*1974*	*1975*	*1976*	*1977*	*1978*	*1979*	*1980*	*1981*	*1982*
EMS–Countries										
Germany	7.2	1.2	−5.0	0.3	1.0	0.3	1.3	−3.3	−6.0	1.7
France	2.5	−6.6	10.0	−2.5	−3.5	0.5	0.7	1.1	−1.9	−2.5
Belgium	0.7	4.1	−4.9	−0.3	2.1	−0.7	−3.1	−6.1	−6.7	−8.1
Netherlands	1.6	−3.4	1.8	2.7	3.2	−1.2	−4.7	−2.2	−2.3	4.7
Denmark	1.4	−3.9	1.2	0.7	2.0	4.4	−2.1	−7.2	−4.2	−2.4
Italy	−2.8	4.2	−6.1	−4.5	−1.5	−2.5	2.6	2.7	−4.5	−1.1
Non–EMS–Countries										
United States	−12.8	−2.8	3.8	2.5	−0.7	−6.1	−0.1	1.6	12.4	9.1
United Kingdom	−12.6	2.0	4.8	−7.4	4.8	4.1	12.3	16.5	3.2	−3.2
Japan	17.4	1.7	−11.6	0.8	5.6	14.5	−11.0	−2.4	1.4	−11.8
Switzerland	10.1	0.3	8.4	4.0	−4.7	16.1	−6.2	−9.2	−0.4	3.9
Sweden	1.3	4.1	0.4	2.5	−3.3	−7.7	2.3	1.2	1.0	−5.2

SOURCE Morgan Guaranty, *World Financial Markets*, August 1983, p. 10.

TABLE 8.2 *Mean absolute yearly change of real exchange rates*

Country	*Pre-EMS* (*1975–78*)	*Post-EMS* (*1979–82*)
EMS-Countries		
Germany	1.7	3.1
France	4.1	1.9
Belgium	2.0	6.0
Netherlands	2.2	3.5
Denmark	2.1	4.0
Italy	3.7	2.7
Average EMS	2.6	3.5
Non-EMS-Countries		
United States	3.3	5.8
United Kingdom	5.3	8.8
Japan	8.1	6.7
Switzerland	8.3	4.9
Sweden	3.5	2.4
Average non-EMS	5.7	5.7

SOURCE Computed from previous table.

when the real exchange rates of the EMS countries ('*avant la lettre*') were about as variable as during the post-EMS period.

A second observation one can make from Tables 8.1 and 8.2 is that the real exchange rates of major non-EMS countries have tended to be substantially more variable not only since 1979 but during the longer period 1973–82. For the United States and the United Kingdom we observe an increase in real exchange rate variability since 1979, similar to the one observed for most EMS countries. For Japan, Switzerland and Sweden we observe a reverse movement since 1979.

These observations suggest the following interpretation. The EMS countries are very open economies and highly integrated with one another. As a result, transaction costs (transport costs and impediments to trade) are low, limiting the divergent movements of nominal exchange rates and price levels. This, in turn leads to smaller movements in real exchange rates, compared with countries that are less integrated.[6] Indeed, real exchange rate changes were less pronounced in EMS countries, than in major non-EMS countries, before and after 1979. This interpretation, however, also suggests that the EMS has been powerless in reducing real exchange rate variability among participating countries. The fact that real exchange rates vary less within the EMS than outside reflects differences in openness and economic integration. This was observed throughout the period 1973–82 and cannot be used as evidence that the EMS succeeded in stabilising real exchange rate movements. If anything, these have become larger since 1979. We conclude that the EMS, although successful in stabilising nominal exchange rates in the very short run (daily, weekly or monthly), has not succeeded in reducing the movements of real exchange rates. As a result, the real value of EMS currencies against each other is as uncertain since 1979 as it was before.

Why have EMS countries been unable to reduce real exchange rate movements? Inflation rates among EMS countries have continued to be widely different (cf. Table 8.3). In fact, it can be seen that inflation rates have been more unequal after 1979 than before. As a result, national price levels have diverged continuously. This has led, as it was true in the Bretton Woods system, to *ex-post* corrections in central rates. Real exchange rate variability in the EMS emerges because nominal exchange rates have not adjusted quickly enough to the underlying trends of national price levels.[7]

It is now well recognised that the ultimate cause of high inflation differentials results from the failure to co-ordinate national monetary policies. This failure is evident from Table 8.4, showing the yearly

TABLE 8.3 *Inflation rates (CPI) in EMS countries*

Country	1974	1975	1976	1977	1978	*Average*[1] 1974—8	1979	1980	1981	1982	*Average*[1] 1979—82
Germany	6.9	6.0	4.3	3.7	2.7	4.7	4.1	5.5	5.9	5.4	5.2
France	13.7	11.8	9.6	9.4	9.1	10.7	10.8	13.3	13.3	11.8	12.3
Belgium	12.7	12.7	9.2	7.1	4.5	9.2	4.5	6.6	7.6	9.0	6.9
Netherlands	9.6	10.5	8.8	6.4	4.1	7.9	4.2	6.5	6.8	6.3	5.9
Denmark	15.2	9.6	9.0	11.1	10.0	11.0	9.6	12.3	11.7	10.0	10.9
Italy	19.1	17.0	16.8	17.0	12.1	16.4	14.7	21.2	17.8	16.6	17.6
Average						10.0					9.8
Standard deviation						3.9					4.8

NOTE [1] compound average growth rate
SOURCE Ungerer *et al.* (1983); and International Monetary Fund, *International Financial Statistics.*

TABLE 8.4 *Growth rates of money stock (M_1) in EMS countries*

Country	*1974*	*1975*	*1976*	*1977*	*1978*	*Average[1] 1974–8*	*1979*	*1980*	*1981*	*1982*	*Average[1] 1979–82*
Germany	10.7	14.3	3.3	12.0	14.5	10.9	2.9	3.9	–1.6	3.2	2.1
France	15.2	12.6	7.5	11.1	11.1	11.5	11.8	6.4	15.9	14.8	12.3
Belgium	6.2	15.7	7.0	8.3	5.9	8.6	2.5	0.2	2.2	3.3	2.0
Netherlands	12.2	19.7	8.2	13.2	4.2	11.5	2.8	6.0	–2.4	5.0	2.7
Denmark	4.7	30.2	6.3	8.0	16.1	12.7	9.9	10.9	11.8	11.4	11.0
Italy	9.4	13.5	18.9	21.4	26.6	18.0	23.7	12.9	9.8	18.0[2]	16.0
Average						12.2					7.7
Standard deviation						3.2					6.2

Notes [1] compound average growth rates
[2] last eleven months only

SOURCE Ungerer *et al.* (1983); and International Monetary Fund, *International Financial Statistics*.

growth rates of the money stocks (M_1) in the EMS countries, before and after 1979. It can be seen that, although the growth rates of the money stock have tended to decline in most countries since 1979, differences in the growth rates across countries have increased.[8] In fact, from 1979 to 1982 there was *de facto* less monetary co-ordination among EMS countries. More ominously the two principal countries of the EMS, France and Germany, have adopted more divergent monetary policies since they joined the EMS. Before 1979 the yearly growth rate of the French money stock was slightly higher than Germany's. During 1979–82 France increased its money stock by 58 per cent against 9 per cent in Germany. It should come as no surprise that, since the inception of the EMS, exchange risk among EMS countries has in fact increased. The major contributing factor to this state of affair is the wider divergence in national monetary policies and inflation rates within the EMS.

In the next sections we raise two different issues, concerning the EMS. First, how do existing EMS arrangements help member countries in raising the effectiveness of their intervention policies in the dollar exchange market? Second, what are the monetary effects of changes in expectations concerning the intra-EMS exchange rates?

IV INTERVENTION POLICIES IN A MULTI-COUNTRY SETTING

In the previous chapter we analysed the effectiveness of foreign exchange market interventions in a single country framework. Here we address the same issue in a model where countries interact with one another. The institutional set up to do this is the EMS.

Individual country models can be linked together in the following way. First, we impose Interest Rate Parity conditions with respect to the Eurodollar interest rate in each country model. The empirical validity of this condition is the subject of Chapter 4. The covered dollar interest rate is defined (see equation 4.1a) as:

$$\log(1+i_k) = \log(1+i^*) + f_k - e_k \tag{8.1}$$

$$\log(1+i_j) = \log(1+i^*) + f_j - e_j \tag{8.2}$$

where subscripts k and j refer, respectively, to country k and j belonging to the EMS; f_k and f_j are the log of the forward dollar rates of currency k and j; e_k and e_j are the log of the spot dollar exchange rates of currency k and j; i^* is the Eurodollar interest rate.

Triangular arbitrage ensures that:

$$e_k = \bar{e}_{kj} + e_j \tag{8.3}$$

and

$$f_k = f_{kj} + f_j \tag{8.4}$$

where $\bar{e}_{kj}$ is the log of the par value rate of currency k in terms of currency j. Within the EMS arrangement this is a fixed value, which is indicated by the bar.[9] And f_{kj} is the log of the forward price of currency k in terms of currency j.

In this section we assume that no changes in the intra EMS exchange rates are expected. This allows us to write:

$$f_{kj} = \bar{e}_{kj} \tag{8.5}$$

Substituting (8.5) into (8.4), and (8.3) and (8.4) into (8.1) yields:

$$\log(1 + i_k) = \log(1 + i_j) \tag{8.6}$$

Equation (8.6) together with (8.2) imply that the forward premium (or discount) on the dollar must be the same for all EMS currencies. Only when expectations of realignment within the EMS exist, can the forward premium on the dollar differ among currencies.

The second link between the different country models has to do with the intra-EMS flows of international reserves resulting from interventions to keep the intra-EMS rates fixed. Thus, for example, when France sells DM and buys FF to keep the DM/FF rate within the band of permissible fluctuations, the international reserve position of Germany increases and that of France declines. This then affects the money base in both countries, except if these reserve movements are fully sterilised. More specifically, in Germany the monetary base rises, in France it declines.

To evaluate the effectiveness of foreign exchange market intervention in this multi-country set-up the model was simulated assuming an unexpected increase in the Eurodollar interest rate. In addition, we assumed an asymmetrical intervention arrangement within the EMS. It is well known that the EMS has evolved *de facto* into a system where the German monetary authorities do most of the intervention in the dollar/DM market, whereas the other EMS countries intervene in their DM exchange market to keep their DM exchange rates within the permissible band of fluctuation. In the simulations reported here we assume such an asymmetrical intervention arrangement.[10]

The simulations are restricted to a three-country group consisting of

Germany, France and Belgium, since we have not yet been able to link all EMS countries. The time paths of the dollar exchange rates following the 1 per cent increase in the Eurodollar interest rate are shown in Figures 8.1 and 8.2: the dollar exchange rate as it evolves within the EMS arrangement is compared with the dollar exchange rate from the individual (unlinked) country simulation.

The most striking aspect of this comparison is that Germany now loses part of its ability to control the dollar/DM exchange rate. This can be seen from Figure 8.1. The increase in the dollar interest rate leads to an immediate depreciation of the DM of 4.3 per cent compared with a depreciation of only 3.4 per cent when Germany is not linked with the other EMS currencies. In France, the depreciation of the FF within the EMS is slightly lower relative to a situation of France intervening alone.

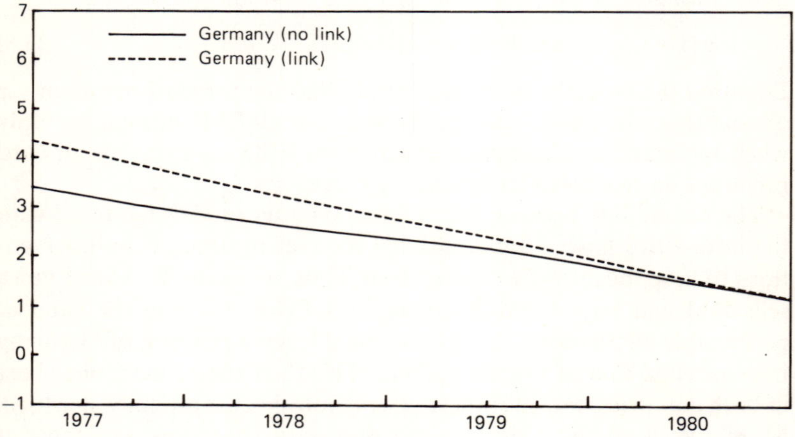

FIGURE 8.1 *Change in dollar/DM rate after* 1 *per cent increase in Eurodollar interest rate* (*annual percentage changes*)

This result can be explained as follows. The sales of DM by France and Belgium tend to increase the German monetary aggregates, reducing, in turn, the loan and deposit rates and bringing upward pressure on the dollar/DM rate. The opposite occurs in France and Belgium. However, our results indicate that this has only a marginal effect on the dollar exchange rate of the currencies of these countries.

The size of these effects is illustrated in Figure 8.3 showing absolute changes of the German loan rate. It can be seen that the loan rate in

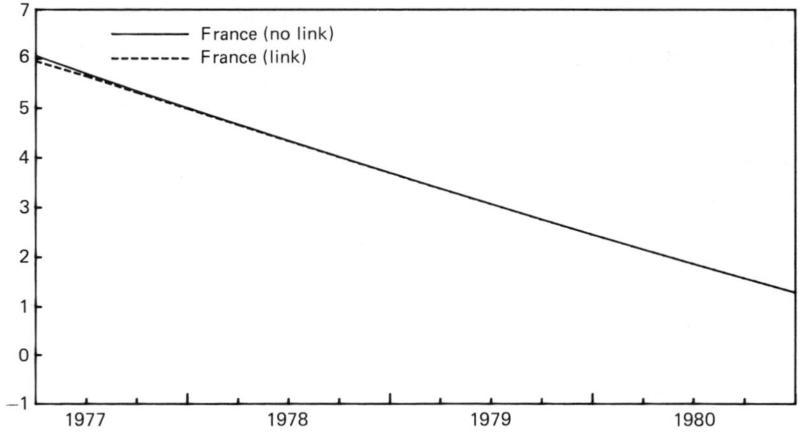

FIGURE 8.2 *Change in dollar/FF rate after 1 per cent increase in Eurodollar interest rate (annual percentage changes)*

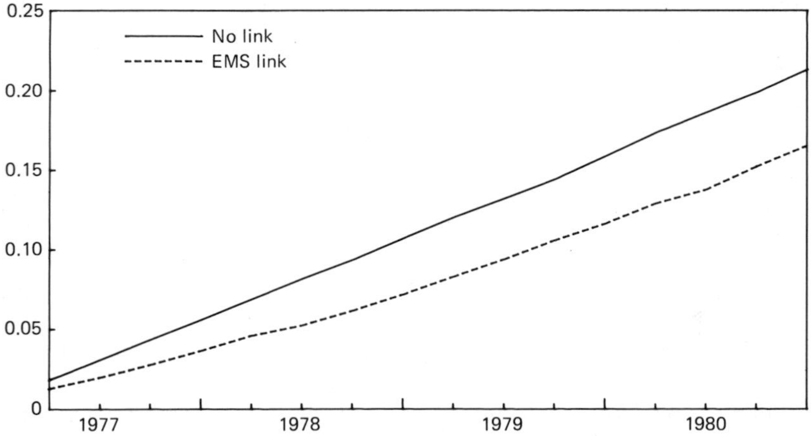

FIGURE 8.3 *Change in loan rate (Germany) after 1 per cent increase in Eurodollar interest rate (absolute changes)*

Germany increases less under the EMS arrangement than in its absence. This follows from the fact that the intervention in the DM market by other EMS countries tends to make the German money market more liquid.

The previous results indicate that existing arrangements make it more difficult for Germany, the leading EMS country, to influence the dollar/DM rate.

V EXPECTATIONS AND MONETARY CONTROL WITHIN THE EMS

In the previous section we discussed how an external shock affects monetary conditions in the EMS countries. The underlying assumption was one of unchanged expectations about the intra-EMS exchange rates. When one drops this assumption the outcome changes substantially. Assume again a 1 per cent increase in the dollar interest rate, and furthermore let this external shock trigger an expected depreciation of one EMS currency *vis-à-vis* the others. We choose Belgium, a small country, and assume that the external shock leads to a 3 per cent expected depreciation of the BF at the terminal date.

What effects do these disturbances have on the different financial variables? To begin with, in our perfect foresight world can this expectational change be absorbed by the EMS without actually changing EMS parity rates? Yes it can, but at substantial costs in terms of internal monetary disturbances. This point is illustrated in Table 8.5, which shows the changes in international reserves of Belgium and Germany in the final period of the simulation, as well as the change in their money base and money stock M_2. There it can be seen that a situation of extreme monetary deflation occurs in Belgium. The size of the intervention by the Belgian monetary authorities is such as virtually to deplete this country's foreign exchange reserves. In addition, the reduction of the money stock is so large that interest rates in Belgium rise by several hundred basis points in the final period. Thus, although technically possible, the maintenance of fixed EMS parities becomes extremely unlikely. There are significant repercussions also for Germany. Despite

TABLE 8.5 *Change in stock of international reserve, the money base and the money stock (M_2); in billions of national currencies*

	Belgium	Germany
International reserves	−263	+16
Money base	−604	+22
Money stock (M_2)	−1388	+25

the fact that Belgium is small, the expectational changes significantly affect monetary conditions in Germany: the German money stock increases by DM 25 bn.

These monetary disturbances within the EMS are not without implications for the dollar exchange rate. This is illustrated in Figure 8.4 depicting the time path of the dollar/DM rate during the simulation period. We compare it with the dollar/DM rate after the same external shock but with stable expectations about the EMS parities. It can be seen that when a realignment is expected, the same 1 per cent increase in the dollar interest rate leads to a stronger depreciation of the DM relative to the dollar. This result follows from the fact that with expectations of a realignment the German monetary authorities are forced to expand their domestic monetary aggregates in a significant way.

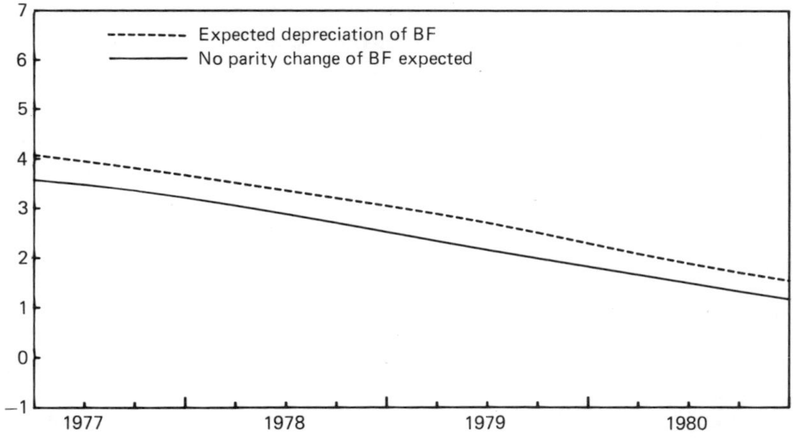

FIGURE 8.4 *Change in dollar/DM rate after* 1 *per cent increase in Eurodollar interest rate* (*Link Belgium–Germany*) (*annual percentage changes*)

VI CONCLUSION

In this chapter we analysed whether the EMS achieved its major objective, namely promoting a greater exchange rate stability. We found that, despite successes in reducing short-term (weekly, monthly) exchange fluctuations, the EMS has failed to reduce the movements of the exchange rates around their purchasing power parities over periods longer than weeks or months. In fact, real exchange rate movements within the EMS were higher after 1979 than during the period immediately preceding it. Although this increase in the real exchange rate variability could have been caused by large supply shocks occurring after 1979, we also found that the degree of monetary co-operation within the EMS declined after 1979. This was, and is most likely to remain, a major source of exchange rate uncertainty within the system. It continues to call into question the long-run survival of the system.

When the EMS was instituted it was hoped that a joint effort in dealing with the dollar problem would have made it easier to alter the dollar exchange rate. Furthermore, it was expected that the EMS countries would be able to insulate themselves more easily from outside disturbances. The results of this chapter allow us to shed some light on these issues. We found that when outside monetary disturbances generate expectations of intra-EMS realignments the monetary disturbances become extreme, making these realignments all but inevitable. In addition, the major EMS country, Germany, finds its ability to influence the dollar/DM rate curtailed substantially as a result of the EMS arrangements. This curtailment is not compensated by other EMS countries gaining significant control over their dollar exchange rates.

NOTES

1. For a more detailed discussion, see IMF Survey (1979) and EC-Commission (1979).
2. The reasons that have led to this situation are explained in De Grauwe and Peeters (1979).
3. Although not an EMS-currency, the pound sterling has been given a special status in the ECU. See EC-Commission (1979).
4. See Masera (1981) and De Grauwe and Van den Bergh (1982).
5. For substantial evidence on this issue see Abraham and Peeters (1981). See also Ungerer, Evans and Nyberg (1983).
6. For a recent formalisation of this idea, see Aizenman (1983).
7. See Fratianni (1980b).
8. We will come back to this issue in Chapter 9.
9. Note that in this analysis we disregard problems resulting from movements of the spot exchange rate within the band.
10. Denote Germany with the subscript k and the second country with j; under this intervention set up equations (7.1) for the two countries are:

$$\Delta BF_j = -\varepsilon \Delta es_j$$

$$\Delta BF_k = -\varepsilon \Delta es_k - \frac{\Delta BF_j}{\bar{e}_{kj}}.$$

9 Monetary Policy in an Interdependent World

I INTRODUCTION

The unifying theme of this chapter is economic interdependence among the industrialised countries and its implications for monetary policies. In Sections I to III we analyse changes in the nature of economic interdependence from the 1960s to the 1970s and offer some explanations for these changes. In doing so, we draw upon the framework of analysis developed in the previous chapters of the book. In Sections IV and V we study the transmission abroad of policy shocks originating in the United States in recent history.

II INTERDEPENDENCE DURING THE 1970s: SOME EMPIRICAL OBSERVATIONS

A critical observation about the nature of economic interdependence since the early 1970s is that business cycles were more correlated across countries during the 1970s than during the 1960s. This came as a surprise to most economists because with the advent of floating exchange rates it was expected that individual countries would be able to shield their economies from foreign monetary shocks. To the extent that business cycles also have a monetary origin, it was generally felt that during a floating exchange rate system business cycles would be less synchronised than during a fixed exchange rate regime where monetary shocks are easily transmitted across countries. Before offering explanations for this phenomenon of increased interdependence, it behoves us to consider in more detail the evidence.

Table 9.1 shows the correlation matrix of the yearly growth rates of real GDP during the 1960s and 1970s. During the 1960s there was very little correlation of GDP growth rates among countries. During the 1970s, however, the correlation coefficients increase dramatically.

TABLE 9.1 *Correlation matrix of yearly growth rates of real GDP (1962–81)*

	US	*Canada*	*Japan*	*France*	*Germany*	*Italy*	*UK*
1962–70							
US	1.00						
Canada	0.95	1.00					
Japan	−0.28	−0.24	1.00				
France	−0.04	0.14	0.10	1.00			
Germany	0.02	0.26	0.14	0.51	1.00		
Italy	−0.34	−0.37	0.20	−0.19	−0.53	1.00	
UK	0.10	0.04	0.56	−0.27	0.12	−0.42	1.00
1971–81							
US	1.00						
Canada	0.67	1.00					
Japan	0.80	0.52	1.00				
France	0.71	0.83	0.59	1.00			
Germany	0.79	0.64	0.72	0.84	1.00		
Italy	0.42	0.47	0.41	0.65	0.80	1.00	
UK	0.77	0.77	0.70	0.79	0.74	0.57	1.00

SOURCE: OECD, *Main Economic Indicators*.

Similar evidence is presented by Swoboda (1983), and Saidi and Huber (1983). Using principal components analysis the former finds that a large part of the variations in real GDP during the 1970s can be explained by an element common to all countries. The common element, moreover, turns out to be substantially more important during the 1970s than during the 1960s. Saidi and Huber (1983) relying on spectral analysis, find that during the 1970s there was substantial coherence between countries' industrial production index and a common (that is, OECD) index of industrial production, especially at frequencies of twenty to sixty months. Again, the coherence is much larger during the 1970s than during the 1960s.

Consider now the evidence about inflation rates: Table 9.2 shows the correlation matrix of yearly inflation rates during the 1960s and the 1970s. Although less pronounced, the facts point in the same direction. The correlation of inflation rates among countries increases from the 1960s to the 1970s in more than half the cases. It is worth noting that, although short-term variations of the price level tended to be more correlated across countries during the 1970s than during the 1960s, the long-term rates of inflation tended to diverge among countries more during the 1970s than during the 1960s. This fact emerges from Table 9.3, which shows that the average inflation rates increase

TABLE 9.2 *Correlation matrix of yearly rates of inflation*

	US	*Canada*	*Japan*	*France*	*Germany*	*Italy*	*UK*
1960–70							
US	1.00						
Canada	0.82	1.00					
Japan	0.19	−0.04	1.00				
France	0.58	0.23	0.48	1.00			
Germany	0.19	0.03	0.56	0.20	1.00		
Italy	−0.22	−0.32	0.49	0.26	0.39	1.00	
UK	0.69	0.46	0.36	0.47	0.72	0.07	1.00
1971–82							
US	1.00						
Canada	0.71	1.00					
Japan	0.26	0.18	1.00				
France	0.80	0.92	0.30	1.00			
Germany	0.15	0.22	0.58	0.24	1.00		
Italy	0.73	0.76	0.33	0.89	0.08	1.00	
UK	0.50	0.37	0.45	0.50	0.13	0.67	1.00

SOURCE: International Monetary Fund, *International Financial Statistics.*

TABLE 9.3 *Mean and standard deviation of yearly inflation rates, 1960–81*

Country	*1960–70*		*1971–81*	
	Mean	*Standard deviation*	*Mean*	*Standard deviation*
US	2.6	1.8	8.1	3.2
Canada	2.6	1.3	8.5	2.8
Japan	5.6	1.4	8.8	6.0
France	4.1	1.5	10.0	2.9
Germany	2.5	0.8	5.2	1.3
Italy	3.8	1.9	14.3	5.3
UK	3.7	1.6	13.6	5.1
Average (across countries)	3.6		9.8	
Standard deviation (across countries)		1.1		3.2

SOURCE: International Monetary Fund, *International Financial Statistics.*

substantially from the 1960s to the 1970s, but the inter-country dispersion of the long-term inflation rates was almost three times higher in the 1970s than in the 1960s.[1] In sum, the empirical evidence on inflation rates is subtle. On the one hand, it confirms our theoretical expectations that in a floating exchange rate system countries can achieve more easily a long-term rate of inflation that is independent from that of the rest of the world. On the other hand the evidence surprisingly reveals a high and positive cross-country correlation of short-term inflation rates, suggesting that individual countries found it difficult to shield their economies from temporary changes in the price level originating in the rest of the world.

III INTERDEPENDENCE DURING THE 1970s: THE COMMON SHOCK EXPLANATION

One explanation of the phenomenon discussed in the previous section is that countries were subjected to large world-wide shocks during the 1970s. The most pronounced of these shocks were the oil-price increases of 1973–4 and 1979–80. Our own empirical analysis of Chapter 3 confirms that these oil-price increases have been significant in adversely affecting the supply of industrial output in the European countries.

Table 9.4 presents the empirical evidence about the output effects of the 'oil shock' in a slightly different form. The table shows the average yearly loss of manufacturing output caused by the oil-price increases of the 1970s. These numbers were obtained by comparing the estimated supply of output assuming no oil-price change with the estimate of the supply of output reported in Table 3.5. The 'oil shock' has caused sizeable reductions in the supply of manufacturing output in four European countries.[2] On the average the loss amounts to 6 to 8 per cent of manufacturing output per year from 1973 to 1980.

TABLE 9.4 *Loss of manufacturing output from 1973 to 1980 (in per cent) caused by oil-price increase*

Country	*Average yearly loss*	*Cumulative loss*
Belgium	5.8	48.8
France	8.1	72.2
Germany	6.7	87.7
Netherlands	7.3	64.0

SOURCE computed from Table 3.5.

Similar evidence emerges in Bruno and Sachs (1979) and in Bruno (1982): in both studies the oil-price increases appear to have played a significant and quantitatively similar role in reducing industrial output in major industrialised countries. This evidence lends support to the hypothesis that the common oil shock has a great deal to do with the increased synchronisation of business cycles during the 1970s.

It is important to note that the flexibility of the exchange rates did not insulate countries from external real disturbances. This point, recognised by economists, was stressed in our theoretical discussion in Chapter 2. It should not be surprising, therefore, that, despite a great flexibility of the exchange rates, European countries were affected in similar ways by the oil shock.

There has been and continues to be a second shock common to most industrialised countries during the 1970s: the substantial increase in taxation of labour income in the form of social security contributions and personal income tax. This phenomenon, which has instigated a wage push with workers attempting to shift the tax on to employers and hence on to consumers, explains in part the reduction of output and employment. The evidence provided in Chapter 3 concerning this tax shock is mixed. For some countries we found a significant negative effect of tax variables on the supply of manufacturing output. For other countries no such effects could be detected. There is evidence, however, that by raising the burden of taxation at about the same time as the oil shocks, the industrialised countries aggravated the adverse output consequences of these shocks.

IV INTERDEPENDENCE DURING THE 1970s: A MONETARY EXPLANATION

A monetary explanation for the observed increased synchronisation of business cycles runs along the following lines: during the 1970s the dollar exchange rate of major currencies exhibited strong cyclical movements, extending over several years. At the same time most industrialised countries intervened heavily in the exchange market. This intervention, discussed in Chapter 7, usually took the form of 'leaning against the wind'. Most countries, however, found it difficult fully to sterilise the monetary effects of their intervention activities. As a result, domestic money stocks of intervening countries tended to fluctuate in the same direction. Thus, although the fixed exchange rate system had been abandoned during the 1970s, major countries continued to intervene so heavily that the system was behaving approximately *à la* Bretton Woods.[3] Put differently, as a result of interventions in the foreign exchange markets the monetary transmission process in the 1970s was similar to that prevailing in the 1960s.

To test this hypothesis we regressed the growth rate of the narrowly defined money stock for each of the four large European countries and Japan against the growth rate of the US money stock. In addition, we regressed the weighted sum of the growth rates of the money stock of these five major industrialised countries against the growth rate of the US money stock.

The equations were specified as follows:

$$\hat{M}_i = \alpha_i + \alpha_i' D_{70} + \beta_i \hat{M}_{US} + \gamma_i \hat{M}_{US}^{70} + \varepsilon \qquad (9.1)$$

where $\hat{M}_i$ denotes the annual growth rate of country *i*'s money stock; α_i, α_i', β_i and γ_i are coefficients to be estimated; $\hat{M}_{US}$ is the growth rate of the US money stock; D_{70} is a vector consisting of zero's for the observations pertaining to 1960–71 and one's for the period 1972–82. Similarly $\hat{M}_{US}^{70}$ is a vector consisting of zero's for the period 1960–71 and the observations of the growth rate of the US money stock during 1972–82. If γ_i is significantly different from zero we reject the hypothesis that the US money stock had the same effect on country *i*'s money stock during the 1970s as compared to the 1960s.

The results of these regressions during the sample period 1960–82 are shown in Table 9.5. It can be seen that γ_i is not significantly different

TABLE 9.5 *Regression results of equation* (9.1), (1960–82)

	α_i	α_i'	β_i	γ_i	$\hat{\rho}$	*SER*	*DW*
UK	0.007	0.017	0.430	−0.047	−0.16	0.025	1.88
	(2.05)	(3.54)	(5.12)	(0.41)	(1.62)	(0.024)	
France	0.020	−0.004	0.379	0.371	0.006	0.025	2.00
	(5.35)	(0.74)	(5.22)	(3.71)	(0.06)	(0.026)	
Germany	0.012	−0.005	0.763	−0.039	−0.069	0.021	2.08
	(4.00)	(1.20)	(11.60)	(0.43)	(0.66)	(0.021)	
Italy	0.028	−0.001	0.827	0.076	−0.10	0.024	1.92
	(8.51)	(0.30)	(10.88)	(0.73)	(0.97)	(0.043)	
Japan	0.030	−0.019	1.228	−0.371	0.088	0.033	1.95
	(5.55)	(2.45)	(12.99)	(2.84)	(0.84)	(0.032)	
Total	0.019	−0.004	0.719	−0.037	−0.022	0.014	1.98
	(9.20)	(1.31)	(16.93)	(0.65)	(0.21)	(0.027)	

SOURCE all the data are from the International Monetary Fund, *International Financial Statistics.*

NOTE The equations were estimated using OLS with a Cochrane–Orcutt procedure.

from zero for the UK, Germany, Italy and for the total group of countries. This means that the US influence on the money stock of these countries has not changed during the 1970s. This is not the case for France, however, where it has increased (γ_i is positive and significantly different from zero). For Japan the US influence declined from the 1960s to the 1970s ($\gamma_i < 0$ and statistically significant).

A possible objection to the above procedure is that the United States is given an unduly large weight at the expense of all other countries. Within the EEC – where the economies are highly integrated and monetary authorities have followed exchange-rate arrangements of one form or another – one would expect the German money supply to be as important as the US money supply in explaining the behaviour of, say, the French money supply.

With this view in mind, we proceeded by regressing each country's money stock growth rate against a weighted average of the six countries' money stock growth rates. We compared the 1960s with the 1970s using a similar method as in the previous estimations.

The equations were specified as follows:

$$\hat{M}_i = \eta_i + \eta_i' D_{70} + \theta_i \hat{M}_{Ei} + \lambda_i \hat{M}_{Ei}^{70} + u \tag{9.2}$$

where $\hat{M}_{Ei} = \sum_{\substack{j=1 \\ j \neq i}}^{7} w_j \hat{M}_j$, i.e. the weighted sum of the growth rates of the money stock of all the countries in the sample (the w_j's are determined by the share of country j's GNP in the total), and $\hat{M}_{Ei}^{70}$ is a vector of zero's for the period 1960–71 and of the money growth rates defined in $\hat{M}_{Ei}$ for the period 1972–82.

The results of estimating equation (9.2) are presented in Table 9.6. We find that the money stocks of Germany, the UK and Italy were as much influenced by the external money stock during the 1970s as during the 1960s. France's money stock was more sensitive to changes of the external money stock during 1972–82 than during 1960–71. Japan's money stock, however, was less influenced by the external money stock during the 1970s. Thus, the results are very similar as in the previous regression with the US money stock. In sum, it is not obvious that monetary interaction across countries was less pronounced in the flexible-rate 1970s than in the fixed-rate 1960s.

A more refined test of the monetary hypothesis involves verifying the channels of transmission that ultimately lead to the noted cross-country correlation pattern. As indicated earlier, the ingredients of this transmission mechanism are the following:

TABLE 9.6 *Regression results of equation* (9.2), 1960–82

	η_i	η'_i	θ_i	λ_i	$\hat{\rho}$	*SER*	*DW*
UK	−0.03	0.020	0.500	−0.015	−0.18	0.025	1.91
	(0.74)	(3.97)	(4.78)	(0.10)	(1.82)	(0.024)	
France	0.011	−0.008	0.480	0.486	−0.014	0.025	2.01
	(2.36)	(1.19)	(5.21)	(3.65)	(0.14)	(0.026)	
Germany	−0.008	−0.002	0.968	0.030	0.009	0.022	1.96
	(1.78)	(0.38)	(10.84)	(0.24)	(0.088)	(0.019)	
Italy	0.009	0.002	1.09	0.124	0.19	0.024	1.87
	(1.87)	(0.36)	(12.85)	(1.06)	(1.89)	(0.032)	
Japan	0.006	−0.012	1.786	−0.601	0.020	0.040	1.99
	(0.75)	(1.13)	(9.22)	(2.40)	(0.18)	(0.034)	

SOURCE International Monetary Fund, *International Financial Statistics*.
NOTE The equations were estimated using OLS with a Cochrane–Orcutt procedure.

1. fluctuations in the dollar rate provoke official interventions in the exchange market;
2. interventions are not completely sterilised and, therefore, alter the money stock;
3. interventions have limited effectiveness on the exchange rate, so that wide movements in the dollar exchange rates persist.

Evidence on points 1 and 2 is provided in Tables 9.7 and 9.8. Table 9.7 shows the correlation coefficients between the yearly and quarterly growth rates of international reserves and the rate of change of the dollar exchange rates. It can be seen that in all countries in the sample an increase (decrease) of their dollar exchange rates coincided on average with a decline (increase) in their international reserves. In other words, when the dollar was depreciating (appreciating) during the 1970s, countries were typically selling (buying) foreign exchange. This evidence is in accordance with the empirical evidence about the intervention policies during the 1970s (read Artus, 1976, for Germany; and Quirk, 1977, for Japan).

Table 9.8 provides evidence concerning the correlation between changes in the international reserves and changes in the money stock. During the 1970s this correlation was positive in all countries, suggesting that increases (decreases) in the stock of international reserves led to increases (decreases) in the stock of money. It should be stressed here that the relation between changes in the stock of international reserves

TABLE 9.7 *Correlation of growth rates of international reserves and rates of change of dollar (1971–82)*

Country	*Yearly*	*Quarterly*
UK	−0.62	−0.35
Belgium	−0.31	−0.34
France	−0.45	−0.37
Germany	−0.75	−0.55
Italy	−0.01	−0.12
Netherlands	−0.04	−0.02
Canada	−0.40	−0.64
Japan	−0.57	−0.55

SOURCE International Monetary Fund, *International Financial Statistics.*

TABLE 9.8 *Correlation of growth rates of international reserves and growth rates of the money stock M_1, yearly data*

Country	*1960–70*	*1971–82*
UK	0.32	0.28
Belgium	−0.48	0.20
France	0.21	0.38
Germany	0.20	0.38
Italy	0.40	0.43
Netherlands	−0.29	0.00
Canada	−0.21	0.03
Japan	−0.32	0.52

SOURCE: International Monetary Fund, *International Financial Statistics.*

and changes in the stock of money is a complex one. We know from theory that an increase in the domestic component of the money stock leads, *ceteris paribus*, to a capital outflow, a decline in the stock of international reserves and a rise in the country's total money stock. If this effect dominates, a negative correlation pattern would be observed in Table 9.8. On the other hand a positive correlation pattern would be observed if the stock of money were to rise because of an inflow of unsterilised international reserves.

The evidence of Table 9.8 suggests that during the 1970s the second effect tended to dominate, in contrast with the evidence of the 1960s when we find as many negative correlation coefficients as positive ones.

The facts of Table 9.8 are also consistent with what we found in Chapter 7. There it was established that, given the structure of the financial system, most countries find it very difficult to sterilise completely the monetary effects of their intervention policies. In sum, many countries have attempted fully to offset official purchases and sales of foreign exchange, but have been unable to do it effectively.

Finally, on point 3 – the relative ineffectiveness of intervention policies – we provided ample evidence in Chapter 7. There it was established that, when large expectational changes occur, interventions in the exchange market are ineffective in changing the fundamental trends in the exchange rates. This evidence is in accord with recent studies such as Obstfeld (1983) and Wonnacott (1983). In sum, there is evidence that the transmission of monetary processes together with the oil shocks can explain why interdependence among nations was higher during the 1970s than during the 1960s.

The nature of the monetary transmission across countries was found to be similar to the one existing during the Bretton Woods system with one important difference. Whereas in the Bretton Woods system exchange rate expectations were frequently tied to the official commitment to support par value rates, the absence of such commitments during the 1970s made exchange rate expectations extremely volatile. Against this background of volatile exchange rate movements, the monetary authorities continued to intervene heavily in the exchange markets. By so doing they kept in place the transmission of monetary impulses *à la* Bretton Woods. At the same time, with intervention policies turning out to be relatively ineffective, the authorities were unable to reduce the swings in exchange rates. Thus, the exchange rate regime of the 1970s combined the disadvantages of the fixed and flexible exchange systems.

It is interesting to note that McKinnon (1982) explains the high monetary interdependence of the seventies by a high degree of currency substitution. This interpretation has been challenged (for example, Dornbusch, 1983a) on the grounds that direct currency substitution is empirically not very important (cf. Brillembourg and Shadler, 1979, and Spinelli, 1983, for empirical evidence). More importantly, the discussion of this chapter highlights the fact that one need not rely on the argument of direct currency substitution to explain the high degree of monetary interdependence observed during the 1970s. Put differently, this high degree of monetary interdependence was the result of the high interdependence of the money *supply* process of the major industrialised countries, which itself was produced by 'leaning against the wind' intervention policies. This explanation does not have to rely on the presumed interdependence of the *demand* for money in different countries (currency substitution), for which the evidence is rather weak.

V US POLICIES, 1979–82, AND THE EUROPEAN ECONOMY

During the period 1979–82 US economic policy was characterised by monetary restriction and fiscal expansion. Many European observers were critical of this policy mix because it was alleged to have detrimental effects on the state of economic activity in the rest of the world, especially in Europe.[4] The core of this European critique went as follows. The US policy mix raised the level of the real interest rates in the world, and in so doing deflated investment and total aggregate demand. In addition, the real appreciation of the dollar resulting from this mix acted as a supply shock to the rest of the world: increasing import prices and setting in motion a cost-push effect in other industrialised countries. In this section we discuss these problems first from a theoretical point of view. In the next section, we provide some empirical evidence about the nature of the transmission of the US policy mix during 1979–82.

What does theory tell us about the way a mix of monetary contraction and fiscal expansion in the United States could affect aggregate demand and supply in Europe? The answer depends on the exchange rate regime. We discuss three different exchange rate regimes – fixed, flexible and managed float – and their implications for European aggregate demand and aggregate supply. The theory used here is based on Mundell's (1963) perfect capital mobility model and on our theoretical model of Chapter 2.[5]

Fixed Exchange Rate Regime

In a fixed exchange rate regime a policy mix of monetary contraction and budgetary expansion in the United States most probably deflates aggregate demand in Europe. A monetary contraction in the United States temporarily raises the real interest rate in this country and attracts capital from Europe; the US current account improves at the expense of Europe's current account. Thus, both the current account and capital account effects tend to reduce aggregate demand in Europe.

The effect of a US budget deficit on aggregate demand in Europe is ambiguous: the capital account and the current account effects work in opposite direction. The budget deficit raises the US real interest rate, attracts capital from Europe, and deflates demand in Europe. But there is a deterioration of the US current account in favour of Europe's, an outcome that expands aggregate demand for European goods. There is a sizeable likelihood that a US policy mix of monetary restraint *and* budget deficits is deflationary for European aggregate demand if European countries peg their currencies to the dollar. We can formalise our argument with Mundell's *IS–LM* model under perfect capital mobility. This is done in Figure 9.1 where the horizontal axis shows European output and the vertical axis the European real interest rate which, under perfect capital mobility, must be equal to the US real interest rate. The US policy shock now does two things. It raises the real interest rate, from r_A to r'_A. The US monetary contraction tends to shift the European *IS*-curve to the left because it produces a current account surplus in the United States, and thus a current account deficit in Europe. The US budgetary expansion has exactly the opposite effect. The net effect on the European *IS*-curve, therefore, is ambiguous and depends on the relative strength of the US monetary contraction and budgetary expansion. In Figure 9.1 we have assumed that they offset each other. What remains is the deflationary effect of the higher real interest rate on European spending, represented by the movement along the *IS*-curve from point *A* to point *B*. Finally, the *LM*-curve must shift upward until it reaches point *B*. This follows from the fixed exchange rate assumption: the European authorities have to sell dollars to keep their dollar exchange rates unchanged.

We can now combine these demand effects of the US policy mix with

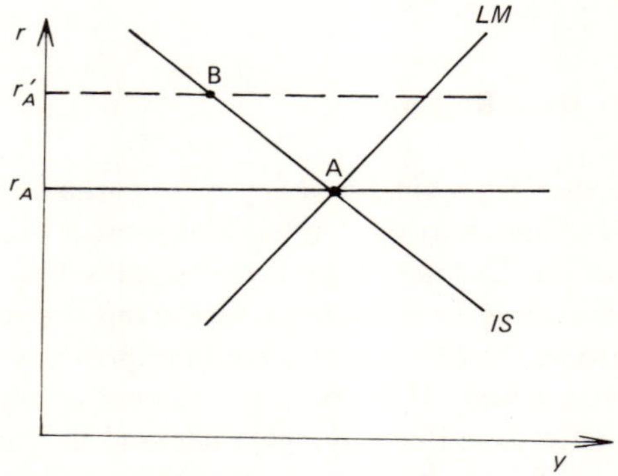

FIGURE 9.1 *US policy mix and aggregate demand in Europe: fixed exchange rates*

the effects on Europe's aggregate supply. This is done in Figure 9.2 showing the aggregate demand and supply schedules in Europe. The vertical axis measures the price level of European goods; the horizontal axis European output. As indicated above, the US policy mix is likely to reduce aggregate demand in Europe. Thus the *D*-curve in Figure 9.2 shifts to the left to *D'*.

The European economy moves from *A* to *B*, the new temporary equilibrium point with a lower output and price level. Implicitly we assume here that the US policy shock was unexpected. As a result, the lower European price level obtained in *B* has not yet been incorporated into wage contracts.

Had the US policy mix been fully anticipated the European aggregate supply curve would have shifted to the right say to point *C*, with the lower European price level immediately incorporated into wage contracts. Note that fully indexed wages, or rigid real wages, yield the same outcome.

Flexible Exchange Rate System

In a flexible exchange rate system the US policy mix of monetary contraction and budgetary expansion affects Europe's output and price level in quite a different way. Let us, first, concentrate on the demand effects using the *IS–LM* representation of perfect capital mobility (see

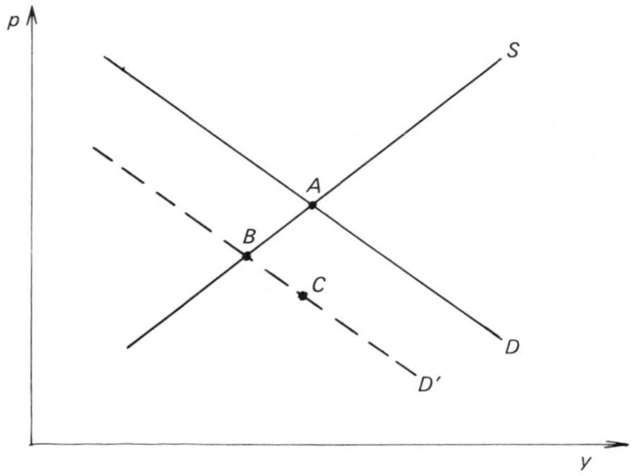

FIGURE 9.2 *Aggregate demand and supply in Europe: fixed exchange rates*

Figure 9.3). The US policy mix raises the real interest rate from r_A to r'_A. At the same time it leads to an appreciation of the dollar. Being in pure floating there can be no net flow of international reserves between the US and Europe and, therefore, there can be no movement in the European *LM*-curve. Thus, the dollar is forced to appreciate (the European currencies to depreciate) enough to move the *IS*-curve to the right until it reaches point *D*. The US policy mix has an unambiguous positive effect on Europe's aggregate demand in a flexible exchange rate system. This effect will be mitigated, however, if we allow for the depreciation of the European currency to raise the price level through higher import prices. This, in turn, reduces the level of real cash balances and shifts the *LM*-curve upwards, bringing the economy to point *F*. If this effect is strong enough the positive demand effect of the US policy mix could disappear, or even become negative.

To analyse the supply consequences of the US policy mix we refer to Figure 9.4. Assuming a weak real cash balance effect the US policy mix raises the level of aggregate demand in Europe from *D* to *D''*. The appreciation of the dollar, on the other hand, raises import prices, shifting the supply curve upwards. In addition, to the extent that the policy mix was expected (or if wages are indexed in Europe) we obtain a further upward shift in the aggregate supply curve. The economy moves to a point like *G* which may be to the right or to the left of the initial point *A*, depending on whether or not the demand shift dominates the supply shift.

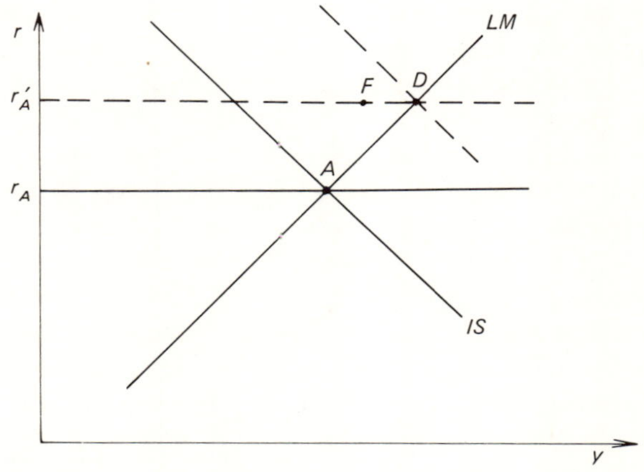

FIGURE 9.3 *US policy mix and aggregate demand in Europe: flexible exchange rates*

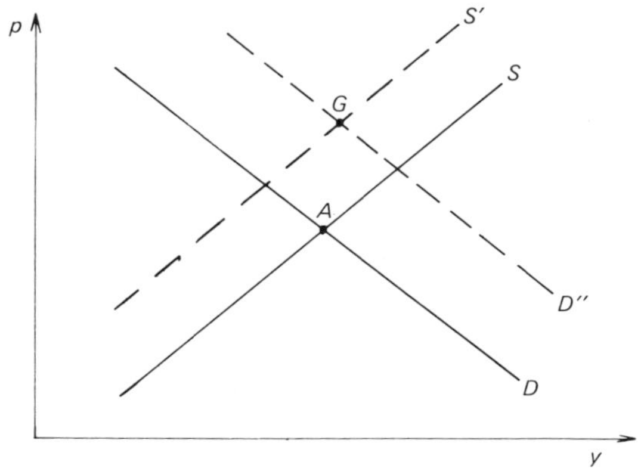

FIGURE 9.4 *Aggregate supply and demand in Europe: flexible exchange rates*

Managed Floating System

The managed floating system combines aspects of the two previously discussed systems. In principle, the effect of the US policy mix on European demand and supply schedules should lie between the two extremes of the fixed and flexible exchange rate system. We show this by combining Figures 9.2 and 9.4 into Figure 9.5. The D_{fix}- and S_{fix}- lines show the outcome of the US policy mix under a fixed exchange rate system.

The D_{flex}- and S_{flex}-lines show the results under flexible exchange rates. By managing the dollar rate successfully the authorities could, in principle, keep the demand and supply lines closer to their initial level. It cannot be excluded in light of the evidence of Chapter 8, that the exchange rate management can fail to influence the dollar exchange rate in any substantial way. This would mean that, despite heavy foreign exchange market interventions resulting in strong monetary contraction, the dollar exchange rate would be little affected.

In that case the supply shift typical of the floating exchange rate regime would be maintained. Thus, when exchange rate management is ineffectual the economy will be located on, or close to, the S_{flex}-line. Note that the S_{flex}-line shown in Figure 9.5 is consistent with a long-run soltion. In the short run S_{flex} is likely to be located to the right of the long-run S_{flex}-curve. As to the demand effects, there are two offsetting forces. The foreign exchange market intervention reduces the money stock (except if successfully sterilised), deflates aggregate demand, and

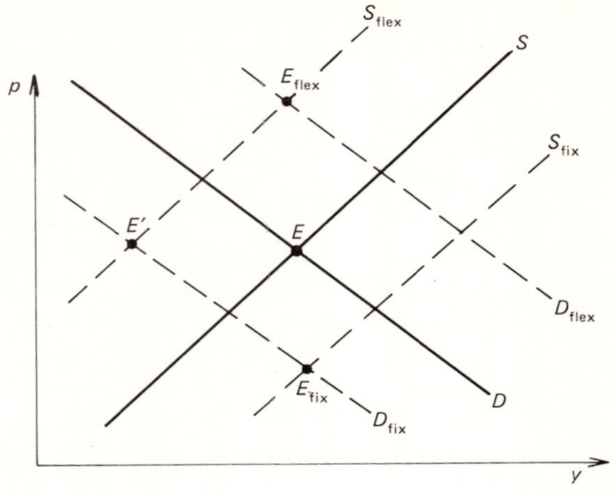

FIGURE 9.5 *Aggregate supply and demand in Europe: managed float*

shows up with a shift to the left of the demand curve, as in the fixed exchange rate system. On the other hand, the appreciation of the dollar (depreciation of the European currency) stimulates aggregate demand in Europe, as in the flexible rate system.

In sum, in a regime of ineffective exchange rate management, the European economy will be located on a point on the S_{flex}-line between the two extreme E' and E_{flex}. If the monetary contraction effect is large relative to the exchange rate effect it will be closer to E'. In the opposite case the economy will be closer to E_{flex} and will resemble the pure floating exchange rate regime. Ineffective exchange rate management combines the disadvantages of the fixed and flexible exchange rate regimes. The reduction of European output results not so much from the US policy mix but rather from an ineffective foreign exchange rate management. In the next section we provide some evidence indicating to what extent this may have happened during the period 1979–82.

VI US POLICIES, 1979–82, AND THE EUROPEAN ECONOMY: SOME EMPIRICAL OBSERVATIONS

We look here at two pieces of evidence, the money stock growth rates and terms-of-trade data. Table 9.9 presents data on the growth rates of the nominal and real money stock during the period of strong dollar depreciation (1976–9) and after 1979. It can be seen that the dollar appreciation since 1979 coincided with monetary deflation in the world.

TABLE 9.9 *Change in the money stock (M_1) foreign exchange reserves and in the dollar exchange rate, in percentage*

	US	*UK*	*Japan*	*France*	*Germany*	*Belgium*	*Netherlands*	*Italy*
1976–9								
ΔM_1 (nominal)	26.3	54.3	22.7	38.1	32.0	17.5	21.2	90.2
ΔM_1 (real)	−0.9	8.4	9.4	4.6	19.0	0.5	10.2	26.4
Δdollar rate	—	−24.7	−35.0	−19.1	−27.7	−20.1	−22.6	−8.1
Δforeign exchange reserves	—	590.0	108.0	267.8	85.6	97.9	84.0	438.9
1980–2								
ΔMl (nominal)	17.4	34.7	17.4	36.6	9.7	6.5	13.9	28.5
ΔMl (real)	−11.7	−6.0	−2.6	−5.1	−6.7	−14.6	−5.4	−22.7
Δdollar rate	—	37.8	20.8	67.3	37.3	67.3	37.7	70.4
Δforeign exchange reserves	—	−47.6	−33.7	−9.4	−16.3	−31.6	33.9	−27.0

NOTE 1. The relevant periods for Japan are 1976–8 and 1978–82. The reason is that the dollar hit its low point against the yen about a year earlier than against the other currencies.

SOURCE IMF, *International Financial Statistics*.

The opposite occurred during the period of dollar depreciation.

This evidence of Table 9.9 confirms two aspects of our hypothesis. First, it confirms again that exchange rate management has been relatively unsuccessful in curbing movements in the dollar exchange rate. Hence it reinforces the conclusion reached in the first part of this chapter. Second, the numbers of Table 9.9 are consistent with the hypothesis that interventions in the dollar exchange markets have been substantial, implying that the monetary transmission, so typical of the fixed exchange rate system, has been kept in place. In terms of Figure 9.5 this means that there were monetary forces pushing the aggregate demand curve downwards in the rest of the world.

To what extent has monetary deflation been offset by the expansionary effect on European aggregate demand resulting from the dollar appreciation? One way to find this out is to analyse the evolution of the terms of trade in European countries. If the exchange rate induced increase in aggregate demand is low, the European economy will be close to point E' in Figure 9.5, implying a deterioration of Europe's terms of trade (the ratio of the price of Europe's output and the price of Europe's imported goods). At E' the dollar appreciation has increased the price of Europe's imports, whereas the price of Europe's output (p) has not changed as a result of the strong demand deflation. The stronger the positive demand effects of the dollar appreciation are the more we move away from E' along the S_{flex}-line, implying a progressively weaker terms of trade effect. At point E_{flex} there is no deterioration of the terms of trade.

Table 9.10 provides some evidence on this point: it shows the change in

TABLE 9.10 *Terms of trade, dollar exchange rates and oil price, 1980–2, per cent change*

Country	*Terms-of-trade changes*[1]	*Dollar exchange rate (+ : appreciation of dollar)*
Belgium	−3.2	+56.1
France	−3.2	+55.3
Germany	−5.0	+33.2
Italy	−4.3	+58.0
Netherlands	+2.0	+34.4
UK	−1.9	+27.0

NOTE 1. Terms of trade changes defined as the per cent change in the ratio of export to import prices.

SOURCE IMF, *International Financial Statistics*.

the terms of trade of the major EC-countries since 1980, the year when the dollar started its upward climb. In five countries there was a deterioration of the terms of trade, although this deterioration was relatively small compared with the magnitude of the dollar appreciation. In one country there was a positive change in the terms of trade.

Thus, although the evidence is highly tentative, it is not inconsistent with the view that the monetary deflation resulting from intervention policies has been offset by the expansionary demand effect of the dollar appreciation. This offsetting tendency, however, was only partial in most countries in the sample, so that it can be said that the management of the dollar exchange rate by European countries tended to combine the disadvantages of the fixed and flexible exchange-rate systems.

In conclusion, the US policy mix of monetary contraction and budgetary expansion of 1979–82 was transmitted to Europe in a very particular way. The European central banks intervened heavily in the dollar exchange market without being able to influence the dollar exchange rate in any significant way. The net effect of this phenomenon was an upward shift of the European supply curve. The impact on the European aggregate demand curve was ambiguous as the monetary deflation, resulting from European dollar interventions, was probably offset by an expansion resulting from the dollar appreciation. Had the dollar exchange rate been allowed to float freely, this monetary deflation could have been avoided. Thus, the evidence provided here supports the idea that the managed floating system has operated to combine the negative aspects of both the fixed and flexible exchange rate systems.

NOTES

1. The standard deviation, and not the coefficient of variation, is the relevant measure of dispersion. Regardless of the value of the worldwide average rate of inflations, the country's 'cost' to return at purchasing power parity with the rest of the world is proportional to the deviation of the country's inflation rate from the world wide rate of inflation.
2. Italy does not appear in the table because the estimated equations failed to detect a significant oil terms-of-trade effect.
3. This point has also been made by Frenkel (1983) who finds that the official demand for international reserves has not changed in any substantial way from the 1960s to the 1970s.
4. Representative spokes men of this veiw are Dornbusch (1983a), Triffin (1983), the Clare group (1983).
5. See also Marston (1983).

10 Summary and Conclusion

The 1970s and the early 1980s have been years of economic turmoil for the European countries. Some difficulties originated from changes in the structure of the productive system; others from financial disturbances. This book has dealt with some aspects of these difficulties. In the first part of the book we directed our attention to the supply side of the economy, and asked the questions how and to what extent the supply of manufacturing output in a group of European countries was affected by changes in the terms of trade, changes in the tax burdens and by unanticipated inflation. As a framework of analysis we developed a theoretical model of the supply side of the economy along the lines of the well-known Lucas model extended to an open economy. The empirical results of the model indicate that changes in relative prices, in particular terms of trade, taking place during 1973–4 and 1979–80, had a strong negative effect on the supply of manufacturing output in the six European countries under investigation (Belgium, France, Germany, Italy, Netherlands, and the United Kingdom). We also found that in a number of these countries the concomitant increase in the tax burdens (social security taxes, personal income taxes) aggravated the problems posed by the terms-of-trade shocks. These increased tax burdens discouraged the use of labour in the industrial production process. The combination of terms-of-trade deterioration and increased taxes goes a long way in explaining the substantial decline of recorded employment in the industrial sectors of these countries.

We did not find strong evidence that the inflationary surprises of the 1970s exerted negative effects on the supply of manufacturing output. When tested on European data we failed to find a link between monetary surprises and the supply of industrial output. This suggests that there may be very little empirical basis for the new business cycle theory, which stresses the importance of unanticipated monetary shocks as a cyclical force.

When the industrial world moved to a system of more flexible exchange rates in the early 1970s, economists and policy-makers were under the impression that such a system would give a greater independence to domestic macroeconomic policies. The experience since 1973 has led to some disappointment. In Parts II and III of this book we focused on this issue. More specifically, we analysed how and to what extent the changed international financial environment since the early 1970s affected monetary policies in Europe. We also studied how the move towards greater exchange rate flexibility affected economic interdependence among the industrialised nations.

In Part II we laid the groundwork for the policy-oriented analysis of Part III of the book. We constructed a theoretical framework to analyse financial interdependence among the major European countries, and to study how the changed environment of the 1970s affected monetary and exchange rate policies. The chosen paradigm is one of imperfect substitutability among assets denominated in different currencies. We subjected this paradigm to extensive empirical testing, and found enough evidence to support it. In other words, our results confirm the notion that the risk characteristics of similar assets denominated in different currencies are quite different in Europe.

The model was estimated and the resulting structure was employed for policy simulations in Part III. We raised questions such as how foreign and domestic disturbances affect the financial side of the economy under different exchange rate regimes. Two conclusions can be drawn from the financial-sector analysis. First, the flexibility of the exchange rates did not insulate domestic financial markets from external monetary disturbances. Despite the greater flexibility of exchange rates, monetary shocks were quickly transmitted across countries. These inter-country effects were substantial, especially when monetary shocks triggered large expectational changes. The volatility of exchange rate changes observed since the early 1970s is probably the most important factor underlying the changed nature of the inter-country transmission of monetary disturbances. Second, the need to control monetary aggregates in Europe increases with the degree of flexibility of exchange rates. Yet we found the financial systems of major countries to be strongly accommodative to exogenous price shocks. This pattern is more apparent the higher the degree of exchange rate flexibility. The implied policy advice is that tighter procedures aimed at controlling monetary aggregates should be set in place.

A question to which we repeatedly turn in this book is the effectiveness of official interventions in the foreign exchange markets. This topic has been studied quite extensively in the recent past. Our analysis goes one step further than much of the literature on this subject in that it is carried out within the context of an econometric model of a group of European countries. Furthermore, we imposed the restriction that expectations about future exchange rates be formed rationally, that is that people use information about the intervention behaviour of the monetary authorities in setting their own expectations. The rational expectations assumption is critical in evaluating the policy effectiveness of exchange rate policies. Our results suggest that as long as exchange rate expectations are stable, foreign exchange market interventions can be useful in some countries. However, when expectations change significantly there is very little that official interventions can accomplish. We also found that it is of relatively little importance whether interventions in the exchange markets are sterilised or not in the face of large expectational changes. Finally, our results imply that monetary authorities may find it easy to sterilise the effects of their interventions on the domestic money base. The authorities have greater difficulty, however, in fully sterilising the effects of their interventions on the domestic money stock. This severely reduces the ability of simultaneously targeting at exchange rates and money stock.

The nature of financial interdependence has changed dramatically since the early 1970s. Within the framework of the financial models of different countries participating in the European Monetary System (EMS), we found that the EMS has not allowed its members to insulate their financial markets better from outside monetary shocks, nor has it made it possible to increase the effectiveness of intervention policies in the dollar exchange markets. Undoubtedly, the EMS has made possible for its members to achieve a greater stability of exchange rates, at least in the short run. An analysis of the medium- and long-run behaviour of the *real* exchange rates of the EMS currencies revealed, however, that these have remained as volatile as before the creation of the EMS. The gain in real exchange rate stability obtained by France and Italy was more than offset by the increase in the variability of the real exchange rates of all other currencies in the system. Lack of progress in reducing real exchange rate variability in the EMS should not come as a surprise, for there has been no progress towards a tighter co-ordination of economic policies in Europe.

The present international monetary arrangements combine features of the fixed and flexible exchange rate regimes. This complicates our understanding of financial interdependence. All too often interdependence is analysed on the assumption that only the polar cases of either fixed or flexible exchange rates exist. In the last chapter of the book we offer some suggestions about the way the system of managed exchange rates has altered the nature of monetary interdependence. Our principal conclusion is that the failure of managing dollar-exchange rates has led to a system that combines the disadvantages of both the fixed and the flexible exchange rate arrangements. As a result, monetary shocks originating in the United States are transmitted to other countries in a way similar to the monetary transmission process under the Bretton-Woods system. What is new in this transmission process, however, is that because of the inability to control the dollar exchange rates, shocks in the United States lead to disturbances in other countries. We illustrated this phenomenon with a case study of the 1979–82 period, and concluded that the macroeconomic disturbances in Europe during this period could be traced not so much to the US policy mix of tight money and large budget deficits, but to an inappropriate response of European monetary and exchange rate policies.

Finally, these results also imply that the high degree of monetary interdependence observed during the floating exchange-rate period can be explained by the interdependence of the money *supply* processes of the major countries. This interpretation offers an alternative to the hypothesis of interdependence of the money *demand* functions in these countries through the phenomenon of direct currency substitution.

Appendix
Data Definitions and Sources

TABLE A.1 *Germany*

Variable symbol	*Definition*	*Source*
A	Banks' borrowings from the central bank, excluding money market bills purchased, end of period (DM million (m)).	MRDBB* 'II Deutsche Bundesbank'; table: 'Assets of the Deutsche Bundesbank',
B	Monetary base (= banks deposits + Federal Post Office deposits + currency), end of period (DM m.)	MRDBB 'II Deutsche Bundesbank'; table: 'Liabilities of the Deutsche Bundesbank'
BE	Excess Reserves (= actual reserves − required reserves), end of period (DM m.)	MRDBB 'IV Minimum reserves'; table: 'Reserve maintenance, total'
BF	International reserves, end of period (DM m.)	MRDBB 'II Deutsche Bundesbank'; table: 'Assets and liabilities of the Deutsche Bundesbank'
BP	Currency in hands of the public, end of period (DM m.)	MRDBB 'I Overall money survey'; table: 'Consolidated balance sheet of the banking system'
BR	Required reserves, end of period (DM m.)	MRDBB 'IV Minimum reserves'; table: 'Reserve maintenance'
BRK	Ratio of liabilities subject to required reserves to total liabilities	$BRK = \dfrac{BRL}{D+T+SD}$

Table A.1 *continued*

Variable Symbols	*Definition*	*Source*
BRL	Liabilities subject to reserve requirements, end of period (DM m.)	MRDBB 'IV Minimum reserves'; table: 'Reserve maintenance'
BTR	Treasury base, end of period (DM m.)	MRDBB 'II Deutsche Bundesbank'; table: 'Assets and liabilities of the Deutsche Bundesbank'
CAB	Current account balance (DM m.)	MRDBB 'IX Foreign trade and payments'; table: 'Important items of the balance of payments'
CPI75	Consumer price index (base: 1975)	IFS**, country table, line 64
D	Sight deposits, end of period (DM m.)	MRDBB 'III Banks'; table: 'Liabilities'
efh	3-month, forward closing exchange rate on last friday of quarter (ch. 4)	Harris Bank, *Weekly Review*
es	Spot exchange rate (DM/$), average of last month of quarter	IFS, country tables, line rf
esh	Spot closing rate on last Friday of quarter (ch. 4)	Harris Bank, *Weekly Review*
FABL	Foreign assets of banks (long term), end of period (DM million)	MRDBB 'IX Foreign trade and payments'; table: 'External assets and liabilities of domestic banks'

FABS	Foreign assets of banks (short term, all banks), end of period (DM m.)	MRDBB 'IX Foreign trade and payments'; table: 'External assets and liabilities of domestic banks'
FLBG	Foreign liabilities of banks (largest banks), end of period (DM m.)	MRDBB 'I Overall monetary survey'; table: 'Consolidated balance sheet of the banking system'
FLBL	Foreign liabilities of banks (long term, all banks), end of period (DM m.)	MRDBB 'IX Foreign trade and payments'; table: 'External assets and liabilities of domestic banks'
FLBS	Foreign liabilities of banks (short term, all banks), end of period (DM m.)	MRDBB 'IX Foreign trade and payments'; table: 'External assets and liabilities of domestic banks'
FP	Forward premium DM/$ (3-months contracts – average of last month of quarter)	MRDBB 'V Interest rates'; table: 'Money market rates in foreign countries'
FR	Free reserves	$FR = BE - A$
IA	Discount rate set by the Deutsche Bundesbank, end of period	MRDBB 'V Interest rates' table: 'Discount rate and Lombard rates of the Deutsche Bundesbank and special interest charged for failure to meet minimum reserve requirements'
IEA	Average rate of interest rate on banks earnings	$IEA = \frac{IL \times L + IS \times SB}{L + SB}$

TABLE A.1 *continued*

Variable symbols	*Definition*	*Source*
π	Expected rate of inflation	Own calculations: $\pi_t = \left[\left(1 + \frac{\pi'_t}{100}\right)^4 - 1\right] \times 100$ $\pi'_t = \frac{\sum_{i=1}^{19} (0.9)^i \hat{P}_{t-i}}{\sum_{i=1}^{19} (0.9)^i}$ $\hat{P}_t = \frac{CPI_t - CPI_{t-1}}{CPI_{t-1}} \times 100$
IL	Loan rate (average of last month of quarter of lending rate on credits in current account of under *DM* 1 m.)	MRDBB 'V Interest rates' table: 'Lending and deposit rates'
IS	Yield on domestic government bonds (average of last month of quarter)	MRDBB 'VI Capital market' table: 'Yield on domestic securities'
IT	Interest rate on 3-months deposits, average of last month of quarter	MRDBB 'V Interest rates' table: 'Lending and deposit rates'
ITMG	Interest rate on 3-month time deposits (ch. 4) End of period	Morgan Guaranty Trust, *World Financial Markets*

K	Total capital flows of banks and public	$K = KLABP + KLLBF + KSLB + KSLP + KSAB + KSAP$
$KLABP$	Long-term investment (= portfolio investments + advances and loans + other capital movements) (DM m.)	MRDBB 'IX Foreign trade and payments' table: 'Capital transactions with the rest of the world'
$KLLBP$	Long-term foreign investment (= portfolio investments + advances and loans + other capital movements) (DM m.)	MRDBB 'IX Foreign trade and payments' table: 'Capital transactions with the rest of the world'
KP	Capital flow of non-banks public	$KP = K + \Delta NFB$
$KSAB$	Variation of external short-term assets of the banks (DM m.)	SBMDB*** – Reihe 3 table 6: '*Kurzfristiger Kapitalverkehr*'
$KSAP$	Variation of external short-term assets of the public (DM m.)	SBMDB – Reihe 3 table 6: '*Kurzfristiger Kapitalverkehr*'
$KSLB$	Variation of external short-term liabilities of the banks (DM m.)	SBMDB – Reihe 3 table 6: '*Kurzfristiger Kapitalverkehr*'
$KSLP$	Variation of external short-term liabilities of the public (DM m.)	SBMDB – Reihe 3 table 6: '*Kurzfristiger Kapitalverkehr*'
L	Bank loans, end of period (DM m.)	$L = LG - LT_1 - LT_2$
LG	Banks' loans, end of period (DM m.)	MRDBB 'III Banks' table: 'Lending to non-banks, by debtor group, maturity and category'
LT_1	Loans on a trust basis (long-term) to private enterprise and individuals, end of period (DM m.)	MRDBB 'III Banks' table: 'Lending to non-banks, by debtor groups, maturity and category'

TABLE A.1 *continued*

Variable symbols	Definition	Source
LT_2	Loans on a trust basis (medium-term) to private enterprises and individuals, end of period (DM m.)	MRDBB 'III Banks' table: 'Lending to non-banks, by debtor group, maturity and category'
NFB	Net foreign assets of banks	$NFB = FABS + FABL - FLBS - FLBL$
M_1	Narrow money	$M_1 = BP + D$
M_2	Broad money	$M_2 = M_1 + T$
OAB	Other assets of banks	$OAB = D + T + SD + A - L - BR - BE - SB - NFB$
OB	Other assets of Central Bank	$OB = B - BTR - BF - A$
OK	Other capital flows	$OK = -CAB - K + \Delta BF$
P	General price level	See CPI 75
S	Stock of government bonds	$S = ST - SDB$
SB	Bond portfolio of banks, end of period (DM m.)	$SB = SBT_1 + SBT_2 + SG$
SBG	Banks' loans to domestic public authorities, end of period (DM m.)	MRDBB 'III Banks' table: 'Lending to non-banks, by debtor group, maturity and category'
SBT_1	Banks' loans to domestic public authorities on a trust basis (long-term), end of period (DM m.)	MRDBB 'Banks' table: 'Lending to non-banks, by debtor group, maturity and category'
SBT_2	Banks' loans to domestic public authorities on a trust basis (medium-term), end of period (DM m.)	MRDBB 'Banks' table: 'Lending to non-banks, by debtor groups, maturity and category'

SD	Savings deposits, end of period (DM m.)	MRDBB 'III Banks' table: 'Liabilities' (internal + external)
SDB	Bundesbank-held government debt, end of period (DM m.)	MRDBB 'VII Public Finance' table: 'Movement in public indebtedness'
ST	Total government debt, end of period (DM m.)	MRDBB 'VII Public Finance' table: 'Indebtedness of public authorities' total
T	Time deposits, end of period (DM m.)	MRDBB 'III Banks' table: 'Liabilities' (internal + external)
YC	Current GNP at market prices (DM m.)	IFS, country tables, line 99e
YPR	Permanent income (DM m.)	Own calculations $YPR_t = \dfrac{\sum_{i=1}^{19} (0.9)^i \overline{Y}_{t-1}}{\left(\dfrac{1}{1+g}\right) \sum_{i=1}^{19} (0.9)^i}$ where $\overline{Y}_{t-1} = YR75$ g = average quarterly growth rate of $\overline{Y}$ during the period for which *YPR* is computed
YR75	Real GNP (DM m.)	IFS, country tables, line 99 a.r.

* Monthly Report of the Deutsche Bundesbank
** *International Financial Statistics*
*** *Statistische Beihefte zu den Monatsberichten der Deutsche Bundesbank*

TABLE A.2 *Belgium*

Variable symbols	*Definition*	*Source*
A	Banks' borrowing from the Central Bank, including export accepts, end of period (BF billion (bn))	Tijdschrift NBB* table: 13.2. a. ACTIVA table: 13.8
B	Monetary base, postal deposits excluded; end of period (BF bn)	Tijdschrift NBB table 13.2.d. PASSIVA
BE	Excess reserves of banks	$BE = RB - BR$
BF	International reserves, end of period (BF bn)	Tijdschrift NBB: table 13.2.a.
BP	Currency in hands of the public, end of period (BF bn)	Tijdschrift NBB table: 13.2.d. PASSIVA
BR	Required reserves of the banks, end of period (BF bn)	Tijdschrift NBB table: 13.2.c.
BRR	Required reserves ratio	$BRR = (BR)/(D+T)$
BTR	Treasury base, end of period (BF bn)	Tijdschrift NBB table: 13.2.a.
CAB	Current account balance = Balance on trade account + transfers (BF bn)	Tijdschrift NBB table: IX.5
CPI75	Consumer price index, period average (base: 1975)	IFS, country tables, line 64
D	Sight deposits, including time deposits till 30 days, end of period (BF bn)	Statistical department of the NBB
efh	3-month forward closing exchange rate on last Friday of quarter (Ch. 4)	Harris Bank, *Weekly Review*

es	Spot exchange rate (FB/US $), end of period	IFS, country table, line ae.
esh	Spot closing rate on last Friday of quarter	Harris Bank, *Weekly Review*
FAB	Foreign assets of banks, end of period (BF bn)	Tijdschrift NBB table: 13.2.c. ACTIVA
FLB	Foreign liabilities of banks, end of period (BF bn)	Tijdschrift NBB table: 13.2.c. PASSIVA
FP	Forward premium on three months of the $ as a percentage of the spot rate, end of period	OECD, *Main Economic Indicators*
FR	Free reserves	$FR = BE - A$
IA	Interest rate on banks' borrowing from central bank = discount rate of the NBB, end of period	Tijdschrift NBB Table 19–1a
π	Expected rate of inflation	Own calculations (see German data-set description)
IEA	Average interest rate on bank credit	See Germany
IL	Interest rate on bank loans, end of period	Morgan Guaranty Trust, *World Financial Markets* 'Commercial Bank Lending rates to prime borrowers'
IS	Interest rate on government securities, long-net yield on state bonds with maturity of 5 to 13 years after taxes (last Wednesday of quarter)	Kredietbank: Statistical department
IT	Interest rate on time deposits at banks, large amounts, end of period	Morgan Guaranty Trust *World Financial Markets*: 'Commercial banks deposit rate'
$ITMG$	Interest rate on 3-month deposits, end of period	Morgan Guaranty Trust, *World Financial Markets*
K	Total capital movements	$K = -\Delta NFB - \Delta NFP$
KP	Capital movements of the private sector (BF bn)	$KP = -\Delta NFP$
L	Total bank loans	$L = LAB + A$

TABLE A.2 *continued*

Variable symbols	*Definition*	*Source*
LAB	Domestic loan assets of the banks on the private sector, export accepts included and loans on other financial institutions not included; end of period (BF bn)	Tijdschrift NBB table: 13.2.c.
M_1	Narrow money stock	$M_1 = BP + D$
M_2	Broad money stock	$M_2 = M_1 + T$
NFB	Net foreign assets of banks	$NFB = FAB - FLB$
NFP	Net foreign assets of the public ($NFP_t = NFP_{t-1} + \Delta NFP_t$) (BF bn)	For ΔNFP_t: Tijdschrift NBB table: IX.2
OAB	Other assets of banks	$OAB = D + T + A - L - BR - BE - SB - NFB$
OB	Other assets of Central Bank	$OB = B - BTR - BF - A$
OK	Other capital flows	$OK = -CAB - K + \Delta BF$
P	General price level	See $CPI75$
RB	Reserves of the banks = money base held by the banks, end of period (BF bn)	Tijdschrift NBB table: XIII.2.a DEPOSITOBANKEN, ACTIVA
S	Total government stock of bonds	$S = SG - BTR$
SB	Bond portfolio of banks (Rentenfonds included), end of period (BF bn)	Tijdschrift NBB table: XIII.2.c
SG	Government debt, currency of the Treasury included, end of period (BF bn)	Tijdschrift NBB table: XVI.3.a + XVI.4.a + XIII.4.a

SP	Public-held government bonds, end of period (BF bn)	Residually calculated: $SP = SG - SB - (SGF - SGFB)$ where (i) SGF = government debt financed on foreign markets source: Statistical department NBB (ii) $SGFB$ = government debt in foreign currency held by the banks source: Banking Commission, annual reports
T	Time deposits, end of period (BF bn)	Tijdschrift NBB table: XIII.2.c.
YC	Current *GNP* at market price (BF bn)	*Cahiers économiques de Bruxelles*, statistical appendix
YPR	Permanent income	Own calculations (see German data-set description)

* Nationale Bank van België

TABLE A.3 *France*

Variable symbols	*Definition*	*Source*
A	Banks' borrowing and discounting from the central bank, end of period (FF million (m.))	BBF* Tableau 38
B	Monetary base, end of period (FF m.)	Own calculation: $B = BP + BR + BE$
BE	Excess reserves of the banks, end of period (FF m.)	BBF Tableau 3 − Tableau 1 + Tableau 9
BF	International reserves, end of period (FF m.)	BBF Tableau 8
BP	Monetary base held by the public, end of period (FF m.)	BBF Tableau 1
BR	Required reserves of the banks, end of period (FF m.)	BBF Tableau 36
BRR	Required reserves ratio, end of period	Own calculation $BRR = \frac{BR}{D+T}$
BTR	Treasury component of the monetary base, end of period (FF m.)	Own calculation $BTR = B - A - BF$
$CPI75$	Consumer price index, end of period (1975 = 100)	IFS, country table, line 64
CAB	Current account balance (FF m.)	BBF Tableau 39
D	Sight deposits, end of period (FF m.)	BBF Tableau 1

ef	Forward exchange rate (FF/\$), end of period	IFS, country tables, line 60 f
efh	3-month forward closing exchange rate on last Friday of quarter (Ch. 4)	Harris Bank, *Weekly Review*
es	Spot exchange rate (FF/\$), end of period	IFS, country tables, line ae
esh	Spot closing rate on last Friday of quarter (Ch. 4)	Harris Bank, *Weekly Review*
FAB_1	Short term foreign assets in FF of the banks, end of period (FF m.)	BBF Tableau 42
FAB_2	Short term foreign assets in foreign exchange of the banks, end of period (FF m.)	BBF Tableau 42
FLB_1	Short term foreign liabilities in FF of the Banks, end of period (FF m.)	BBF Tableau 42B
FLB_2	Short term foreign liabilities in foreign exchange of the banks, end of period (FF m.)	BBF Tableau 42A
FP	Forward premium, end of period	Own calculation $FP = \frac{ef - es}{es} \times 400$
FR	Free reserves	$FR = BE - A$
IA	Central Bank discount rate, end of period	Morgan Guaranty Trust, *World Financial Markets*: 'Central bank discount rates'
π	Expected rate of inflation	Own calculations See: German data-set description
IEA	Interest rate on banks domestic earnings assets	$IEA = (IL \times L \times IS \times SB)/(L + SB)$
IL	Interest rate on banks loans, end of period	Morgan Guaranty Trust, *World Financial Markets*: 'Commercial bank lending rates to prime borrowers'
IS	Interest rate on bonds, end of period	BBF Tableau 32

TABLE A.3 *continued*

Variable symbols	*Definition*	*Source*
$ITMG$	Interest rate on 3-month time deposits. End of period (Ch. 4)	Morgan Guaranty Trust
IT	Interest rate on time deposits, end of period	BBF Tableau 31
K	Total capital flows	$K = KBS + KBL + KPL + KPS$
KBL	Long term external capital flows of the banks, (FF m.)	*Statistiques et études financières, Ministères de l'économie et du budget*
KBS	Short term external capital flows of the banks, (FF m.)	*Statistiques et études financières, Ministères de l'économie et du budget*
KP	Capital flow of non-bank public	$KP = K + \Delta NFB$
KPL	Long term external capital flows of the public (FF m.)	*Statistiques et études financières, Ministères de l'économie et du budget*
KPS	Short term external capital flows of the public (FF m.)	*Statistiques et études financières, Ministères de l'économie et du budget*
L	Banks' loans, end of period (FF m.)	BBF Tableau 10
M_1	Money stock, end of period (FF m.)	BBF Tableau 1
M_2	Money stock, end of period (FF m.)	BBF Tableau 2
NFB	Net foreign assets of banks	$NFB = FAB_1 + FAB_2 - FLB_1 - FLB_2$
OAB	Other assets of banks	$OAB = D + T + A - BR - BE - SB - L - NFB$

OB	Other assets of banks	$OB = BR + BE + RP - BTR - BF - A$
OK	Other capital movements	$OK = -CAB - K + \Delta BF$
P	General price level	See $CPI75$
S	Stock of bonds, end of period (FF m.)	*Statistiques et études financières, Ministères de l'économie et du budget*
SB	Bond portfolio of banks, end of period (FF m.)	BBF Tableau 9
SP	Public-held government bonds, end of period (FF m.)	$SP = S - SB$
YC	Current GNP at market prices (FF m.)	IFS, country tables, line 99e
YPR	Permanent income (FF bn)	Own calculations (see German Data Description)
$YR75$	Real GNP (FF bn)	IFS, country tables, line 99 a.r.

* *Bulletin Trimestriel de la Banque de France*

TABLE A.4 *Italy*

Variable symbols	*Definition*	*Source*
A	Banks' borrowing from the Central Bank, end of period (lire bn)	BBI*, *Base Monetaria* table: *'Creazione di base monetaria'*
B	Monetary base, end of period (lire bn)	BBI, *Base Monetaria* table: *'Situazione Riassuntiva'*
BE	Excess reserves, end of period (lire bn)	BBI, *Base Monetaria* table: *'Situazione Riassuntiva'*
BF	Stock of international reserves (= foreign component of the monetary base) end of period (lire bn)	BBI, *Base Monetaria* table: *'Situazione Riassuntiva'*
BP	Monetary base held by the public, end of period (lire bn)	BBI, *Base Monetaria* table: *'Situazione Riassuntiva'*
BR	Required reserves of the banks, end of period (lire bn)	BBI, *Base Monetaria* table: *'Situazione Riassuntiva'*
BRR	Required reserves ratio	$BRR = BR/(D+T)$
BTR	Treasury component of the monetary base (lire bn)	BBI, *Base Monetaria* table: *'Situazione Riassuntiva'*
CAB	Current Account Balance	OECD, *Main Economic Indicators*
$CPI75$	Consumer price index, end of period (base: 1975 = 100)	IFS, country table, line 64
D	Sight deposits, end of period (lire bn)	BBI, *Conti Finanziari* table: *'Attività Liquide del Pubblico'*
ef	3-month forward exchange rate, end of period	IFS, country table, line 60 f

efh	3-month forward closing exchange rate on last Friday of quarter (Ch. 4)	Harris Bank, *Weekly Review*
es	Spot exchange-rate (Lira/$), average of last month of quarter	BBI, *Bilancia dei pagamenti* table: '*Corso dei cambi tasso medio di deprezzamento della Lira, prezzo dell'oro*'
esh	Spot closing rate on last Friday of quarter (Ch. 4)	Harris Bank. Weekly Review
FAB	Foreign assets of banks, end of period (lire bn)	BBI, *Bilancia dei pagamenti* table: '*Posizione verso l'estero ed in cambi delle aziende di credito*'
FLB	Foreign liabilities of banks, end of period (lire bn)	BBI, *Bilancia dei pagamenti* table: '*Posizione verso l'estero ed in cambi delle aziende di credito*'
FLBD	Foreign liabilities of banks: deposits, end of period (lire bn)	BBI, *Bilancia dei pagamenti* table: '*Posizione verso l'estero ed in cambi delle aziende di credito*'
FP	Forward premium, end of period	$FP = \frac{ef - es}{es} \times 400$
FR	Free reserves	$FR = BE - A$
IA	Interest rate on banks' borrowings from central bank, end of period	BBI, *Tassi d'interesse* table: '*Tassi del mercato monetario e finanziario*'
IEA	Interest rate on domestic earnings assets of banks	$IEA = (IL \times L + IS \times SB)/(L + SB)$
π	Expected rate of inflation	See: German data-set description
IL	Interest rate on bank loans, end of period	Morgan Guaranty Trust, *World Financial Markets* 'Commercial Bank Lending Rate to Prime Borrowers'
IS	Interest rate on bonds of '*Istituti di credito Mobiliare*', average of last month of quarter	BBI, *Mercato Finanziario* table: '*Indice e rendimento netto dei valori mobiliari*'

Table A.4 *continued*

Variable symbols	*Definition*	*Source*
IT	Interest rate on demand deposits, end of period (lire bn)	BBI, *Tassi d'interesse* table: '*Tassi passivi medi*'
$ITMG$	Interest rate on 3-month time deposits. End of period (Ch. 4)	Morgan Guaranty Trust, *World Financial Markets*
K	Total capital movements	BBI table: '*Bilancia dei pagamenti valutaria*'
KP	Capital flows of non-bank public	$KP = K + \Delta NFB$
L	Loans of the banks, end of period (lire bn)	BBI, *Aziende di Credito* table: '*Impieghi sull' interno*'
NFB	Net foreign assets of banks	$NBF = FAB - FLB$
OAB	Other assets of banks	$OAB = D + T + A - L - BR - BE - SB - NFB$
OB	Other assets of Central Bank	$OB = B - BTR - BF - A$
P	General price level	See $CPI75$
S	Stock of government bonds	$S = SDF - BTR$
SB	Bond portfolio of banks, end of period (lire bn)	BBI, Aziende di credito table: 'Titoli in Lire'
SDF	Cumulated government deficit (+) or surplus (−), end of period (lire bn)	$SDF = \Sigma DF$ See DF
YC	Current GNP at market prices (lire bn)	IFS, country tables, line 99a
YPR	Permanent income (lire bn)	See German data-set description
YR	Real GNP	$YR = YC/CPI75$

* Bollettino of the Banca d'Italia

TABLE A.5 *The Netherlands*

Variable symbols	*Definition*	*Source*
A	Banks' discount and borrowings from central bank, end of period (millions of guilders)	QSDNB* table:1.1
B	Monetary base, currency held by the public plus reserves of commercial banks, end of period (millions of guilders)	IFS, country tables, line 14
BE	Excess reserves	$BE = B - BP - BR$
BF	Stock of international reserves (= foreign component of the monetary base) end of period (millions of guilders)	QSDNB table:2.1 table:1.1
BP	Currency held by the public, end of period (millions of guilders)	QSDNB table: 2.1
BR	Required reserves of the banks, end of period (millions of guilders)	Annual report of the DNB
BRR	Required reserves ratio	$BRR = BR/(D+T)$
BTR	Treasury base	$BTR = B - BF - A$
CAB	Current account balance	$CAB = CCB - CCB(-1)$
CCB	Cumulated current account balance, end of period (millions of guilders) $= \sum CB$	For CB: QSDNB table: 6.2
$CPI75$	Consumer price index, period average (base: 1975)	IFS, country tables, line 64
D	Sight deposits, end of period (millions of guilders)	QSDNB table: 2.1

TABLE A.5 *continued*

Variable symbols	*Definition*	*Source*
EA	$EA = DEA_1 + DEA_2$	QSDNB table: 2.1
	A. DEA_1 = total credits from banks to domestic government and private sector with exception of long-term credits from non-bank money-creating institutions to government and private sector, end of period (millions of guilders)	
	$DEA_1 = SK^{HB}_{Rijk} + SK^{HB}_{LO} + LK^{HB} + (SL+IL)^{HB} + (SK+LK)^{OGI}$	
	SK^{HB}_{Rijk} = short and medium term credits from commercial banks to government	'Universal banks': col. 6
	SK^{HB}_{LO} = short term credits from commercial banks to the local authorities	'Universal banks': col. 7
	LK^{HB} = short term credits from commercial banks to the private sector	'Universal banks': col. 8
	$(SL+IL)^{HB}$ = investment on the capital market from commercial banks	
	(a) bonds and domestic participations	'Universal banks', col. 9 + 10 + 11 + 12 + 13
	(b) mortgage loans	col. 20
	(c) private loans	col. 16 + 17 + 18 + 19
	(d) investment in real estate	col. 21
	$(SK+LK)^{OGI}$ = credits from registered credit institutions to the domestic sectors	

	(a) government (short and medium term)	'Other money-creating institutions': col. 6
	(b) local authorities (short term)	col. 7
	(c) private sector (short term)	col. 8
	B. $DEA_2 = SL^{OGI} + LL^{OGI}$ = long term credit from the registered credit institutions to the public and private sectors, end of period (millions of guilders)	
	SL^{OGI} = Investments on the capital market from registered credit institutions to the public sector	col. $9+10+11+12+13$
	LL^{OGI} = Investments on the capital market from registered credit institutions to the private sector	col. $16+17+18+19+20+21$
ef	Forward exchange rate (FL/$), end of period	OECD, *Main Economic Indicators*
efh	3-month forward closing exchange rate on last Friday of quarter (Ch. 4)	Harris Bank, *Weekly Review*
es	Spot exchange rate (FL/$), end of period	OECD, *Main Economic Indicators*
esh	Spot closing rate on last Friday of quarter (Ch. 4)	Harris Bank, *Weekly Review*
FABA	Foreign assets of banks, end of period (millions of guilders)	QSDNB table 2.1
FABB	Foreign assets of 'other money-creating institutions'	QSDNB table 2.1
FLBA	Foreign liabilities of the banks, end of period (millions of guilders)	QSDNB table 2.1
FLBB	Foreign liabilities of 'other money-creating institutions', end of period (millions of guilders)	QSDNB table 2.1

TABLE A.5 *continued*

Variable symbols	*Definition*	*Source*
FP	Forward premium	Own calculations $FP = \frac{ef - es}{es} \times 400$
FR	Free reserves of banks	$FR = BE - A$
IA	Interest rate on banks' borrowing from central bank, average of the period	QSDNB table 9.1: 'Official Interest Rates'
IEA	Interest rate of banks domestic earnings assets	$IEA = (IL \times L + IS \times SB)/(L + SB)$
π	Expected rate of inflation	See German data-set description
IL	Interest rate on bank loans, average of last 2 months of quarter	Morgan Guaranty Trust, *World Financial Markets*
IS	Interest rate on Government bonds, average of last month of quarter	QSDNB table 9.2: 'Market Interest Rates'
IT	Interest rate on time deposits (at banks), average of last 2 months of quarter	QSDNB table 9.2
$ITMG$	Interest rate on 3-month time deposits, end of period (Ch. 4)	Morgan Guaranty Trust, *World Financial Markets*
ITT	Interest rate on call money, average of last 2 months of quarter	QSDNB table 9.2
K	Total capital flows of banks and public	$K = -\Delta NFB - \Delta NFP$
KP	Capital flows of non-bank public	$KP = -\Delta NFP$
L	Bank loans to the public	$L = EA - SB$

M_1	Money supply, end of period (millions of guilders)	QSDNB table 2.1
M_2	Money supply, end of period (millions of guilders)	QSDNB table 2.1
NFB	Net foreign assets of banks	$NFB = FABA + FABB - FLBA - FLBB$
NFP	Net foreign assets of non-banks, end of period (millions of guilders)	QSDNB table 6.3
OB	Other assets of Central Bank	$OB = B - BTR - BF - A$
OAB	Other assets of banks	$OAB = D + T + A - BR - BE - SB - L - NFB$
OK	Other capital flows	$OK = -CAB - K + \Delta BF$
P	General price level	See $CPI75$
S	Stock of government debt, end of period (millions of guilders)	QSDNB table 5.1
SB	Bond portfolio of banks, end of period (millions of guilders)	QSDNB table 2.1
	$SB = SB_1 + SB_2$	
	A. $SB_1 = SL_1^{HB} + SL_2^{HB} + SK_{Rijk}^{OGI} + SK_{LO}^{OGI} + SK_{Rijk}^{HB} + SK_{LO}^{AB}$	
	SL_1^{HB} = Investments on the capital market from commercial banks (included government fonds)	'Universal banks': col. 9 + 10
	SL_2^{HB} = Investment on the capital market from commercial banks: private loans to government	col. 16
	SK_{Rijk}^{OGI} = Credit from the registered credit institutions to government (short and medium term)	'Other money-creating institutions': col. 6

TABLE A.5 *continued*

Variable symbols	*Definition*	*Source*
SK_{LO}^{OGI}	= Credit from the registered credit institutions to local authorities (short term)	'Other money-creating institutions': col. 7
SK_{Rijk}^{HB}	: See EA	
SK_{LO}^{HB}	: See EA	
B. SB_2	= Investments on the capital market from the registered credit institutions to central government and local authorities	'Other money-creating institutions': col. 9 + 10
SP	Government bonds in hands of public	$SP = S - SB$
T	Time deposits	$T = M_2 - M_1$
YC	Current GNP at market price (millions of guilders)	OECD: *Main Economic Indicators*
YPR	Permanent income (billions of guilders)	See German data-set description

* Quarterly Statistics, Dutch National Bank

TABLE A.6 *United Kingdom*

Variable symbols	*Definition*	*Source*
A	Banks borrowing from the Bank of England. Includes market advances to the discount houses, loans to customers and support loans to deposit-taking institutions. Measurement is at close of business third Wednesday of the month concerned (record for December) (£ million (m.))	Bank of England Statistical Abstract Table 5 and various issues of the BEQB*
B	Monetary Base (= Total notes and coin + Bankers deposits at the Bank of England). End of period (£ m.)	BEQB, March 1981 Table B
BE	Reserves – Notes and Coin held by banks and Bank deposits at the Bank of England. End of period. (£ m.)	BEQB, March 1981
BF	Balance for official financing which includes changes in official reserves, net transactions with overseas monetary authorities and foreign currency borrowing by the central government under the exchange cover scheme. (£ m.)	Balance of Payments Summary. Table *Economic Trends* Annual Supplement 1982
BP	Notes and Coin held by the Non-bank Private Sector. End of period (£ m.)	BEQB, March 1981
BTR	Treasury base, end of period (£ m.) = Net holdings of public sector securities by the central bank	*Financial Statistics*, May 1981 Table 6.3 and various back issues
CAB	Current account balance (£ m.)	*Economic Trends* 1982, Annual Supplement A
CPI75	Consumer Price Index 1975 = 100	Derived as the implicit deflator of consumers' expenditure from *Economic Trends*, Annual Supplement 1982.

TABLE A.6 *continued*

Variable symbols	*Definition*	*Source*
D	Sight deposits, end of period (£ m.)	Derived as $M_1 - BP$
DS	Special deposits including supplementary special deposits (£ m.)	Same as for *B*
es	Spot exchange rate (£/$)	*Financial Statistics*, January 1982 Table 13.2 and various back issues. Collected as £/$ and inverted
FAB	Foreign currency assets of the banking sector end of period (£ m.)	Financial Statistics, 1981 Table 6.1 and various back issues
FLB	Foreign currency liabilities of the Banking Sector, end of period (£ m.)	Same as for *FAB*
FP	Forward premium/discount on dollars (three months) in London, expressed as percentage per annum. Middle market rate as recorded by the Bank of England during the late afternoon of the last working day of the period	BEQB, March 1981, Table 18 and various back issues and B. of E. Statistical Abstract 1 Table 25 and B. of E. Statistical Abstract 2 Table 28
IEU	Three month Eurodollar deposit rate in London, Middle market rates, late afternoon of the last working day of the quarter	Same as for *FP*
π	Expected annual rate of inflation	Own calculations
IL	Loan rate, end of period	*Economic Trends*, Annual Supplement Table 192 and 193
ILA	Local authority interest rate, end of period	*Economic Trends*, Annual Supplement, pp. 175/196

IS	Yield on domestic government bonds taken as yield on 3 1/2 % war loan	BEQB, March 1981, Table 9 and various back issues B. of E. Statistical Abstract 1 and 2, Table 30
IT	Interest rate on time deposits – taken as the inter bank deposit rate, mid way between lowest bid and highest bid at the end of period	Same as for *IEU*
IA	Treasury bill rate, end of period	BEQB, Various
L	Bank lending to the non-bank private sector net of foreign currency lending – end of period (£ million)	*Financial Statistics*, August 1981
LO	Lending in sterling to overseas	Same as *L*
M_1	Notes and coin in circulation with the non-bank public plus sterling sight deposits adjusted for breaks (£ million)	Bank of England (B. of E.)
M_2	Broad Money Stock	Own calculations, $M_2 = M_1 + T = M - MF$
M	Non-bank private sector component of sterling M3 including domestic despsits in foreign currency end of period (£ million)	*Financial Statistics*, August 1981
MF	Holding of bank deposits in foreign currency by the NBPS	Same as *M*
NDA	Net domestic assets	Own calculations, $NDA = M_2 + SP - L$
NFB	Net foreign assets of the banks	Own calculations, $NFB = FAB - FLB +$ lending in foreign currency to the domestic sector
NFP	Net foreign assets of the public, overseas assets less overseas liabilities	*Financial Statistics*, August 1981
NWP	*NBPS* Financial sector net worth (£ m.)	*Financial Statistics*, August 1981, $NWP = NDA + NFP + RESID$
OSL	Other sterling liabilities	*Financial Statistics*, August 1981

TABLE A.6 *continued*

Variable symbols	*Definition*	*Source*
S	Stock of government bonds	Own calculations, $S = SP + SB$
SB	Bank lending to the public sector less public sector debt held by the B. of E. and banking sector deposits at the B. of E. (£ million) end of period	*Financial Statistics*, Nov. 1981, Table 6.1 and various back issues
SP	Public sector long-term debt plus fixed price public sector debt, end of period (£ m.)	*Financial Statistics*, August 1981
T	Time deposits (£ m.)	Own calculations, $T = M - MF - M_1$
YPR	Permanent or expected real income	Own calculations

* *Bank of England Quarterly Bulletin*

TABLE A.7 *List of variables and sources used in the real sector* (in Chapter 3)

Variable symbol		*Definition*	*Source*
es		See financial sector (B, G, I, F, N) for UK: spot exchange rate, end of period	*International Financial Statistics*, country tables, line ae
G	(i)	Total government expenditures	OECD, *National Accounts of OECD Countries*, vol. II, Table 9, lines 12 and 23
	(ii)	Total government revenues	
GDP		See financial sector (B, G, I, F, N) for UK: gross domestic product at current prices (purchasers' values)	OECD, *National Accounts of OECD Countries*, vol. I, June 1982
IEU		Eurodollar rate on 3-months deposits. End of period	Morgan Guaranty Trust, *World Financial Markets*
IEUH		Interest rates on a 3-month Eurodollar rate, bid closing data of last Friday of quarter (Ch. 4)	Harris Bank, *Weekly Review*
M (M_1)		See financial sector (B, G, I, F, N) for UK: exclusive money stock, (yearly average)	*International Financial Statistics*, country tables, line 34
P_d	(i)	Wholesale Price Index (F, I, N, UK)	(i) *International Financial Statistics*, country tables, line 63
	(ii)	Domestic goods prices (B, G)	(ii) UN, *Monthly Bulletin*
	(iii)	Value added in manufacturing deflator	(iii) OECD, *National Accounts of OECD Countries*, Table 2a, 2b
P	(i)	See financial sector	

TABLE A.7 *continued*

Variable symbols		*Definition*	*Source*
P_m	(ii)	*CPI*: goods less food	(ii) OECD, *Consumer Price Indices Sources and Methods and Historical Series*, March 1980. Completed when necessary.
P_0	(iii)	Food and Services Consumer Price Index. Calculated as $P_0 = [P - (\lambda_1 P_d + \lambda_2 P_f)]/\lambda_3 = [P - \lambda_0 P_m]/(1 - \lambda_0)$	
P_f^*		World index for price of exports of manufactured goods (in US dollars)	UN, *Monthly Bulletin*, Special Table: c
P_h^*		Saudi Arabia petroleum price (US $/barrel)	*International Financial Statistics*, Commodity Price Table, line 76aa
τ		$\dfrac{\text{Total transfer payments of general gov.}}{\text{Nominal GDP}}$	G. Warren Nutter, *Growth of Government in the West*, American Enterprise Institute, 1978, Table B.1, period 1950–69. OECD, *National Accounts of OECD Countries*, Table 9, period 1970–80 (items 17 + 18 + 19 + 20 + 21)
t_w^1		$\dfrac{\text{Social security contributions by employers 'Société-Quasi-Société'}}{\text{Total wage bill SQS} - \text{numerator}}$	EC – databank
t_w^2		$\dfrac{\text{Social security contributions by workers}}{\text{denominator of } t_w^1}$	EC – databank

USM_1		United States Money Supply	*International Financial Statistics*, country tables, line 70
W		Wages: Hourly Earnings	*International Financial Statistics*, country tables, line 65
W used for tax wedge		$\frac{\text{denominator of } t_w^1}{\text{numbers employed in industry}}$	EC–databank
WPHO		Saudi Arabia Petroleum Price (US/$) barrel	*International Financial Statistics*, Commodity Price Table, line 76aa
WPF		World export index-manufactured goods	UN *Monthly Bulletin*, Special Table c
XC		Value of Exports, Current prices	*International Financial Statistics*, country tables, line 70
Y	(i)	Index of Industrial Production	(i) *International Financial Statistics*, country tables, line 66
	(ii)	Index of Industrial Production – Manufacturing	(ii) OECD, *Main Economic Indicators*
	(iii)	Value added in manufacturing	(iii) OECD, *National Accounts of OECD Countries*, 1950–79, Table 2b

Bibliography

Abraham, J. and T. Peeters (1981) 'La scène monétaire internationale en 1981', in J. Abraham and M. Vanden Abeele (eds) *European Monetary System and International Reform* (University of Brussels).

Aizenman, J. (1983) 'Modelling Deviations from Purchasing Power Parities' *National Bureau for Economic Research Working Paper*, no. 1066.

Aliber, R. Z. (1973) 'The Interest Rate Parity Theorem: a Reinterpretation', *Journal of Political Economy*, vol. 81, no. 6.

Al-Khouri, S. and S. M. Nsouli (1978) 'The Speed of Adjustment of the A to the Desired Money Stock: a Comparative Study, *European Economic Review*, vol. 11, no. 2.

Amano, A. (1983) 'Exchange Rate Modelling in the EPA World Economic Model' in P. De Grauwe and T. Peeters (eds), *Exchange Rates in Multicountry Econometric Models* (London: Macmillan)

Arango, S. and M. I. Nadiri (1981) 'Demand for Money in Open Economies' *Journal of Monetary Economics*, vol. 7, no. 1.

Argy, V. (1978) 'A Comment on the Korteweg, Fratianni and Fourçans Papers' in K. Brunner and A. H. Meltzer (eds), *The Problem of Inflation*, Carnegie-Rochester Conference Series on Public Policy, vol. 8.

Argy, V. (1982) 'Exchange Rate Management in Theory and Practice', *Princeton Studies in International Finance*, no. 50.

Argy, V. and E. Spitäller (1980) 'The Joint Determination of Changes in Output and Prices in the Seven Main Industrial Countries', *Weltwirtschaftliches Archiv*, Band 116, Heft 1.

Artus, J. (1976) 'Exchange Rate Stability and Managed Floating. The Experience of the Federal Republic of Germany', *IMF Staff Papers*, vol. 23, no. 2.

Barrett, R. J., M. R. Gray and M. Parkin (1975) 'The Demand for Financial Assets by the Personal Sector of the UK Economy', in G. A. Renton (ed.) *Modelling the Economy* (London: Heinemann).

Barro, R. (1981) *Money, Expectations and the Business Cycle* (New York: Academic Press).

Basevi, G. and P. De Grauwe (1977) 'Vicious and Virtuous Circles: A Theoretical Analysis and a Policy Proposal for Managing Exchange Rates', *European Economic Review*, vol. 10, no. 3.

Benjamin, D. and L. Kochin (1979) 'Searching for an Explanation of Unemployment in Inter-war Britain', *Journal of Political Economy*, vol. 87 no. 3.

Bewley, R. A. (1981) *The Portfolio Behaviour of the London Clearing Bank 1963–1971* (Manchester School).

Bilson, J. F. O. (1978) 'The Monetary Approach to the Exchange Rate: Some Empirical Evidence', *IMF Staff Papers*, vol. 25, no. 1.
Bilson, J. F. O. (1979a) 'Comment' in R. Dornbusch and J. A. Frenkel (eds), *International Economic Policy: Theory and Evidence* (Baltimore: The Johns Hopkins University Press).
Bilson, J. F. O. (1979b) 'The "Vicious Circle" Hypothesis', *IMF Staff Papers*, vol. 26, no. 1.
Brainard, W. C. and J. Tobin (1968) 'Pitfalls in Financial Model Building', *American Economic Review*, vol. 58, no. 2.
Branson, W. (1982) 'A Model of Exchange Rate Determination with Policy Reaction: Evidence from Monthly Data', Paris: (Colloque International sur les Dévelopements Récents de la Modélisation Macroéconomique, CEPREMAP).
Braun, A. R. (1976) 'Indexation of Wages and Salaries in Developed Economies', *IMF Staff Papers*, vol. 23, no. 1.
Brillembourg, A. T. and S. Schadler (1979) 'A Model of Currency Substitution in Exchange-rate Determination, 1973–78', *IMF Staff Papers*, vol. 26, no. 3.
Brunner, K. and A. H. Meltzer (1964) 'Some Further Investigations of Demand and Supply Functions for Money', *Journal of Finance*, vol. 29, no. 2, part 1.
Brunner, K. and A. H. Meltzer (1966) 'A Credit Market Theory of the Money Supply and an Explanation of Two Puzzles in US Monetary Policy', *Rivista internazionale scienze economiche e commerciali*, May.
Brunner, K. and A. H. Meltzer (1968) 'Liquidity Traps for Money, Bank Credit and Interest Rates', *Journal of Political Economy*, vol. 76, no. 1.
Brunner, K., Cukierman, A. and A. H. Meltzer (1980) 'Stagflation, Persistent Unemployment and the Permanence of Economic Shocks', *Journal of Monetary Economics*, vol. 6, no. 4.
Bruno, M. (1982) 'World Shocks, Macroeconomic Response, and the Productivity Puzzle', *National Bureau of Economic Research Working Paper*, no. 942.
Bruno, M. and J. Sachs (1979) *Macroeconomic Adjustment with Import Price Shocks: Real and Monetary Aspects* (Stockholm: Institute for International Economic Studies).
Bruno, M. and J. Sachs (1982) 'Energy and Resource Allocation. A Dynamic Model of the "Dutch Disease"', *National Bureau of Economic Research Working Paper*, no. 852.
den Butter, F. A. G. and M. M. G. Fase (1981) 'The Demand for Money in EEC Countries', *Journal of Monetary Economics*, vol. 8, no. 2.
Cagan, P. (1965). *The Determinants and Effects of Changes in the Stock of Money, 1875–1900* (New York: Columbia University Press).
Chetty, V. K. (1969) 'On Measuring the Nearness of Near-moneys', *American Economic Review*, vol. 59, no. 3.
Clare-group (1983) 'World Recession and World Debts', *Midland Bank Review*.
Coghlan, R. (1980) *The Theory of Money and Finance* (London: Macmillan).
Darby, M. R. (1972) 'The Allocation of Transitory Income among Consumer Assets', *American Economic Review*, vol. 62, no. 5.
Darby, M. R. (1981) 'The Real Price of Oil and the 1970s World Inflation', *National Bureau of Economic Research, Working Paper*, no. 629.
De Grauwe, P. (1982) 'The Exchange Rate in a Portfolio Balance Model with a

Banking Sector', *Journal of International Money and Finance*, vol. 1, no. 3.
De Grauwe, P. and T. Peeters (1979) 'The EMS, Europe and the Dollar', *The Banker*, April.
De Grauwe, P. and P. Van den Bergh (1982) 'Foreign Exchange Market Intervention using an ECU-indicator', in M. Summer and G. Zis (eds), *European Monetary Union* (London: Macmillan).
Dooley, M. and P. Isard (1982) 'A Portfolio-balance Rational Expectations Model of the Dollar–Mark Exchange Rate', *Journal of International Economics*, vol. 12, no. 3/4.
Dornbusch, R. (1983a) 'Equilibrium and Disequilibrium Exchange Rates', *Zeitschrift für Wirtschafts und Sozialwissenschaften*, 1.
Dornbusch, R. (1983b) 'Exchange Risk and the Macroeconomics of Exchange Rate Determination', in R. Hawkins, R. Levich and C. Wihlborg (eds), *The Internationalisation of Financial Markets and National Policy*.
EC-Commission (1979) 'The European Monetary System – Commentary, Documents', *European Economy*, no. 3.
Fair, R. C. (1979) 'Analysis of a Macro-econometric Model with Rational Expectations in the Bond and Stock Market', *American Economic Review*, vol. 69, no. 4.
Fair, R. C. and J. B. Taylor (1983) 'Solution and Maximum Likelihood Estimation of Dynamic Non-Linear Rational Expectations Models', *Econometrica*, vol. 51, no. 4.
Fleming, J. M. (1962) 'Domestic Financial Policies under Fixed and Floating Exchange Rates', *IMF Staff Papers*, vol. 9, no. 3.
Fourçans, A. (1978) 'Inflation and Output growth: The French Experience, 1960–75', in K. Brunner and A. H. Meltzer (eds), *The Problem of Inflation*, Carnegie-Rochester Conference Series on Public Policy, vol. 8.
Frankel, J. A. (1982) 'In Search of the Exchange Risk Premium: A Six-Currency Test Assuming Mean-Variance Optimization', *Journal of International Money and Finance*, vol. 1, no. 3.
Fratianni, M. (1976) 'Domestic Bank Credit, Money and the Open Economy', in M. Fratianni and K. Tavernier (eds), *Bank Credit, Money and Inflation in Open Economies* (Berlin: Duncker & Humbolt).
Fratianni, M. (1978) 'Inflation and Unanticipated Changes in Output in Italy', in K. Brunner and A. H. Meltzer (eds) *The Problem of Inflation*, Carnegie-Rochester Conference Series on Public Policy, vol. 8.
Fratianni, M. (1980a) 'Money, Wages and Prices in Italy', *Banca Nazionale del Lavoro Quarterly Review*, no. 135.
Fratianni, M. (1980b) 'The European Monetary System: a Return to an Adjustable Peg', in K. Brunner and A. H. Meltzer (eds), *Monetary Institutions and Policy Processes*, Carnegie-Rochester Conference Series on Public Policy, vol. 13.
Fratianni, M. and L. M. Wakeman (1982) 'The Law of One Price in the Eurocurrency Market', *Journal of International Money and Finance*, vol. 1, no. 3.
Frenkel, J. A. (1978) 'A Monetary Approach to the Exchange Rate: Doctrinal Aspects and Empirical Evidence', in J. A. Frenkel and H. G. Johnson (eds), *The Economics of Exchange Rates* (Reading: Addison Wesley).
Frenkel, J. A. (1983) 'International Liquidity and Monetary Control', *National*

Bureau of Economic Research Working Paper, no. 1118.
Friedman, M. and A. J. Schwartz (1963) *A Monetary History of the United States 1867–1960* (Princeton: National Bureau of Economic Research).
Genberg, H. (1981) 'Effects of Central Bank Intervention in the Foreign Exchange Market', *IMF Staff Papers*, vol. 28, no. 1.
Giavazzi, F., M. Odekon and C. Wyplosz (1982) 'Simulating an Oil Shock with Sticky Prices', *European Economic Review*, vol. 18, no. 1/2.
Goldfeld, S. (1973) 'The Demand for Money Revisited', *Brookings Paper on Economic Activity*, 3.
Gourieroux, C., J. J. Laffont and A. Monfort (1982) 'Rational Expectations Models: Analysis of the Solutions', *Econometrica*, vol. 50, no. 1.
Haas, R., P. Hooper, R. Meese, G. Stevens and R. Tryon (1980) 'Exchange Rate Determination in a Multi-Country Model', Federal Reserve Board, August.
Harris Bank, *Weekly Review* (Chicago) various issues.
Holden, K. and D. A. Peel (1979) 'The Determinants of the Unemployment Rate: Some Empirical Evidence', *The Statistician*, vol. 46, no. 6.
Hooper, P., R. D. Haas, S. A. Symansky and L. Stekler (1982) 'Alternative Approach to General Equilibrium Modelling of Exchange Rates and Capital Flows: the MCM Experience', *International Finance Discussion papers*, no. 213.
Hooper, P., R. D. Haas and S. Symansky (1983) 'Revision of Exchange Rate Determination in the MCM' in P. De Grauwe and T. Peeters (eds), *Exchange Rates in Multicountry Econometric Models* (London: Macmillan).
Howard, D. H. (1982) 'The British Lending Systems Demand for Cash Reserves', *Journal of Monetary Economics*, vol. 9, no. 1.
HMSO Green paper (1980) *Monetary Control*, Cmnd, 7858.
Hunt, B. F. and P. A. Volker (1981) 'A Simplified Portfolio Analysis of the Long-run Demand for Money in Australia', *Journal of Monetary Economics*, vol. 8, no. 3.
IMF, *International Financial Statistics* (Washington: International Monetary Fund) various issues.
IMF (1979), 'The European Monetary System', *Supplement to IMF Survey*, March.
Korteweg, P. (1978) 'The Economics of Inflation and Output Fluctuations in the Netherlands, 1954–75: a Test of Some Implications of the Dominant Impulse-cum-Rational Expectations Hypothesis', in K. Brunner and A. H. Meltzer (eds), *The Problem of Inflation*, Carnegie-Rochester Conference Series on Public Policy, vol. 8.
Korteweg, P. (1980) 'The Economics of Stagflation: Theory and Dutch Evidence', *Zeitschrift für die gesamte Staatswissenschaft*, Heft 1.
Korteweg, P. and P. D. van Loo (1977) *The Market for Money and the Market for Credit* (Leiden: Martinus Nijhoff Social Sciences Division).
Krueger, A. O. (1983) *Exchange-rate Determination* (Cambridge University Press).
Ladenson, M. R. (1971) 'Pitfalls in Financial Model Building: Some Extensions', *American Economic Review*, vol. 61, no. 1.
Laidler, D. (1980) 'The Demand for Money in the United States: Yet Again', in K. Brunner and A. H. Meltzer (eds), *On the State of Macroeconomics*,

Carnegie-Rochester Conference Series on Public Policy, vol. 12.

Leiderman, L. (1981) 'Monetary Accomodation and the Variability of Output, Prices, and the Exchange Rates', in K. Brunner and A. H. Meltzer (eds), *Monetary Regimes and Protectionism*, Carnegie-Rochester Conference Series on Public Policy, vol. 16.

Levich, R. M. (1983) 'Empirical Studies of Exchange Rate Determination and Market Efficiency', *National Bureau of Economic Research Working Paper*, no. 1112.

Lucas, R. E. (1973) 'Some International Evidence on the Output–Inflation Tradeoffs', *American Economic Review*, vol. 63, no. 3.

Lucas, R. (1975) 'An Equilibrium Model of the Business Cycle', *Journal of Political Economy*, vol. 83, no. 6.

Marston, R. C. (1983) 'Stabilization Policies in Open Economies', *National Bureau of Economic Research Working Paper*, no. 1117.

Masera, R. (1981) 'The First Two Years of the EMS: The Exchange Rate Experience', *Banca Nazionale del Lavoro, Quarterly Review*, no. 138.

Matthews, K. and P. Minford (1980) 'Private Sector Expenditure and Financial Asset Accumulation in the UK.', *Journal of Money, Credit and Banking*, vol. 12, no. 4, part I.

Matthews, K. and J. Thompson (1982) 'A Model of the UK Financial Sector: The Non-bank Private Sector', *International Economics Research Paper*, no. 36, (Leuven, Centre for Economic Studies).

Mayer, H. and H. Taguchi (1983) 'Official Intervention in the Exchange Markets: Stabilizing or Destabilizing', *BIS Economic Papers*, no. 6.

McCallum, B. T. (1976) 'Rational Expectations and the Natural Rate Hypothesis: Some Consistent Estimates', *Econometrica*, vol. 44, no. 1.

McKinnon, R. I. (1982) 'Currency Substitution and Instability in the World Dollar Market', *American Economic Review*, vol. 72, no. 3.

Meese, R. A. and K. Rogoff (1983) 'Empirical Exchange Rate Models of the Seventies: Do They Fit out of Sample?', *Journal of International Economics*, vol. 14, no. 1/2.

Melitz, J. and H. Sterdyniak (1979) 'An Econometric Study of the British Monetary System', *Economic Journal*, vol. 89, December.

Minford, P. (1983) *Unemployment. Cause and Cure* (Oxford: Martin Robertson).

Minford, P., K. Matthews and S. A. Marwaha (1980) 'Terminal Condition, Uniqueness and Solution of Rational Expectations Models' (University of Liverpool, mimeo).

Morgan Guaranty Trust Co, *World Financial Markets* (New York) various issues.

Mundell, R. (1963) 'Capital Mobility and Stabilization Policy under Fixed and Flexible Exchange Rates', *Canadian Journal of Economics and Political Science*, vol. 29.

Mussa, M. (1981) 'The Role of Official Intervention', *Occasional Paper 6*, Group of Thirty (New York).

Muth, J. F. (1961) 'Rational Expectations and the Theory of Price Movements', *Econometrica*, vol. 29, no. 3.

Nutter, G. W. (1978) *Growth of Government in the West* (Washington: American Enterprise Institute).

Obstfeld, M. (1983) 'Exchange Rates, Inflation and the Sterilization Problem: Germany, 1975–81', *European Economic Review*, vol. 21, March–April.

OECD (1980) *Consumer Price Indices: Sources and Methods and Historical Series* (Paris: Organisation for Economic Co-operation and Development).

OECD (1981a) *National Accounts of OECD-countries, 1950–1979, Volume I, Main Aggregates* (Paris: Organisation for Economic Co-operation and Development).

OECD (1981b) 'Long-Term Trends in Tax Revenues of OECD Member Countries', *Studies in Taxation* (Paris: Organisation for Economic Co-operation and Development).

OECD, *Main Economic Indicators* (Paris: Organisation for Economic Co-operation and Development) various issues.

Officer, L. H. and T. D. Willet (1970) 'The Covered-arbitrage Schedule: a Critical Survey of Recent Developments', *Journal of Money, Credit and Banking*, vol. 2, no. 2.

Parkin, M. (1970) 'Discount House Portfolio and Debt Selection Behaviour', *Review of Economic Studies*, vol. 37, no. 4.

Parkin, M., M. R. Gray and R. J. Barrett (1970) 'The Portfolio Behaviour of Commercial Banks' in K. Hilton and D. Heatfield (eds), *Econometric Models of the UK* (London: MacMillan).

Parkin, M. and G. Copplestone (1978) *A Model of the Financial Sector of the United Kingdom: Some Preliminary Results* (University of Western Ontario, mimeo).

Quirk, P. (1977) 'Exchange Rate Policy in Japan: Leaning Against the Wind', *IMF Staff Papers*, vol. 24, no. 3.

Saïdi, N. and G. Huber (1983) 'Postwar Business Cycles and Exchange Rate Regimes: Issues and Evidence', presented at Konstanz Seminar on Monetary Theory and Monetary Policy.

Sato, K. (1967) 'A Two Level Constant-elasticity of Substitution Production Function', *Review of Economic Studies*, vol. 34, no. 2.

Saving, T. R. (1977) 'A Theory of the Money Supply with Competitive Banking', *Journal of Monetary Economics*, vol. 3, no. 3.

Spinelli, F. (1983) 'Currency Substitution, Flexible Exchange Rates, and the Case for International Co-operation: Discussion of a Recent Proposal', *IMF Staff Papers*, vol. 30, no. 4.

Strotz, R. H. (1957) 'The Empirical Implications of a Utility Tree', *Econometrica*, April.

Stulz, R. M. (1983) 'Currency Preferences, Purchasing Power Risks and the Determination of Exchange Rates in an Optimizing Model' (University of Rochester, mimeo).

Swoboda, A. K. (1983) 'Exchange Rate Regimes and US-European Policy Interdependence', *IMF Staff Papers*, vol. 30, no. 1.

Tosini, P. (1977) 'Leaning Against the Wind: A Standard for Managed Floating', *Princeton Essays in International Finance*, no. 126.

Triffin, R. (1983) 'The Rehabilitation of the World Monetary System is an Indispensable Prerequisite to Ending the World Recession' (mimeo).

UN, *Monthly Bulletin of Statistics* (New York: United Nations) various issues.

Ungerer, H., O. Evans and P. Nijberg (1983) 'The European Monetary System: The Experience, 1979–82', *IMF Occasional Paper*, no. 19.

Wallis, K. F. (1980) 'Econometric Implications of the Rational Expectations Hypothesis', *Econometrica*, vol. 48, no. 1.

White, W. R. (1975) 'Some Econometric Models of Deposit Bank Portfolio Behaviour in the UK.' in G. A. Renton (ed.) *Modelling the Economy* (London: Heinemann).

Wickens, R. M. (1982) 'The Efficient Estimation of Econometric Models with Rational Expectations', *Review of Economic Studies*, vol. 49, no. 155.

Wonnacott, P. (1983) 'US Official Intervention in the Exchange Market for DM: Theoretical Issues and Empirical Evidence', *Princeton Studies in International Finance*, no. 51.

Index

Abraham, 172
accommodation, monetary, 145, 149, 150, 157
Aizenman, 172
Aliber, 69
Al-Khouri, 123
Amano, 123
AR, 46, 47
Arango, 91, 122
Argy, 21, 157
ARIMA, 30, 31, 46, 47
ARMA models, 23, 38, 39
Artus, 148, 180

balance of payments, 16, 70, 96, 106, 136
Bank of England, 113
Barret, 113
Barro, 44
Bewley, 113
Bilson, 53, 88
Box-Jenkins, 46
Brainard, 103, 113
Branson, 148
Braun, 7
Bretton Woods, 163, 177, 181, 195
Brillembourg, 182
Brunner, 74, 84, 88
Bruno, 21, 43, 44
bubble, 86
business cycle, 1, 44, 173, 177, 192
  equilibrium theory of the, 44

Cagan, 88
cash-balances, 11
central rates, 160
  bilateral, 159
Clare group, 191
clearing banks, 113
Coghlan, 123
comparative advantage, 78
competition and credit control, 120
controls, foreign exchange, 106
co-ordination, 194
Copplestone, 113
cost-push, 144
credit ceilings, 87
currency substitution, 182, 195

Darby, 21, 91, 122
De Grauwe, 71, 88, 172
devaluation, 16
Dooley, 54, 67
Dornbusch, 65, 182, 191

EC-Commission, 172
Economic Planning Agency, 97
Eurocurrency, 57, 62, 67, 98
  assets, 54
  market, 53
Eurodollar, 54, 93, 98, 99, 123, 154, 166
  interest rate, 153, 167, 168
  uncovered rate, 100
European Currency Unit (ECU), 159, 160, 172
European Monetary Co-operation Fund, 160
European Monetary System (EMS), 2, 159, 160, 161, 168, 171, 172, 194
  arrangement, 160
  countries, 163, 166
  country, 170
  parities, 170
Evans, 172
exchange market, 80
exchange rate
  effective, 161, 162
  fixed, 2
  fixed regime, 182
  fixed and flexible, 187

exchange rate (*contd.*)
  fixed and flexible arrangements, 195
  fixed and flexible regimes, 194
  flexible, 2, 192
  flexible system, 185
  floating, 143, 173, 187
  floating system, 176
  managed, 3, 194
  management, 186, 187, 188
  nominal, 163
  policies, 194
  real, 161, 163, 172
  real variability, 194
  regimes, 153, 193
  stability, 171
exchange systems, fixed and flexible, 181, 191
expectations
  inflationary, 1
  rational, 1, 2, 21, 30, 32, 33, 40, 85, 87, 88, 99, 100, 101, 121, 143, 144, 149, 194

Fair, 157
Federal Reserve, 123
Federal Reserve Board, 97
Fisherian, 65
Fleming, 70
floating, 149, 150, 153
  flexible and managed, 182
forward
  discount, 154
  dollar, 166
  market, 57
  premium, 54, 66, 87, 99, 102, 123, 136, 145
Frankel, 54, 65, 67, 69
Fratianni, 21, 45, 59, 69, 84, 88, 172
Frenkel, 88, 191
Friedman, 88, 91
Fourçans, 21
full-information estimation, 104

Genberg, 148
Giavazzi, 44
Goldfeld, 122
Gray, 113
Green Paper, HMSO, 123
Gourieroux, 88

Haas, 123
Harris Bank, 57
Holden, 45
Hooper, 123
Huber, 174
Hunt, 104

IMF Survey, 172
income
  permanent, 91, 92, 106, 111, 116, 123
  transitory, 91, 92, 106
indexation, 11, 12, 33
indexation clauses, 10
indicator of divergence, 160
inflation surprises, 43
information set, 10, 30
Isard, 54, 67
IS-curve, 184, 185
interdependence, 193
  financial, i, 1, 193, 194
  monetary, 3
interest rate
  covered, 101, 116
  uncovered, 101
interest-rate parity, 53, 54, 55, 63, 67, 84, 98, 112, 151, 152, 166
intermediate good, 8, 11, 17, 18, 21, 47
intermediate products, 16
intervention, 145, 148, 177, 179, 193
  exchange market, 83, 143, 186, 187
  foreign exchange market, 167
  non-sterilised, 148, 155, 157
  official, 120, 159, 160
  policies, 152, 156, 181
  sterilised, 87, 83, 84, 148, 149, 150, 152, 153, 155, 156, 157

Kochin, 45
Korteweg, 21, 45, 91, 106

Ladenson, 103, 104
Laffont, 88

lagged endogenous variable, 103, 104, 109
Laidler, 122
leaning against the wind, 148, 149, 157, 177
Leiderman, 21
Levich, 66, 67, 69, 99
LM-curve, 184, 185
Lucas, 8, 11, 23, 42, 44, 192
  supply, 21, 36
  supply equation, 1, 33
  supply function, 10
  supply of output, 22

McCallum, 45
McKinnon, 181
market efficiency, 57, 67, 69, 87, 99
Marston, 21, 191
Masera, 172
Matthews, 112
Mayer, 148
Meese, 88
Meltzer, 74, 84, 88
minimum variance portfolio, 65
Minford, 45
monetary approach, 53
monetary co-operation, 172
monetarist model, 75
Monfort, 88
Mundell, 70, 182
  IS–LM model, 183
Mussa, 157

Nadiri, 91, 122
non-traded goods, 20, 33
Nsouli, 123
Nyberg, 172

Obstfeld, 148, 181
Odekon, 44
OECD, 174
Officer, 53
oil shock, 1, 44, 161, 176, 177
oil tax, 22
open-market operations, 83
overshooting, 145, 153, 157

Parkin, 113
partial adjustment mechanism, 104
Peel, 45
Peeters, 172
perfect foresight, 121, 144, 149, 157
portfolio balance, 2, 53, 70, 75, 87, 90
PPP, 66
price-taker, 10
price-takership, 19
principal components analysis, 174
Public Sector Borrowing Requirement (PSBR), 119
purchasing power parity, 144, 171, 191

Quirk, 148, 180

random walk, 27, 86, 87, 101
realignment, 171
regime
  floating, 97
  managed, 97
reserve
  excess, 105, 136
  free, 105
  required, 136
reserve requirement, 72, 74, 80, 85, 87, 154, 155
risk
  exchange, 62
  neutrality, 67
  political, 62, 67
  premium, 54, 65, 66, 67, 84, 112, 161
risk-averse, 54
risk-aversion, 65
Rogoff, 88

Sachs, 21, 43, 44
Saidi, 174
Sato, 114
Saving, 73
Schwartz, 88
SDR, 160
Shadler, 182
snake, arrangements, 160
spectral analysis, 174
Spinelli, 182

spot
  dollar exchange rate, 166
  exchange market, 83
  exchange rate, 86, 87, 97, 98, 111
  market, 57
  rate, 65
stagflation, 17
sterilisation, 154
Strotz, 114
Stulz, 65
substitutability, 1, 193
  imperfect, 54, 65, 67, 70, 84, 87, 98
  perfect, 53, 54, 75, 80–1, 82, 84
substitutes, perfect, 80
Swoboda, 174

Taguchi, 148
tax burdens, 1, 8
tax wedge, 8, 19, 22, 28, 30, 33, 36, 42, 43
Taylor, 157
terminal condition, 121, 144, 153, 155
terms of trade, 7, 11, 16, 17, 19, 20, 21, 22, 26, 27, 30, 33, 38, 42, 43, 188, 190, 191, 192
Theil, inequality coefficients, 122, 123
Thompson, 112
three-stage least squares, 104, 117
Tobin, 70, 72, 103, 113
Tosini, 148
triangular arbitrage, 167
Triffin, 191
two-stage least squares (2 SLS), 104, 105, 117

underground, 19, 20
Ungerer, 172
utility tree, 114

Van den Bergh, 172
Van Loo, 91, 106
vector autoregression (VAR), 30, 31, 38, 39
vector autoregressive models, 23, 49
Volker, 104

wage indexation, 1, 7, 22, 36
Wakeman, 59, 69
Wallis, 12, 30
wedge, 10
White, 113
white-noise, 11, 47, 85
Wickens, 30
Willett, 53
Wonnacott, 148, 181
World Financial Markets, 57
Wyplosz, 44

yields, covered, 53